Second Language Writing
Series Editor, Paul Kei Matsuda

SECOND LANGUAGE WRITING
Series Editor, Paul Kei Matsuda

Second language writing emerged in the late twentieth century as an interdisciplinary field of inquiry, and an increasing number of researchers from various related fields—including applied linguistics, communication, composition studies, and education—have come to identify themselves as second language writing specialists. The Second Language Writing series aims to facilitate the advancement of knowledge in the field of second language writing by publishing scholarly and research-based monographs and edited collections that provide significant new insights into central topics and issues in the field.

The Politics of Second Language Writing

In Search of the Promised Land

Editors
Paul Kei Matsuda
Christina Ortmeier-Hooper
Xiaoye You

Parlor Press
West Lafayette, Indiana
www.parlorpress.com

Parlor Press LLC, West Lafayette, Indiana 47906

© 2006 by Parlor Press
All rights reserved.
Printed in the United States of America

SAN: 254-8879

Library of Congress Cataloging-in-Publication Data

The politics of second language writing : in search of the promised land / editors, Paul Kei Matsuda, Christina Ortmeier-Hooper, Xiaoye You.
   p. cm. -- (Second language writing)
 Includes bibliographical references and index.
 ISBN 1-932559-33-7 (hardcover : alk. paper) -- ISBN 1-932559-11-6 (pbk. : alk. paper) -- ISBN 1-932559-37-X (adobe ebook)
  1. Language and languages--Study and teaching. 2. Rhetoric--Study and teaching. I. Matsuda, Paul Kei. II. Ortmeier-Hooper, Christina, 1972- III. You, Xiaoye, 1974-
 P53.27.P65 2006
 808'.040711--dc22
                        2006020017

Cover design by Paul Kei Matsuda
Printed on acid-free paper.

Parlor Press, LLC is an independent publisher of scholarly and trade titles in print and multimedia formats. This book is available in paper, cloth and Adobe eBook formats from Parlor Press on the World Wide Web at http://www.parlorpress.com or through online and brick-and mortar bookstores. For submission information or to find out about Parlor Press publications, write to Parlor Press, 816 Robinson St., West Lafayette, Indiana, 47906, or e-mail editor@parlorpress.com.

Contents

Preface *vii*

The Politics of L2 Writers in U.S. K-12 Schools 3

1 Writing Development and Biliteracy 5
   Danling Fu and Marylou Matoush

2 Reforming High School Writing: Opportunities and Constraints for Generation 1.5 Writers 30
   Kerry Enright Villalva

The Politics of L2 Writing Support Programs 57

3 The Legacy of First-Year Composition 59
   Ilona Leki

4 Improving Institutional ESL/EAP Support for International Students: Seeking the Promised Land 75
   Ryuko Kubota and Kimberly Abels

5 No ESL Allowed: A Case Exploring University and College Writing Program Practices 94
   Angela M. Dadak

6 The Role(s) of Writing Centers in Second Language Writing Instruction 109
   Jessica Williams

The Politics of English Writing for Academic and Professional Purposes 127

7 Understanding Context for Writing in University Content Classrooms 129
   Wei Zhu

8 EAP and Technical Writing Without Borders: The Impact of Departmentalization on the Teaching and Learning of Academic Writing in a First and Second Language   *147*
   Guillaume Gentil

9 Different Writers, Different Writing: Preparing International Teaching Assistants for Instructional Literacy   *168*
   Kevin Eric DePew

10 Globalization and the Politics of Teaching EFL Writing   *188*
   Xiaoye You

The Politics of Second Language Writing Assessment   *203*

11 The Politics of Implementing Online Directed Self-Placement for Second Language Writers   *205*
   Deborah Crusan

12 Investing in Assessment: Designing Tests to Promote Positive Washback   *222*
   Sara Cushing Weigle

The Politics of the Profession   *245*

13 Mapping Postsecondary Classifications and Second Language Writing Research in the United States   *247*
   Jessie Moore Kapper

14 Institutional Politics in the Teaching of Advanced Academic Writing: A Teacher-Researcher Dialogue   *262*
   Christine Norris and Christine Tardy

15 Shifting Sites, Shifting Identities: A Thirty-Year Perspective   *280*
   Stephanie Vandrick

Coda   *295*

16 Toward a Promised Land of Writing: At the Intersection of Hope and Reality   *297*
   Barbara Kroll

Contributors   *306*
Editors   *310*
Index   *311*

Preface

The "Promised Land"... is one in which each and every NNES [Nonnative English-Speaking] student at an English-medium campus would have access to programs of study and support systems that are designed to promote mastery and excellence in academic English in ways that most address the local and specific needs of those students, whoever they may be and at whichever campus they are studying.

—Barbara Kroll

Scholarship on second language writing has grown exponentially over the last few decades. While a majority of work done in second language writing addresses instructional issues, the focus of much of this scholarship is on what happens in the classroom as opposed to how the institutional contexts outside the classroom shape instructional practices. Although classroom issues are important, such narrow focus on the classroom is problematic because instruction is always situated in and shaped by larger institutional contexts. No amount of theoretical knowledge will be useful in shaping classroom practice unless we also understand how classroom practices are shaped by institutional policies and politics. To help remedy this imbalance, the 2004 Symposium on Second Language Writing brought together second language writing specialists in the United States and Canada to explore the intersection of institutional policies and politics and classroom practices.

As we heard the reports of various efforts and struggles involved in negotiating the balance between theoretically sound and ethical instructional practices on the one hand and the demands of institutional policies and politics on the other hand, we came to realize that none of us had it easy; we were not alone as we searched desperately for the Promised Land, to borrow Barbara Kroll's phrase from her Symposium presentation, which quickly became the running theme of the two-day event. After the Symposium, we asked the presenters to develop their presentations into manuscripts suitable for print publication, and this volume is the result.

The Politics of Second Language Writing: In Search of the Promised Land is the first edited collection to present a sustained discussion of classroom practices in larger contexts of institutional politics and policies. We refer here to policies on assessment, placement, credit, class size, course content, instructional practices, teacher preparation, and teacher support and to politics in terms of the relationships and interaction between second language writing professionals and their colleagues at the program, department, school, college, and university levels and beyond. Authors in this collection explore—through critical reflections and situated descriptions of their instructional practices in larger institutional contexts—how instructional policies and politics affect instructional practices. Such descriptions would provide an understanding of how classroom practices are not neutral, pragmatic spaces but ideologically saturated sites of negotiation.

The primary audience for *The Politics of Second Language Writing* includes those who are involved in the teaching, research, and administration of second language writing. By including contextualized descriptions and discussions, this collection provides insights that will help second language writing specialists understand and critically reexamine how institutional policies and politics shape instructional practices. The secondary audience includes members of programs and departments where second language writing courses and programs are located—which include second language specialists and composition specialists who do not necessarily see second language writing as their area of expertise. This book focuses largely on situations at North American institutions, where, perhaps because of the influence of composition studies, the interest in exploring issues of institutional contexts has been most conspicuous. However, we hope this publication will inspire similar discussions focusing on other parts of the world.

As we prepare this volume, we have also come to a greater awareness of the politics of second language writing research: The field has grown most significantly in the United States over the last three decades; it has predominantly dealt with writing in English rather than in other second languages; and all contributors to this first volume on the politics of the profession are based largely in the United States. While we address this political imbalance in a small way with the inclusion of chapters by Guillaume Gentil and Xiaoye You, we acknowledge the limitation of this volume and hope more efforts will be made to consider the politics of second language writing in other geopolitical contexts.

Overview

This volume is organized roughly by the level of instruction: K-12 education, language support programs in higher education, English for academic and professional purposes, assessment, and the politics of the profession. Part 1, "L2 Writers in U.S. K-12 Schools" explores the dynamics and politics that affect the writing development and writing opportunities of second language writers in middle school and high school. In Chapter 1, Danling Fu and Marylou Matoush argue that political pressure of the "English Only" movement has undermined the value of biliteracy for nonnative English speaking students. The chapter describes Fu's research on the writing development of the Chinese-speaking students in a middle school located in New York's Chinatown, demonstrating how first language literacy can help students in their second language writing development, noting that writing development takes place in four transitions, as students progress from their first language to second language writing proficiency. In Chapter 2, Kerry Enright Villalva explores the dynamics and politics that are at play in a U.S. high school and the effects of those elements on the writing opportunities given to Generation 1.5 students. Using an ecological framework, Villalva demonstrates the various facets of the institutional ecology of one high school, and examines how the systems within the school provide both opportunities and constraints for the student writers in her research study. She concludes that, even as the school strove to reform some of its practices to provide richer opportunities for its students, the strengths and challenges that were unique to second language writers were not taken into account. These neglected opportunities have important ramifications for how these students will develop the advanced academic writing skills that they will need to further their education beyond high school.

Part Two, "The Politics of L2 Writing Support Programs," examines the institutional support systems at universities and colleges and their role in providing assistance to L2 writers. In Chapter 3, Ilona Leki critiques the negative legacy of first-year composition programs and their impact on L2 writers. She examines the focus of those composition classes and the obstacles they often present, institutionally, for second language writers, noting that the class often seems to elevate writing skills above the other communicative skills that L2 students often need to survive in academic institutions. She also provides interesting insights into how L2 writers are trapped in the institutional quagmire that first-year composition often presents. Finally, she calls on second language writing specialists to remain vigilant to the trends in L1 composition that may threaten to compromise and further complicate L2 writers' efforts on the university and college campus. In Chapter 4, "Improving Institutional ESL/EAP Support for International Students: Seeking a Promised Land," Ryuko Kubota and Kimberly Abels pick up on the metaphor used by Barbara Kroll and explore the efforts of faculty members to work together to enhance English language instruction and support for international students at their university. The chapter reflects on two years of effort by the ESL committee to negotiate institutional history and politics in order to persuade the university to increase the level of services and opportunities for its international and Generation 1.5 students. In Chapter 5, "No ESL Allowed: A Case Exploring University and College Writing Program Practices," Angela M. Dadak explores the consequences and unexpected alliances that emerged when her university made the decision to phase out its intensive English program for ESL students, while at the same time reaffirming its commitment toward becoming a global university. Dadak reveals the paradoxical nature of the university's stance and its surprising effects on institutional and departmental politics during the time of transition. In Chapter 6, "The Role(s) of Writing Centers in Second Language Writing Instruction," Jessica Williams argues that writing centers often serve as a primary site of learning for a significant number of L2 writing clients. Her research explores the views of writing center administrators and staff members to learn more about the kinds of support and the quality of support that writing centers provide L2 writers at the university level. Her article provides important insights into the role of university writing centers in the academic experiences of L2 writers.

Section Three, "The Politics of English Writing for Academic and Professional Purposes," explores various political dimensions of teaching and learning English writing for academic and professional purposes. In Chapter 8, "Understanding Context for Writing in University Content Classrooms," Wei Zhu examines both purposes and factors for writing assignments in EAP programs in a large American university. She finds that besides assessment, writing in the content classroom is used to prepare students for success in their disciplines and careers, to address course goals and content, and to foster individual development. Professors in different disciplines consider writing assignments according to the class size and time needed to design and grade assignments, as well as the nature of the discipline or course. In Chapter 9, "EAP and Technical Writing without Borders: The Impact of Departmentalization on the Teaching and Learning of Academic Writing in a First and Second Language," Guillaume Gentil focuses on how departmentalization has hindered students' development of academic and professional biliteracy in a Canadian university. He argues that the disciplinary L1/L2 division of labor needs to be adjusted in response to the increasing presence of immigrant and refugee ESL students and Generation 1.5 students in North American universities. In Chapter 10, "Different Writers, Different Writing: Preparing International Teaching Assistants for Instructional Literacy," Kevin Eric DePew points out the prevailing lack of attention to the writing component in preparing international teaching assistants (ITAs) in American universities. He suggests that writing, particularly writing in the multimodal environment, should be made a significant component in ITA mentoring. In Chapter 11, "Globalization and the Politics of Teaching EFL Writing," Xiaoye You examines English writing instruction in two Chinese universities in relation to the discourse of globalization. He suggests that English literacy has been redefined, more geared toward international communication and competition, in some non-English-dominant countries, and that heightened institutional stipulations on teaching English writing are sometimes hard to meet in classroom instruction.

Part Four, "The Politics of Assessment," explores the realm of assessment, both in terms of placement and in terms of the writing classroom. In Chapter 11 "The Politics and Policies of Implementing Online Directed Self-Placement for Second Language Writers," Deborah Crusan examines the current history of her institution's assessment tools for placement, reminding us about the inherently political nature of assessment. Crusan describes the gatekeeping nature of assessment, particularly in the placement of L2 writers, as she describes her university's decision to re-evaluate its assessment procedures in favor of directed self-placement (DSP) and online directed self-placement (ODSP). Crusan raises important questions of how L2 writers are positioned and considered within this ongoing discussion at her open admissions university. In Chapter 12, "Investing in Assessment: Designing Tests to Promote Positive Washback," Sara Cushing Weigle focuses on a major issue with timed impromptu essays in externally mandated tests in postsecondary institutions—the separation of assessment from instruction. She introduces an alternative test designed for ESL students at Georgia State University that has quite successfully connected writing assessment with values of teaching academic writing, thus yielding positive washback effects in classroom instruction.

Part Five, "The Politics of the Profession," focuses on the professional work of second language writing. In Chapter 13, "Mapping Postsecondary Classifications and Second Language Writing Research in the United States," Jessie Moore Kapper analyzes the geographical and educational contexts of second language writing scholarship in the United States through mapping. She finds that doctoral universities in the Carnegie classifications produced 75 percent of the scholarship that she has sampled; therefore, she suggests more attention and collaboration be devoted to underrepresented settings, such as K-12, two-year colleges, and community programs. In Chapter 14, "Institutional Politics in the Teaching of Advanced Academic Writing: A Teacher-Researcher Dialogue," Christine Norris and Christine Tardy reflect upon their experiences teaching and researching a graduate-level EAP course at Purdue University. In their dialogue, they discuss how institutional policies on placement, credit, and grading as well as the teacher's institutional roles and identities have influenced decisions in the classroom; they also highlight the inadequacy of the applied linguistics model for teaching advanced academic writing. In Chapter 15, "Shifting Sites, Shifting Identities: A Thirty-Year Perspective," Stephanie Vandrick reflects upon the evolution of ESL and ESL writing at the University of San Francisco over the last three decades. She points out that some major changes with the institutional status of ESL and ESL writing resulted from unionization, changes of administration, institutional stance on internationalism and multiculturalism, the enrollment profile, and individual faculty members' efforts. Consequently the changes with ESL's institutional status have led to new identities for the ESL/L2 writing discipline, faculty, and students.

The volume concludes with a coda, "Toward a Promised Land of Writing: At the Intersection of Hope and Reality." In this chapter, Barbara Kroll juxtaposes ideal institutional practices and obstacles in promoting NNES students' mastery and excellence in academic English at English-medium campuses. In reality, as she suggests, second language specialists need to negotiate with administrators to overcome five major obstacles to reach the "promised land." These obstacles include identifying students who may benefit from English language assistance, designing effective placement tests to sort students into appropriate classes, offering a variety of English courses suitable to students' needs, enforcing English language requirements in different departments and colleges, and setting reasonable tuitions for NNES students.

Acknowledgments

First and foremost, we thank Dave Blakesley of Parlor Press for supporting this project and for his ongoing editorial guidance in producing this volume. We are also grateful to the contributors for sharing their work and for responding promptly and thoughtfully to all queries, and to the anonymous reviewers for providing constructive feedback that helped shape this project. We also thank Tony Silva, the co-founding chair of the Symposium on Second Language Writing. Without his many years of hard work and mentorship, this volume would not have come into existence. Finally, we thank our families for their undying love, support and understanding. We love you, too.

The Politics of Second Language Writing

The Politics of L2 Writers
in U.S. K-12 Schools

1 Writing Development and Biliteracy

Danling Fu and Marylou Matoush

Children who immigrate to the United States and those born to recent immigrants from non-English speaking countries, like immigrants of all ages, live in the "borderlands" (Anzaldua, 1987) where two languages and two cultures come together. Such settings offer numerous opportunities to transition between languages and cultures, for immigrants find that they need to be able to move fluidly from one group or situation to another without significant misunderstanding or loss of identity. The fact that over one half of the world's population is bilingual (Kohnert, 2004) suggests that bilingualism not only helps serve transitional needs but that becoming at least partially bilingual is not as overwhelmingly difficult or potentially confusing as one might suspect. Further, the fact that the acquisition of a second language has historically been a mark of erudition among the educated elite suggests that, at some level, bilingualism is a socially and culturally desirable goal. Despite this, in the United States bilingualism represents, at best, a necessary but mostly transitional state for those who cannot be counted among the socially or academically privileged. The political push for "English Only" in the U.S. obliterates many opportunities. It not only affects most new immigrants at the personal level but also serves to place them at a distinct linguistic and cultural disadvantage by determining the nature of the educational programs that serve children in American schools across the country.

This strong differential in language status between official and subordinate languages that currently exists in the U.S. often carries direct consequences particularly for low-income speakers of the subordinate languages (Tse, 2001). Opportunities for educational success, economic advancement, and sense of self worth as an "American" must be weighed against keeping open lines of communication with one's immediate or extended family, neighbors, and cultural affiliates. Because the majority of immigrant children come from low-income families, most have little choice but to adopt English as their language of preference if they hope to flourish in this country. Further, although first generation immigrant children may find themselves serving as bilingual translators for their parents, neither they nor their children are apt to be afforded the opportunity to further develop their native language skills beyond those required by domestic situations and so a shift to monolingual English within the first three generations is prevalent (Anderson, 2001; Tse, 2001). The current demand for new immigrant students to pass the same standardized tests as their native-English speaking peers after one (Florida) or three years (New York) in the country pushes these students into English monolingual status, which results in an ever faster loss of their primary language.

Over the past two decades the number of English language learners (ELLs) in the U.S. over the age of five has grown from 23 million to 47 million, or by 103 percent (U.S. Census Bureau, 2003). In fact, in the U.S. one out of every five students (20 percent) resides in a home in which a language other than English is spoken. By the year 2030, this number is expected to double to reach roughly 40 percent of all students. Because educational advancement in the U.S. is closely tied to English proficiency, students from linguistically and culturally diverse backgrounds are approximately three times more likely to be low achievers than high achievers and two times more likely to drop out than their native-English speaking peers (The Urban Institute, 2005). Such data alert educational researchers to the urgency of the need for exploration of effective instructional approaches designed specifically to accommodate the unique needs of this ever growing and very diverse population. However, research as well as research funding for studies pertaining to diverse English language learners remains severely limited. The ratio of studies about diverse learners in special education compared to that of studies about diverse English language learners is an alarming 108:4 (Ame, 2004).

Research on writing development from first language to English among nonnative English speaking students is sparse. Writing, because of its association with high status academic pursuits, is often taught formally with an emphasis on the distinct, abstract, decontextualized formal properties of correct written English. As a result, limited English proficiency is often associated with deficits and the need for remediation. For this reason, most ESL programs in the United States focus their instruction on grammar skills, vocabulary building, content reading, or speaking and listening. Little attention is paid to writing development and a focus on writing as a tool for thinking and communication among English language learners is a rarity. This focus on the surface structure of English may lead to ELLs' achieving enough English proficiency to compose proper English sentences in correctly formatted monolingual papers, but it does not support them as competent writers and thinkers who are able to draw upon their vast array of sociolinguistic, sociocognitive, and sociocultural understandings to satisfy their communicative, intellectual, or social needs. However, when ELLs, especially those enrolled in the transitional bilingual and ESL programs, are made to quit writing in their first language to demonstrate proficient standard English, their development as individuals who are able to make flexible use of written language as a tool for thinking and expressing themselves is often hindered.

This study examines the transitional moves in the writing development of Chinese speaking students enrolled in a New York Chinatown middle school and discusses their use of codeswitching and language mixing in light of this difficult situation. It illustrates that writing development among students already literate in subordinate languages takes place in roughly four transitions as the students move from first language to accomplished second language usage. We argue that these transitions—which can be identified as moving from "First Language Usage" to "Code-Switching" to "Trans-Language Usage," during which English words appear in the native language syntax, and finally, to "Approaching Standard English"—not only represent a natural route to contextualized English proficiency, but reflect sociolinguistic performances that can be associated with biliteracy.

Background

There is a lack of research on the transitional moves of English language learners in their writing development from their first language to English. While this lack of research may be attributed, in part, to a lack of foresight with respect to issues relative to the rapid burgeoning of a subordinate language speaking population, it may also be attributed to a set of beliefs that Luis Moll (2001) calls "official nationalism" (p. 13), for the idea that the United States must remain monolingual in order to maintain its identity and coherence appears to prevail and is reflected in our educational policies. As a result, even those few programs that are purportedly bilingual have English proficiency rather than bilingualism as their goal (Crawford, 2004; Moll, Saez, & Dworin, 2001).

Although long-term (6 to 12-year) bilingual or dual language programs are more effective for supporting the academic achievement of English language learners (Tomas & Collier, 2004), over 90 percent of the bilingual/ESL programs in New York City are transitional ones. This means that after two or three years in ESL or transitional bilingual programs, ELLs are expected to be tested out and then be mainstreamed into regular classrooms. Yet, not only are such test results suspect (Crawford, 2004), but according to Thomas and Collier (1987) it takes at least two or three years for ELLs to develop their communicative language proficiency (CLP) and five to seven years to develop their cognitive academic proficiency (CAP), in part because academic language is more abstract and less closely tied to familiar contexts.

In other words, although there is a great degree of between-child and within-child variation, academic language development usually takes approximately twice as long as conversational language development. Yet, children are placed in transitional programs that are predicated on the idea that they will acquire academic language and knowledge at approximately the same rate as it would ordinarily take them to become conversationally fluent. Supportive services are often withdrawn when students have reached conversational fluency, but not necessarily academic parity. Schools that rely on such practices not only underestimate, but restrict cognitive and academic growth among ELLs, yet it seems unlikely that this situation will change in the near future (Crawford, 2004, Cummins, 1981, 1993; Thomas & Collier, 1997).

Crawford (2001) emphasized that the Improving America's Schools Act of 1994 included proficient bilingualism and biliteracy and so officially cracked open the door for the more equitable education of subordinate language speaking students. Unfortunately, as Crawford (2001) also pointed out, subsequent *No Child Left Behind* legislation once again slammed that door shut by eliminating bilingualism and biliteracy as goals and by narrowing the focus to academic outcomes on standardized tests, thereby situating bilingualism as a deficit condition requiring remediation.

A remaining possibility for changing subordinate language knowledge from a deficit condition to an asset leading to potential bilingualism resides in the contextualization of language and literacy acquisition in terms of previously acquired "funds of knowledge" (Moll, 2001). There is evidence that each of us acquires such funds of knowledge as we go along immersed in language-saturated environments. Tomasello (2000) attributed language learning to a compelling need to understand the communicative intent of others within the context of daily life. Krashen (2003) pointed out that humans "pick-up" language without necessarily being aware that we are doing so in the course of describing the acquisition-learning hypothesis. He acknowledged that language can be consciously learned, but stated that "research strongly supports the view that both children and adults can subconsciously acquire . . . both oral and written language" (p. 1). Taken together, the views of these two theorists suggest that humans naturally acquire language in compelling social contexts. This phenomena was observed in two girls as they became literate in two languages "without formal instruction in *both*" (p. 99). Reyes (2001) dubbed it "spontaneous biliteracy" and contrasted it with "sequential biliteracy" (p. 97) or the successful use of first language and literacy knowledge as an aid to literacy learning in a second language.

Reyes's observations of these two children led her to question the idea that biliteracy must be sequential; an idea that Reyes attributes to Cummins (1981) has been largely undisputed for two decades. Her question leads us to examine existent prohibitions against encouraging children to move flexibly between languages utilizing whatever funds of knowledge they have previously acquired. While Cummins's ideas concerning "sequential biliteracy" justify bilingual or dual language programming based on the abstract and decontextualized nature of academic language, "spontaneous biliteracy" serves to justify biliteracy based on prior contextualized social knowledge as a legitimate goal. By that we mean that spontaneous, idiosyncratic experimentation or problem solving with the lexical or semantic aspects of two languages, and possibly with their syntactic aspects as well, seemingly arises from a child's "funds of knowledge" about language and literacy (Moll, 2001, p. 18).

Young, "spontaneously biliterate" children, such as those observed by Reyes (2001), and older, "sequentially biliterate" students, such as those observed in the course of this study, both demonstrate idiosyncratic experimentation with various aspects of two languages in the form of codeswitching and/or language mixing. This finding suggests that rather than being simply evidence of a deficit, or a source of potential confusion between languages, such activity may represent a natural manifestation of the type of cognitive, linguistic, and social flexibility necessary for active and empowered borderland exchanges, for "code choices are not just choices of content, but discourse strategies" (Meyers-Scotton, 1993, p. 57).

> . . . studies have shown that code switching by fluent bilinguals is rule-governed and is used in a highly controlled way. It is used to convey subtle meanings, to show identification with speakers of the other language, and to accommodate the listeners. It is also used as an indicator of dual identity. Code switching is often evidence of linguistic creativity and sophistication and it is no cause for alarm. (Cloud, Genesse, & Hamayan, 2000, p. 63)

Becoming bilingual and biliterate is much more complex than simply learning to speak, read, and write in two languages. It not only involves a transformation process that appears to require a greater degree of cognitive, social and linguistic flexibility than monolinugalism, but also potentially affords a greater degree of cognitive, social and linguistic freedom of choice. We would argue that it is questionable to deny bilingual children the opportunity to learn how to take advantage of their previously acquired linguistic funds of knowledge in ways that will enhance both language acquisition and cultural understandings because of political bias. Denying them learning opportunities that ultimately provide them with voiced opportunity seems tantamount to discrimination of a most insidious kind.

Research Methodology

This research is on ELLs' writing development. It was part of a longitudinal study along with a professional development project which took place from 1997 to 2002 in a New York Chinatown middle school that housed 1,400 mostly Chinese students from 6th to 8th grade, 43 percent of whom had lived in this country for two years or less. The professional development project was designed to promote reading and writing workshops for the newly arrived ELLs and the research question came first from the concerns raised by the school ESL faculty: "How can we let ELLs write to express, to communicate and to present their knowledge to read for meaning when they haven't developed basic English language skills?" The researcher, who was also a literacy consultant, worked side by side with classroom teachers to search for effective ways to help ELLs develop as readers and writers while developing their English language skills.

This kind of research is defined as scholarship of engagement (Boyer, 1996). Rather than going to a setting with specific research questions and purpose, the researcher, who was first invited as a staff developer, helped the school make changes or reform the existing programs for improving newly arrived ELLs' school achievement. With the support of school administrators, the researcher worked closely with the school faculty in search for effective ways of teaching through her involvement as a participant observer. She observed the teaching, working with students, communicating with parents, debriefing and planning with teachers and meeting with faculty and administrators as a whole. Instead of remaining an outsider or objective researcher, she actively participated in the process of school improvement, which started with individual teachers with the understanding that what was tried successfully would be promoted school-wide. This kind of research represents an innovative way for a researcher and teacher-educator to engage in helping schools improve instruction, while concurrently conducting research, currently a highly recommended tactic that fosters scholarship of engagement in the field of teacher education (Boyer, 1996).

Research questions arose from the challenges teachers experienced in the course of trying out novel strategies and new approaches. Through carefully observing teaching and learning, and examining the students' backgrounds as well as the existing program, the researcher helped teachers more closely examine their students' progress as writers, revise their teaching, and search for ways to meet the needs of diverse learners. In addition to collecting student's work in each ESL and bilingual classroom in which the researcher worked, all the teachers with whom she worked were contributors of data collection. They constantly shared with her their students' information, descriptions of learning behavior, or examples of their students' work, some of which puzzled them with challenging issues and others of which demonstrated the success of their instruction.

Data were categorized, coded, and analyzed according to the following questions, which came from the challenges the ESL and Bilingual teachers encountered when they taught their ELLs to write for expressive and communicative purposes:

- How can ELLs write before they master basic English language skills?
- How long should ELLs continue to write in their first language?
- When should they be helped to make transitions from their first language to English writing?
- What would the transitional stages of ELLs' writing development look like?
- How should each transitional stage be assessed in ELLs' writing development?
- How can we, ESL and bilingual teachers, help ELLs develop academic English proficiency effectively through writing within the limitation of a transitional ESL and bilingual program?

Research Findings

Four Transitional Stages

This research on ELLs writing development illustrates that students spontaneously demonstrate roughly four transitions as they move from first language to accomplished second language usage. These transitions are identified as moving from "First Language Usage" to "Code-Switching" to "Trans-Language Usage" and finally, to "Approaching Standard English" (see Figures 1 to 4). The transitions ELLs make in their writing development parallel the process used by people acquiring a new spoken language. For example, when we travel abroad we often use one or two words we know, or speak the local language mixed with English words and attempt to speak any way we can to make ourselves understood. In that situation, speaking a broken language is much better than only using gestures or being mute, which represents an initial step in language acquisition. That is how we acquire spoken

Writing Development and Biliteracy

language and use language for genuine communicative purposes. The results of this study suggest that that is also how ELLs acquire the communicative ability in written language.

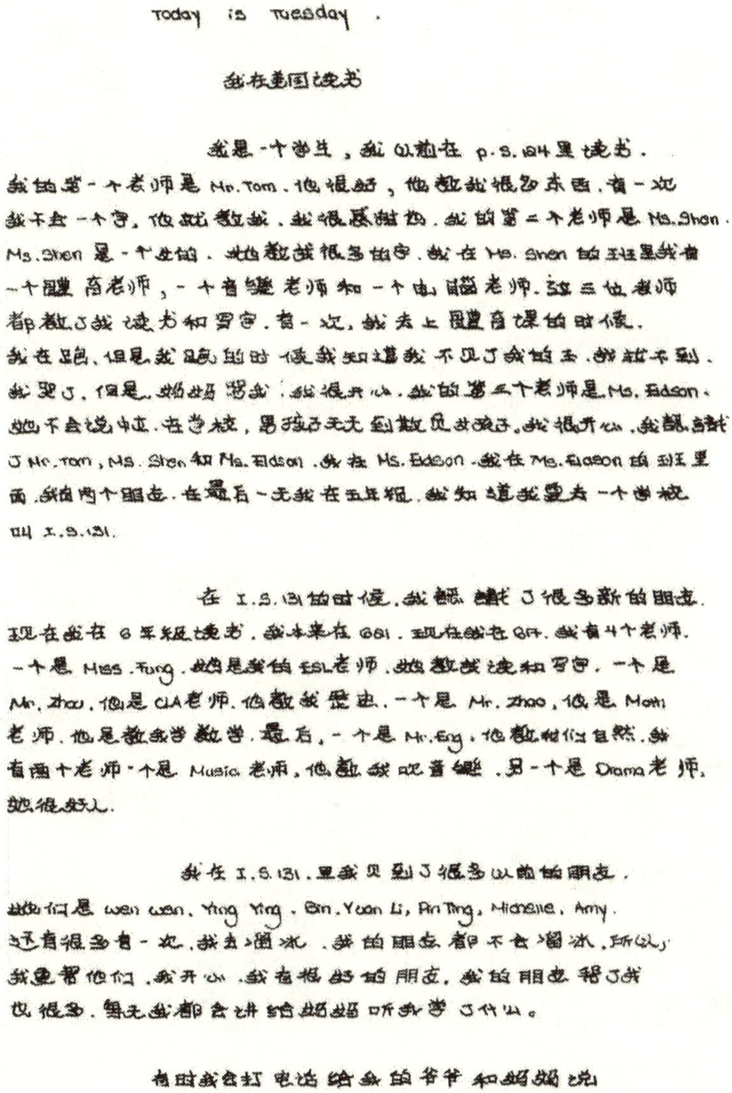

Figure 1.

Today is Firday, I in Home 来 到 School. 到 了 School, I 坐 in chair 等 teacher. Teacher 来了, I 就 go 排队.

到了班上, teacher 叫 I and Lin Ge go computer 里 听 English, I and Lin Ge 就 坐 in chair up 听.

过了one儿, teacher 叫 We go 排队. We 就 go 排队, teacher 就 带 We go computer 室.

到了computer室, We two 个 two 个 the 进 go. Teacher 就走了, computer teacher 教 We 打 computer.

到了Ten点Ten分, teacher 来 接 We. Computer Teacher 叫 We 把 computer 关上, 然后 one 个 one 个 the 走 出去, teacher 叫 带 We 回到 班 上.

到了班上, I go 跟 teacher talk. Ms. Huang class, teacher talk Yes. I and Lin Ge 就 go Ms. Huang class.

到了 Ms. Huang class, I 就 把 Yesterday 借 the book 放 in box. 然后 坐下来 听 Ms. Huang talk, Ms. Huang talk 完后, Ms. Huang get We one 张 纸 里 写着 Family, 还有画. 然后 又 ger one 张,

Figure 2.

"My friend in America"
in my school still this and my very good friend. He is my in school pass January only friend. in school he and me inseparable friend. we is same class schoolmate. he name is Li yau. he English compare good. My incapable make homework time. Li you teach my make home work. go home, Li you and my piece play basketball. every day we city piece go play. sometimes we play electron. sometimes we be park play got. we be piece very happy. he is my best friend

Figure 3.

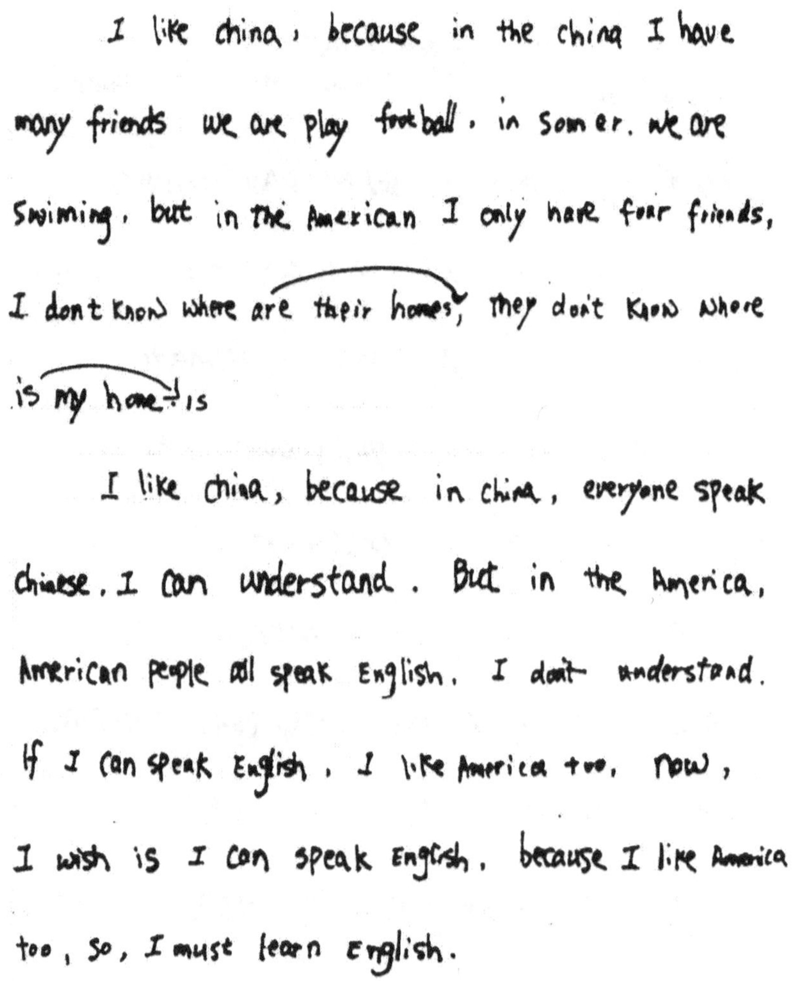

> I like china, because in the china I have many friends we are play football. in som er. we are swimming. but in the American I only have four friends, I don't know where are their homes, they don't know where is my home is
>
> I like china, because in china, everyone speak chinese. I can understand. But in the America, American people all speak English. I don't understand. If I can speak English, I like America too. now, I wish is I can speak English. because I like America too, so, I must learn English.

Figure 4.

Most of our ELLs in the school worked hard in their learning and were eager to become readers and writers in English. They knew that their ability to make it in this new world depended on the development of their English language skills. Though they were given freedom to write in their first language in both their ESL and bilingual classes, they chose to express themselves in English whenever they could. Teachers also felt the pressure. While we do not doubt that long-term bilingual or dual language programs are more effective for literacy achievement for ELLs, in our Transitional Bilingual programs, the teachers constantly face the challenge of helping their ELLs to make effective transitions from their learning in the first language and to develop both communicative and academic English proficiency within two to three years. It is important to recognize that nearly all ELLs live in and are schooled in a dual language environment. They use their first language at home, among their peers, in the community and in their bilingual classes. They learn English at school and live in our English-dominant world. Living in a dual language environment, it is natural for them to code-switch in their daily conversation and writing. Recognizing this, in our transitional bilingual program, the teachers introduced English terminology, vocabulary and phrases while teaching ELLs content knowledge in their first language. Then, teachers welcomed the use of English words and phrases in the ELLs' first language dominant-writing and accepted code-switching or the mixed usage of both languages (see Figure 2). Teachers believed this not only helped students develop their English language skills, but encouraged the development of the social, cognitive, and linguistic flexibility associated with bilingualism.

We found that the eleven- to thirteen–year-old new ELLs code-switch naturally as soon as they learn some English vocabulary. They sometimes found that it was easy to use English words to express their life experiences in this country. Those words or phrases tend to be ones that have more condensed or more general meanings in English, such as "shopping," "have a party," and "uncle or aunt," or new concepts such as "yard sale" and "flea market." The translation of these words into Chinese either would require rather complicated language and the loss of general meaning (e.g., Chinese has words meant to specifically distinguish between various paternal or maternal "uncles" and "aunts") or might lead to the loss of the original flavor of words and phrases, such as "yard sale" or "flea market." Such usage not only reflects rather sophisticated bilingual understandings pertaining to each language but can also lead to insight concerning the importance of word choice and the special voice a language/culture contains.

At some point, syntactic transformations, like lexical ones, are evident in the students' writing. Often their written English sounded "broken," because English words were used in the syntax of the native language (see Figure 3). This trans-language transformation signals that the writers or speakers usually think in their first language and translate the meaning into English, and the word-for-word translation can sound foreign to English-speakers. All language learners go through this stage before they develop fluency in a new language. As ELLs' writing develops from the first language to English, teachers should accept and value this necessary transition and natural developmental stage, rather than looking at it as deficit or incorrect usage of English language.

Nonlinear Patterns of Development

When we talk about development or use words "stages" or "transitions," it is easy to interpret the movement as linear and to assume that all ELLs develop as writers from their first language to English along this linear pathway. However, as we looked at the students work holistically, we found this was not true. Using the students' writing as data there is a strong indication that their progression from the first language to second language usage is not necessarily linear as the four transitional stages appear. In writing, when we stress on content more than language usage, students move back and forth among the four transitions depending upon the complexity of the topics and their particular communicative strengths and needs.

Let's look at specific examples of student work on the topic of spring (see Figures 5 to 8).

Spring

In spring, snow begins to melt, and the weather is warmer. Most time it rains, but some plants begin to grow. The grass is green, the flowers grow very beautiful. The tree's leaf is green and the tree has so many leaf.

Today it isn't rains, the sun is shinning, the weather is nice. I go to park with my sisters, in the park some old men sit on the chair and play chess, some children are plant flowers and trees. In the park has many things to play, but I don't play in there because I have to learn how to plant flowers. I like the flowers in spring.

In China, my sister planted many kinds flowers. There are many kinds of flowers. there are rose, daffodil, lily, and pansy in the garden. Some flowers are bud and some flowers are bloom. When the flowers are bloom, it is beautiful.

Figure 5.

Writing Development and Biliteracy

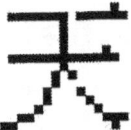

在春天,那美麗的花來,孩子他們也在公園玩,人人穿著衣服也變成更少的,多數的鳥也飛來,天空也變成藍色當時的時間真正的熱的,那天空的太陽真正的熱的,美麗的花來蝴蝶也飛來,人人 快樂的去玩,學校也 放孩子他們不去學校,

Spring

When the spring is come the beautiful flowers are come and the children who play in the park to play and the people who wear the less clothes and many birds come and the school are close and children who do not go to school and people who was very happy that are go to play because in summer people who play in the beach.

Figure 6.

Spring is the first 季节 of a year, the spring make the mother earth. When the spring was come there have the beautiful flowers and the 翠绿的 tree and it also have the 快乐的 birds come back to our city, and everyday we can hear the bird singing and the cat dancing and dog 蹦蹦跳跳 . When we go outside we can 眺望着 the tree and the flower that 迎风摇摆 are in the sky and the spring make us very happy.

Figure 7.

C1A

Spring

　　春天到来了，大地到处都充满了生气。早晨，我刚刚下床，睁开眼睛一看，一切都好像刚刚睡醒似的，欣欣然，张开了眼。河里的水涨得满满的。小鱼在水里游来游去，好像在说："春天到来了，春天到来了！"

　　走过一些，一棵棵苹果树对挺立在地面上，苹果树上的叶子经过春雨的清洗后，好像显得一尘不染。

　　再走过一些，湖边的柳树也经过春雨的清洗后，叶子也一尘不染。柳树的枝上长绿油油枝芽，一阵春风吹来，把柳树吹得一摆一摆，好像在欢迎春天的到来而遍遍地舞。

　　湖里的荷花长得非常美丽，像一顶顶帽子那样。湖里的青蛙在荷花里跳来跳去，好像在开心地跳舞。

　　又走过一些，到了马路上，一眼看去是绿油油的稻田，老战青树尤，农民都忙忙碌碌地插林。

　　再走过一些，是一望无际的森林，森林里的树都随春雨的冲洗下，长得非常之绿和非常茂盛。

　　最后走一些，是一条村庄，村庄的屋在春雨的冲洗下，变得一尘不染像刚刚建成的。

　　啊！春天真美呀！
　　我爱春天。
　　我更爱春天的景色。

Figure 8.

These are samples of the ELLs writing about spring in four various language styles: in only English; in English with Chinese characters; in two languages; and in Chinese. It is easy to determine that the students who wrote in Chinese were those with the least English proficiency. Yet, according to the teacher, many of the students who wrote in Chinese were able to write equally well in English, and a few even had better English proficiency than those who chose to write in English. When we saw the level of the Chinese writing among the students' work, we realized that the reason that many of the students chose to write in Chinese was that they were unable to express themselves as they wanted to in English. Here is the translation of one example of the Chinese writing pertaining to spring.

Spring

Spring has arrived,
And the world is filled with a
New sense of life.
Every morning,
I awake and open my eyes,
Just as this world opens its eyes.
I stroll through apple trees,
So stiff and rigid,
Its leaves cleansed of all filth
By the brisk spring showers.
As I walk further,
I pass willow trees by a lake.
The spring rain also falls on them,
With their dustless leaves
And shiny green buds.
Their branches waft,
Riding the warm spring wind,
Acting as if they are dancing
A welcome jig for spring
And in the lake,
There are beautiful lotus flowers
Each wearing its pretty bloom hats,
Frogs jump to and fro amongst them,
Seemingly dancing free from care.
And even further,

I arrive at a road,
I look up and catch a green vastness
Of rice patties,
Sprinkled with farmers,
Busily planting this time of year.
As I continue my journey,
I wander to some edgeless woods,
The trees there appear sturdy and healthy
After a brisk Spring shower,
At last,
I arrive at a village,
Where houses are rinsed by Spring rain,
So that they look as if they've just been built.
Ah, the beauty of Spring!
I love Spring,
But even more so the beauty it brings.

It was obvious that, the reason that this writer chose to write this poem in Chinese was that he was unable to express himself in English with the same level of sophistication that he could in his native language. His spring fever definitely took him back to his home village in China through this poem and the images that he expressed in the poem undoubtedly came to him in Chinese.

Looking through the students' writing portfolios, we discovered nonlinear pattern in the writing collections of other students. At the beginning of the year many students started writing in English and that writing was close to standard English. These pieces were about topics related to what they had learned and enjoyed most during the previous year and what they had done during the summer. As the school year moved on, they were assigned to retell and summarize their readings and to make comparisons between the topics under study. For example, they were asked to compare the Revolutionary War with the Civil War. As the writing topics became too complicated for them to express themselves adequately in English, the students chose to write in their first language. Some even wrote their reading responses in Chinese to the English books they read, indicating that they'd understood what they'd read but that their receptive abilities in their new language exceeded their expressive skills.

The work of these students illustrates that once we give them freedom and value in whatever language they would like to use to express themselves, or when they realize our emphasis is on what they say rather than only using English correctly, they would focus their attention on the content and ideas in their writing rather than correct usage of the new language. Students usually know what teachers expect them to do, depending upon how we value their work and how we teach them to write. As a matter of fact, when the students are encouraged to and therefore willing to choose language usage based on how they feel able to express themselves, it is a very good sign. Making use of such freedom of choice means that their focus is on the deep structure of their writing, that the ideas they want to express take precedence over the simple use of a second language for the sake of practicing it.

Close Observation of Transitional Moves

Expecting ELLs to move only forward in a linear manner is counter productive if we hope students to grow in their understandings of biliteracy. Unfortunately, transitional moves are often identified as incorrect usage and seen as deficits, deficiencies, or limited proficiency in English language learners. We tend to, or often are advised to, only teach ELLs to write in Standard English. This is similar to forbidding children to use invented spelling or nonstandard dialects during the writing process despite the fact that "according to linguists no language or dialect is inherently better or worse than others" (Tse, 2001, p. 41). If we don't value what and how ELLs write in the transitional stages, but only aim at teaching them to write correctly or learn Standard English, these students won't develop into writers with depth of thinking and logical thought. Even when their English becomes proficient, few of them would have confidence as writers of English, which may mean that on the surface they may speak correctly, or closely resemble their English-speaking peers, but they may lag behind in their overall literacy skills, as thinkers, writers and readers. We have to look at all their work as a whole to gain a deep understanding of the semantic choices that they have been able to make in terms of the lexical and syntactic insights they develop.

To effectively guide ELLs' writing development in a new language, teachers need to learn to assess their students' work from a developmental perspective, attempting to see the logistics behind language errors (Shaughnessy, 1977) and understand the conceptual, linguistic, and social nature of transitions from one language to another. We need not only to legitimate each transition in the development but also to provide support and guidance to enable the students to develop their writing skills in each transitional stage so that they can move fluidly between stages in the name of bilingualism and biliteracy rather than simply aiming for correctness of English language usage.

The teachers in the school where this study was conducted not only provided time, choice and guidance in helping their ELLs develop their writing competency and skills in English but also worked to understand the logistics behind the "language errors" made in the transition from one language to another and to see them not as "errors," but to value them as the precursors of flexible dual language word choice and phraseology. Armed with such understandings, they knew better how to guide ELLs, when to push them to the next level, what specifically to teach them, and when to leave them alone to continue their own language explorations so that they might gain an appreciation of bilingual and biliterate practice as an enriched state to be valued and enjoyed.

With this practice and appreciation of the students' biliteracy, our ELLs were gradually approaching writing in Standard English through the use of biliterate transitions during frequent practice in writing and reading in both languages. Many are able to reach this point within one year, although some took two to three years according to their previous educational background and their first language literacy level. Hopefully, by recognizing the natural transitions that students make and by actively encouraging the bilingual interplay of language we will help not only ELLs but also policy makers and educational researchers begin to recognize the advantages of biliteracy.

Implications for Further Research

The development of a body of research pertaining to bilingual writing development is of utmost importance. For, according to social-psycholinguistic theory, we learn the culture the language carries with it as we acquire a new language. When we learn to speak or write with a new tool, we transform ourselves not only linguistically but conceptually. We learn not only the new words and expressions, but the new ways with those words and new meanings carried through them and embedded within them. On both surface and deep levels, we are different speakers and thinkers when we speak a new language.

In this sense, we should explore further what the "bi" in bilingual and biliteracy really means at all levels of language or literacy proficiency. We need to explore the transitions between languages, and between languages and literacy, with a focus on biliteracy rather than simply on English language acquisition. The latter often results in a discontinuity of the first language development in reading, writing, and speaking. There are undeniable differences in the learning needs of ELLs who are literate in their first language and those who are not. We need to explore the differences that promoting the utilization of previously acquired funds of oral language knowledge might make within children as well as between children. We need to explore those differences with an eye to acknowledging the advantages of biliteracy as the more empowering outcome.

Implications for Instruction

We understand the bilingual educators who recommend strict separation of language usage in long-term (6 to 12 years), one-way or two-way bilingual or dual language programs. Their fear of weakening subordinate language learning as the dominant language takes over and is understandable when viewed from the luxurious position of programming aimed at the maintenance of the equal development in two languages. The view that language programs should systematically and forcefully protect the subordinate language is one with which we concur. Yet, the opposite effect is caused by a strict separation of languages in ESL/bilingual transition programs where English proficiency is the goal in academic settings and subordinate language speakers experience increasingly narrow opportunities to develop their native language skills. This is attested to by the language loss across the first generations of immigrants in the U.S., who are considered by schools to be "English language learners" rather than speakers of other languages who are in the process of becoming bilingual.

We also agree that ELLs should be encouraged to write in their first language, for writing contains a deep structure activity that involves thinking. However, if we hope to protect subordinate languages and to promote biliteracy, we must plan the writing programs across the subject areas and to encourage writing development as bilingual thinking. Restricting students to writing in their limited English, or forbidding them to code-switch in their writing (in either their first language or second language writing) prevents them from fully expressing their thoughts and emotions. When this happens, not only does writing become a frustrating activity but students will begin to conceive of writing as useful only for language practice. Young adult learners, in particular, are easily bothered by language practice in basic forms that does not enable them to express themselves and communicate with others. Writing must be acquired within the context of students' current "funds of knowledge" (Moll, 2001) if it is to be understood as a tool for thoughtful communication. We can help students express themselves in meaningful ways by valuing moves back and forth between languages according to the complexity of the writing topics, the depth and fluency of what the writers want to say with their writing, and their need to develop understandings via language interplay. We can help them recognize the advantages of biliteracy, and, as they learn to value each language for its unique characteristics, we can help them recognize the value of word choice and voice. When we stress thinking, content, and ideas rather than language practice in students' writing and allow them to move back and forth between languages until they are able to express what they want to say properly in that language, they will not only gradually develop as proficient writers in conventional English but will also have the added advantage of being able to express themselves in a unique biliterate voice.

REFERENCES

Ame, C. (2004, September). Opening address. The TNC (Teaching of New Era) Second Language Learner's Conference, East Lansing, MI.

Anderson, R. T. (2004). First language loss in Spanish-speaking children: Patterns of loss and implications for clinical practice. In B. A. Goldstein (Ed.), *Bilingual language development and disorders in Spanish-English speakers* (pp. 187–213). Baltimore, MD: Paul H. Brookes Publishing Co.

Anzaldua, G. (1987). *Borderlands/La frontera: The new mestiza.* San Francisco: Aunt Lute Books.

Boyer, E. (1996). The scholarship of engagement. *Journal of Public Outreach, 1*(1), 11–20.

Cloud, N., Genesee, F., & Hamayan, E. (2000). *Dual language instruction: A handbook for enriched education.* Boston, MA: Heinle & Heinle Publishers.

Collier, V. (1987). Age and rate of acquisition of second language for academic purposes. *TESOL Quarterly, 21,* 617–641.

Crawford, J. (2004). *No child left behind: Misguided approach to school accountability for English language learners.* National Association of Bilingual Education. Retrieved May 21, 2006, from http://www.nabe.org/documents/policy_legislation/NABE_on_NCLB.pdf

Cummins, J. (1981). The role of primary language development in promoting educational success for language minority students. In California State Department of Education (Ed.), *Schooling and language minority students: A theoretical framework* (pp. 3–49). Los Angeles: California State University, Evaluation, Dissemination and Assessment Center.

Cummins, J. (1993). Bilingualism and second language learning. *Annual Review of Applied Linguistics, 13,* 51–70.

Farnan, N., Flood, J., & Lapp, D. (1994). Comprehending through reading and writing: Six research-based instructional strategies. In K. Spangenberg-Urbschat & R. Pritchard (Eds.), *Kids come in all languages: Reading instruction for ESL students* (pp. 64-80). Newark, DE: International Reading Association.

Fu, D. (2003). *An Island of English: Teaching ESL in Chinatown.* Portsmouth, NH: Heinemann.

Gutierrez, K. D., Baquedano-Lopez, P, & Alvarez, H. (2001). Literacy as hybridity: Moving beyond bilingualism in urban classrooms. In M. Reyes & J. H. Halcon (Eds.), *The best for our children: Critical perspectives on literacy for Latino students* (pp. 122–141). New York: Teachers College Press.

Kohnert, K. (2004). Processing skills in early sequential bilinguals. In B. A. Goldstein (Ed.), *Bilingual language development and disorders in Spanish-English speakers* (pp. 77–104). Baltimore, MD: Paul H. Brookes Publishing Co.

Krashen, S. D. (2003). *Explorations in language acquisition: The Taipei lectures.* Portsmouth, NH: Heinemann.

Moll, L. C. (2001). The diversity of schooling: A cultural-historical approach. In M. Reyes & J. H. Halcon (Eds.), *The best for our children: Critical perspectives on literacy for Latino students* (pp. 13–28). New York : Teachers College Press.

Moll, L. C., Saez, R., & Dworin, J. (2001). Exploring biliteracy: Two student case examples of writing as a social practice. *Elementary School Journal, 101*(4), 435–449.

Myers-Scotton, C. (2004). *Social motivations for codeswitching: Evidence from Africa.* Oxford, UK: Oxford University Press.

Reyes, M. (2001). Unleashing possibilities: Biliteracy in the primary grades. In M. Reyes & J. H. Halcon (Eds.), *The best for our children: Critical perspectives on literacy for Latino students* (pp. 96–121). New York: Teachers College Press.

Shaughnessy, M. P. (1977). *Errors and expectations.* London: Oxford University Press.
The Urban Institute (2005). High concentration of limited-English students challenges implementation of No Child Left Behind Act. Retrieved May 21, 2006, from http://www.urban.org/url.cfm?ID=900884
Thomas, W. P., & Collier, V. (1997). *School effectiveness for language minority students: NCBE resource collection series, No. 9.* Washington, DC: National Clearinghouse for Bilingual Education.
Tomasello, M. (1999). *The cultural origins of human cognition.* Cambridge, MA: Harvard University Press.
Tse, L. (2004). *Why don't they learn English? Separating fact from fallacy in the U.S. language debate.* New York: Teachers College Press.
Walter, J. (2005). *Bilingualism: The sociopragmatic-psycholinguistic interface.* London: Lawrence Erlbaum Associates.

2 Reforming High School Writing: Opportunities and Constraints for Generation 1.5 Writers

Kerry Enright Villalva

In the literature on college composition classrooms, bilingual students who have been schooled mostly in the United States in English-only classrooms are beginning to receive more attention. These students, often referred to as Generation 1.5, present unique challenges to instructors in that they generally speak English effortlessly, particularly in informal situations, but they lack academic proficiency in English, most notably when it comes to school-based writing tasks. We know very little, however, about the schooling and writing experiences of Generation 1.5 youth before they reach the college composition classroom. Harklau (2002) describes a need in particular for "more comparative research on the differing institutional 'ecologies' of high school and college literacy" (p. 154). Although this chapter does not compare different high school settings, it does provide a detailed description and analysis of one institutional ecology, adding to the literature on secondary writing contexts for second language writers (Harklau, 1994; Valdés, 1999) and providing data for future comparisons.

This chapter presents the case of a high school classroom that appeared to be ideal for the second language writing development of Generation 1.5 students. Cerro Vista High School[1] was a reform-oriented school in the San Francisco Bay Area with policies that seemed promising for the advancement of bilingual students who were orally fluent in English but still developing academic proficiency in writing. The study described here centered on the experiences of high school seniors engaged in their senior exhibition project—a year-long research and writing project required for graduation. This chapter reports findings in response to the following research questions:

- How do different aspects of the institutional ecology influence instructional practices around writing for the senior exhibition at this school site?
- How do these systemic influences impact the writing possibilities for Generation 1.5 writers in terms of opportunities and constraints?

Case studies on the senior exhibition experiences of one transnational and four Generation 1.5 Latino students revealed how a variety of institutional policies and reform efforts impacted their second language writing opportunities and development. An ecological framework incorporates data from individual student case studies (oral and written texts, interview data, school records, observations), the focal classroom (classroom practices, curricula, teacher interviews), the school (school documents, reports, policies, reform efforts), the state (requirements for student placement, teacher licensure, standards use), and the nation (the standards movement).

Ecological Framework

This project employed an ecological framework to study the writing experiences of Generation 1.5 students and the systemic factors that influenced them. The term *ecology* implies a systematic approach to context and interdependent relationships within and among systems. The framework for this study draws from ecological theories of literacy, language acquisition, and human development. Ecological approaches to research emerged in these areas as the need to account for context in new ways became apparent. This framework is based on an understanding that literacy is social practice (Barton, 1994; Barton & Hamilton, 2000; Heath, 1983), rather than a series of psychological processes involving individuals and written texts. This framework is also grounded in an understanding of language as fluid and dynamic.

Ecological theories of language acquisition challenge many traditional assumptions in language research (Leather & van Dam, 2002a), being concerned with relationships and interactions, and with context as an object of study rather than as supporting information in a study (Fettes, 2002; Kramsch, 2002; Leather & van Dam, 2002b; van

Lier, 2000, 2002). While writing studies often explore what a person can do under particular circumstances, the circumstances themselves often are neglected. Classroom contexts, learner experiences beyond the focal site or circumstance, institutional climate and policies, and local or national politics are often excluded from such studies.

To account for these factors, some language theorists, including van Lier (2000, 2002) and Leather and van Dam (2002), draw from ecological theories in human development, particularly from the work of Urie Bronfenbrenner, who defined context as a series of nested and overlapping systems that influence the development of an individual in different ways over time. Bronfenbrenner's (1993; 1995) bioecological model seeks to explain how the development of an individual is related to a variety of contextual factors, not always within that person's direct experience. The strength of Bronfenbrenner's theory for this study is that he articulates the types of "systems" within and around a young person's experience, and this articulation of systems can support an analysis of the systemic influences on the second language writing development of students in particular school settings. See Figure 1 for an illustration of Bronfenbrenner's systems.

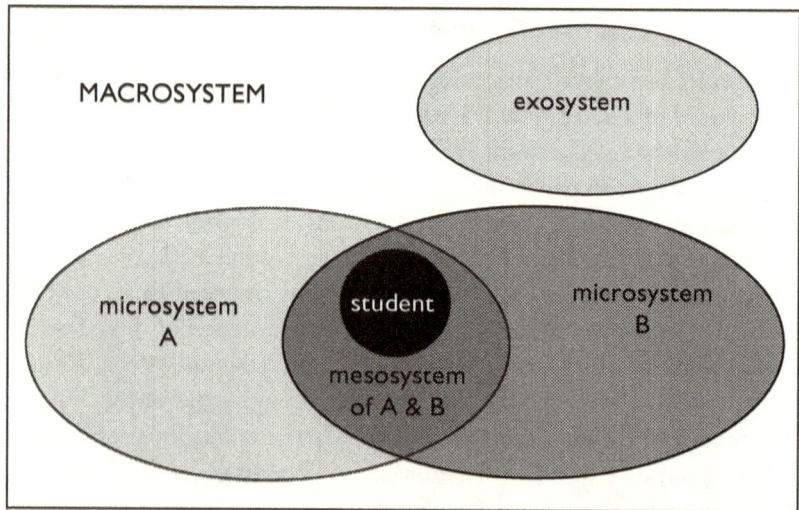

Figure 1. Ecological framework representing the experience of a student.

The system at the core of an individual's experience is the *microsystem*, a pattern of activities, roles, and interpersonal relations experienced by the developing

> person in a given face-to-face setting with particular physical, social, and symbolic features that invite, permit, or inhibit, engagement in sustained, progressively more complex interaction with, and activity in, the immediate environment. (Bronfenbrenner, 1993, p. 15)

The microsystem is at the center of the young person's immediate daily experience, such as home, or a school program. A *mesosystem* represents overlap or "linkages and processes" between two microsystems, and considers how these linkages might encourage or discourage development for the young person (p. 22). *Exosystems* consist of overlap between a young person's microsystem and a related system just outside of his or her experience, but one which has an indirect influence over his or her daily experience (p. 24), such as a parent's workplace, a sibling's friendship network, or the school district office. Finally, a *macrosystem* accounts for broader social, political, and cultural influences, and is defined as

> the overarching pattern of micro- meso- and exosystems characteristic of a given culture, subculture, or other extended social structure, with particular reference to the developmentally instigative belief systems, resources, hazards, lifestyles, opportunity structures, life course options and patterns of social interchange that are embedded in such overarching systems. (p. 25)

Bronfenbrenner's ecological perspective illustrates the dynamic fluid relationships between systems at all levels, which overlap and shift, each responding to changes in another due to their interdependence. As such, it is a useful model to describe how systemic influences can impact the writing development of Generation 1.5 writers in this study.

The Study

Data used in the analysis of this institutional ecology for Generation 1.5 students come from a more comprehensive study that examined the inquiry, understanding, literacy practices, and writing development of five Latino bilingual students and five native English-speaking students as related to their senior exhibition projects. See Villalva

(2006) for analyses of the literacies and inquiry processes of two Latina students, and Villalva (2003) for detailed case studies of two bilingual and two monolingual students. Cerro Vista was an ethnically and linguistically diverse school where white English speakers were in the majority (60 percent), but almost one in three students was from a home where a language other than English was spoken. Bilingual students were of Hispanic, Asian, Pacific Islander, and Filipino ethnicities. Two thirds of these bilingual students were still officially designated as having limited English proficiency.

This study was framed partly in response to concerns by teachers and administrators that the school-wide senior exhibition project might demand a level of skill and/or support that the school did not provide at the time to students who spoke English as a second language. The school-wide senior exhibition project was developed by a group of committed teachers to raise academic standards and avoid remediation of "at-risk" students. One of these teachers, Mr. Quinn, welcomed me into his classroom as the site for my research. Along with his involvement in institutionalizing the senior exhibition at Cerro Vista High School, Mr. Quinn was one of two teachers running the Social Action Academy, an interdisciplinary partnership involving his English classes and Ms. Hammerstein's social studies classes. Mr. Quinn was also a teacher in the AVID (Advancement via Individual Determination) program, a cohort-based college prep and study skills program for young people with potential to be the first generation in their families to attend college. Most reform efforts at Cerro Vista High School seemed to have Mr. Quinn's involvement, from conceptualization to leadership in implementation.

A connection to reform efforts was not a criterion for selection of the focal classroom in this study, however. Rather, selection was contingent upon enrollment of a cluster of Generation 1.5 Latino students. School staff sorted through demographic data to identify all seniors who spoke a home language other than English, had been enrolled in ESL classes at some point in their academic career, were currently designated as orally fluent in English, and were enrolled in mainstream classes. For the purposes of this study, these students were considered the school-wide pool of Generation 1.5 seniors. From that list, I limited the potential bilingual participants to those who spoke Spanish as a first language. Partly, I chose this population because the number of Latino students is rising significantly in U.S. schools (Waggoner,

1999), and there is a need for research that informs their unique needs. Also, since Spanish is my second language, it could help me to establish rapport with these students as well as to note features in their oral and written literacy practices that might be influenced by their native language experience and development. Five out of seven Generation 1.5 Latinos had self-selected into Mr. Quinn's English class—a class which focused on social action through an integrated curriculum with a social studies teacher and through student-designed group projects that were meant to serve the local community in some way.

Data collection for this study was conducted over the course of the 2001–2002 academic year. The breadth of school-based data, which included interviews with students, teacher and administrators, school demographic data, school handbooks and policy manuals, and classroom materials related to the senior exhibition, provided a wealth of information to examine influences at the levels of the microsystem (individual classroom and program contexts), mesosystem (interactions between microsystems), and exosystem (school policies, departmental decisions). My position at the university as the Crosscultural Language and Academic Development (CLAD) Coordinator ensured that I was aware of state policies and national priorities in education, particularly for language minority students. This allowed me to examine macrosystemic influences on the writing practices in Mr. Quinn's room as well.

Institutional Contexts: Programs and Policies

This section provides a brief description of four program and policy areas that were central to the writing experiences of Generation 1.5 students at Cerro Vista High School. I present them here in order of the breadth of Generation 1.5 students impacted by them in their senior year. They include school-wide placement policies for English language learners, a description of the senior exhibition and its history at Cerro Vista, the Social Action Academy in which all focal students were enrolled, and the AVID program. See Table 1 for a brief description of each program and its involvement of second language writers. The description of these programs sets the stage for the analysis and findings presented in the subsequent section.

Table 1. Program Descriptions and Relevance for L2 Writers

	Description	Areas of Overlap	Involvement of L2 Writers
Senior Exhibition	Year-long research and writing project required of all seniors. Culminated in a 15-page essay and an oral presentation before a panel, both evaluated by standardized rubrics.	Senior exhibition required particular strategies and heuristics taught in AVID.	All seniors were required to do a senior exhibition project, including bilingual students. Only Newcomers had flexibility in terms of process and product.
Social Action Academy	Collaborative partnership between English and Social Studies teachers with integrated curriculum focusing on social action and community service. Cohort-based, two-year involvement (junior/senior years).	Half of the Social Action students were seniors engaged in their s. Several were also enrolled in AVID. The Social Action English teacher was also an AVID teacher.	Five of the seven Latino Generation 1.5 seniors self-selected enrollment in the Social Action Academy.
AVID	Advancement via Individual Determination. Nationwide program for potential first-generation college attenders. Cohort-based three-year involvement. Focused on academic skills and college admissions.	AVID devoted some time to supporting the senior exhibition of seniors, and introduced some of the required strategies in students' sophomore and junior years.	Almost all of the AVID students were bilingual, demonstrating an unstated policy of using this program to support bilinguals who were orally fluent in English.

School-Wide Placement Policies for English Language Learners

At Cerro Vista High School, only newcomer students were in ESL (Newcomer) and sheltered content classes. Beyond the newcomer-level of English proficiency, bilingual students were integrated into mainstream classes, usually clustered within the classrooms of content teachers who had received special training in sheltered methods to adapt their instruction for these populations. This placement policy, like many of the school's reform efforts described in this chapter, suggested the belief that the school's failure of many students was the result of limited rigor in their academic experience and limited support to meet the demands of a challenging curriculum. In practice, however, teachers were accustomed to the ethnic diversity of the students at Cerro Vista but sometimes neglected to consider the linguistic diversity of the students enrolled in their classes. Although class rosters had labels articulating the proficiency level of students in the class, teachers did not always know what the labels meant since the system was not transparent.

Students were labeled N, F, L, M, or R—Newcomer, Fluent, Limited, Mainstreamed, Redesignated. As a former ESL teacher, even I needed the system explained to me several times to understand the nuances of each designation since some labels appeared to focus on language proficiency while others appeared to focus on placement type. Regardless of official label or designation, all seniors were required to successfully complete their senior exhibition projects in order to graduate, although slight modifications were made for Newcomer students.

The Senior Exhibition

The senior exhibition, or "Senior Ex," as the students called it, extended throughout the senior year and could be on any topic the student chose, pending teacher approval. Students selected a topic early in the senior year, researched it, and drafted a 15-page essay over the course of the year. The project was in its fourth year at the time of this study. It was the result of a cadre of reform-minded teachers who met regularly as a book club to reflect on works like *The Power of Their Ideas* (Meier, 1995) and *Horace's Hope* (Sizer, 1996). Ultimately, the teachers became committed to translating the ideas from their readings into new practices at their school. The same year that they approached their principal about the possibility of a senior exhibition, the social studies department decided to focus its work in the coming year on supporting students through writing and research. Conditions were right for the birth of Cerro Vista's senior exhibition project, which was implemented school-wide the following year as an integrated English/social studies project required of all seniors.

The Social Action Academy

The classroom that served as the focal site of this study was the English classroom of the school's Social Action Academy. According to the Student Handbook,

> Social Action is an interdisciplinary study of social studies and literature spread over two years, and focusing on issues of social change. Students apply to be in this academy during their Sophomore year, and will stay with the same English and Social Studies teachers during their Junior and Senior years. The curriculum meets the state, district, and school requirements for U.S. History, American Government, Economics, English 5–6 and English 7–8. . . . Students are expected to have an interest in social action and community service, and will participate and construct community service learning projects.

The academy had a total of 63 students during the year of the study. Although instruction was usually delivered in fairly traditional classrooms of 31 or 32 students, the students were clustered or divided periodically according to the instructional task at hand. At times they met as a full group of 63 to gather into social action interest groups and plan or provide updates on their service projects. Occasionally the classes were divided according to graduating class, juniors meeting with the history teacher for instruction and guidance on their required junior-year research projects and seniors meeting with the English teacher to focus on their senior exhibition projects.

AVID (Advancement via Individual Determination)

AVID is an academic support program implemented in schools internationally for young people who traditionally are underrepresented on college campuses. Students in the AVID program are recruited by school faculty and administrators based on a particular academic and family profile, targeting students who demonstrate the ability to be academically successful but might not have a family legacy of college attendance and may require extra school-based support. The program is cohort-based, and students are generally involved for at least three years. While students take a college preparatory sequence of classes, they enroll in AVID as their elective to work on study skills, academic writing, test-taking skills, and orientation to the college admissions process (AVID Center, 2006). At Cerro Vista, students in their first year of AVID were tutored by seniors who were AVID students, so there was also a sense of cross-cohort mentoring.

In the next section, I describe how each of these programs and policies influenced the instructional practices of teachers and writing opportunities of Generation 1.5 students in Cerro Vista High School classrooms. Examples from the focal classroom illustrate findings based on the research questions.

Instructional Practices and Writing Opportunities: Findings and Analysis

All of the seniors in Mr. Quinn's English class were working on their senior exhibition projects throughout the year of this study. Five of these young people were Latino Generation 1.5 students. Of these five, two were also enrolled in the AVID program. As such, it is possible to analyze how systemic influences at several levels impacted general school policies and specific classroom practices in the focal classroom. Although I use Bronfenbrenner's (1993; 1995) terms to describe interactions across levels of the students' experience with regard to writing for the senior exhibition, it is important to note that Bronfenbrenner did not conceive of his model for this type of analysis, but instead was interested in questions of human development well beyond a child's school experience. His model is still useful to help articulate the broad range of political and institutional influences on the instruction and evaluation of writing for this study, however.

Each of the findings in this section initially respond to the research question: How do different aspects of the institutional ecology influence instructional practices around writing for the senior exhibition at this school site? The findings represent three kinds of influences on instructional practices: macrosystemic influences, internal mesosystemic influences, external mesosystemic influences, and cohort-based microsystems. After each description of an influence on writing instruction, I explore its impact on writing opportunities for Generation 1.5 students in response to the question: How do these systemic influences impact the writing possibilities for Generation 1.5 writers in terms of opportunities and constraints?

Macrosystemic Influences: Standardization

A significant influence on writing instruction at Cerro Vista was the result of national and state forces—the macrosystem represented by the standards and accountability movements. This macrosystemic influence resulted in widespread standardization of writing instruction at Cerro Vista High School. In the case of the senior exhibition, it meant that all students were required to meet the same standards as defined by Expected Schoolwide Learning Results, ESLRs. ESLRs were specific outcomes based on state and national English Language Arts standards. The ESLR demonstrated by successful completion of the senior exhibition essay was entitled Effective Communicator of Oral Language, and, in the terms of its rubric, included evaluation of "Presentation" (thesis, evidence, analysis, perspectives), "Content" (language, paragraph structure, spelling, punctuation, grammar, and citation) and "Senior Exhibition" (central question, expert interview, assignment completion). For the senior exhibition essay, all 12th grade English teachers worked together to develop the rubric for the ESLR on written language (see Table 1) so that a consistent set of academic standards would be in place for all seniors. Each draft of the senior exhibition essay was returned by the student's caseload teacher with a copy of the rubric and comments about the student's progress according to these standards.

Articulation and support for these writing skills was standardized school-wide through the distribution of the Senior Exhibition Guidelines handbook, which had more than 40 pages of instructions, timelines, and examples to support students through the writing process. In the focal classroom, the handbook was used as a resource or reference but was rarely used during class lessons. Its content was consistently addressed in class, however, and was echoed in the teacher's written feedback to students on their essay drafts, as well as in writing conferences. The content in the handbook focused primarily on the timeline, elements to be included in the project, and organization of the paper. Organization, in particular, was prescriptive and was prioritized for Generation 1.5 students in the focal classroom. According to the Guidelines and the ESLR rubric, paragraphs, for example, must "consistently use topic sentences stemming from the thesis, following by evidence and analysis tied back to thesis."

Impact of Standardization on Writing Opportunities

The standardization of writing instruction presented both opportunities and constraints for Generation 1.5 writers. It promoted coherence of terms and priorities across classrooms so that Generation 1.5 writers had multiple opportunities to work towards the outcomes prioritized by the English department. For Belinda and Leesa, two focal students, this meant that they could approach English teachers other than their own and receive feedback or guidance that aligned closely with that of their current English teacher. A major constraint of this standardization, however, is that only the product was evaluated by the standardized rubric. A student's engagement in the writing *process* was excluded for the most part, beyond turning in benchmark assignments such as evidence of interviews or essay drafts. For Generation 1.5 students, this emphasis on product over process was especially problematic, since their written products often had "flaws" that became the exclusive focus of written feedback and writing conferences with the teacher. Belinda represented an example of this problem. Her struggle to organize her text became the exclusive focus of writing conferences and written feedback, leaving problems in her inquiry process and framing of argument unaddressed.

The following influences on instructional practices were the result of interactions or overlap between one microsystem of the young person's experience and another—either interactions between school programs or interactions between a school program/policy and the home.

Internal Mesosystemic Influences: Integration and Overlap between Programs

Internal mesosystemic influences were instances in which people or programs within the institution intentionally created overlap between school microsystems with a particular purpose or outcome in mind. One instance of this kind of overlap involved the integration of AVID techniques and strategies into the English and social studies curricula throughout the school. Specific writing strategies and formatting styles required in AVID became embedded in the writing instruction related to the senior exhibition. For example, the notes in the research journal that students had to submit for their senior exhibitions were required to be Cornell-style, a particular note-taking program taught in all AVID classes. Also, senior exhibition teachers taught all of their students an AVID paragraph-writing heuristic in which students typed all topic sentences in boldface, underlined evidence and analysis, and used italics for sentences that "tied back" to the thesis statement. Although not all teachers required that this format be used throughout the essay, all teachers did evaluate the use of this paragraph structure, which was explicitly noted in the ESLR rubric.

Another internal mesosystemic influence on writing instruction involved the process by which the senior exhibition became a de facto graduation requirement. To ensure that every Cerro Vista student experienced the academic rigor and long-term personal engagement of the project, key members of the English and social studies faculties decided that it must be a graduation requirement. The principal allowed the departments to integrate the senior exhibition into the curricula for social studies and English to such an extent that any student who earned below a "C" on the paper would fail both classes. As such, successful completion of the senior exhibition became a de facto graduation requirement since both classes had to be passed in order to graduate. This decision was made to avoid the necessity of seeking school board approval, a tedious and difficult process required to add "official" graduation requirements. The impact of this policy on writing instruction was significant because it transformed the senior exhibition into a high stakes project with a final grade that could determine a student's graduation date. The high stakes nature of the assignment made it essential that a student's written text meet minimum standards on the standardized evaluation rubric and became another factor that encouraged a focus on product over process.

Impact of Overlap on Writing Opportunities

The overlap between AVID and senior English classes was important in the lives of many Generation 1.5 students because these students were often among those enrolled in the AVID program. AVID makes no claims about addressing issues of second language acquisition and was not developed with immigrant students in mind. However, one young person in my study, Leesa, told me that all of the other students in her AVID class were bilingual. She could not recall having one white person in her AVID class. It appeared that Cerro Vista faculty and staff had adapted the AVID student profile in their recruitment efforts to target and support bilingual students at their school. As AVID students, Generation 1.5 students received extra support for the writing of their senior exhibition essays. They also were exposed to required senior exhibition writing strategies prior to their senior years since they were AVID strategies, and AVID classes started in their sophomore year. However, the embeddedness of AVID strategies in senior writing curricula was also problematic for Generation 1.5 students. Although the AVID enrollment profile was modified to include bilingual students, the curriculum was not adapted for attention to bilingualism and the challenges or strengths of bilingual writers. Since heuristics and other writing supports in the senior exhibition were drawn almost exclusively from the AVID program, Generation 1.5 students rarely received feedback and support tailored to their linguistic and academic experiences.

Having the senior exhibition as a graduation requirement presented writing opportunities and constraints for Generation 1.5 students. Struggling writers often are rarely enrolled in honors-track English classes in high school. Lower-track English classes often focus on discrete skills, with few opportunities for long-term research and writing projects. By having the senior exhibition as a graduation requirement, participation in this type of writing was ensured for all students, including Generation 1.5 students. The flexible topic choice meant that students from linguistically and culturally diverse backgrounds had the opportunity to choose topics of personal relevance, which made academic growth and success more likely.

However, many students and teachers focused on the high stakes nature of the assignment and imposed constraints on their senior exhibition activities to ensure success according to the rubric. For example, Belinda sought a "typical" topic that she knew many students had previously addressed successfully: the media's influence on teenage girls' body image. She was much more concerned with successfully managing the "structure" of her paper than with a coherent response to her research question. Supports embedded in the project encouraged this orientation, tending to facilitate correctness in the product more than strength of argument, as noted in the next section.

External Mesosystemic Influences: Parental Concerns

External mesosystemic influences provoked changes within the institution, but were initiated by individuals outside the institution—in this case, parents of Cerro Vista students. Many parents were incited over the imposition of a new graduation requirement and academic demand that students in neighboring schools did not face. In response to parental concerns, several supports were built in to the senior exhibition experience that impacted writing instruction at Cerro Vista.

The first change to the senior exhibition was institutional and school-wide: Cerro Vista High School changed its bell schedule from traditional 50-minute class periods to longer "block" periods with a short tutorial period built into the day for individual consultation with teachers. Every Senior English and social studies teacher became responsible for approximately 40 "caseload" students whom he or she would guide through the senior exhibition process. The following year, a curricular change was also instituted in the English and social studies courses to introduce students to the academic demands of the senior exhibition earlier in their school experience. The junior American Dream project was a small research and writing project, narrow in focus, which introduced the basic skills required in a research paper to all students in their junior year, before they reached the high stakes of the senior exhibition. The final support embedded in the senior exhibition project was the requirement that students find a mentor, preferably someone with expertise in their topic of inquiry, to support their work throughout the project. The mentor could not be an immediate family member, but no other restrictions were placed on mentor selection. Ultimately, mentors were responsible for providing feedback to students on two to three drafts of their research paper. Types of mentors and degrees of involvement varied widely.

Impact of Parent Concerns on Writing Opportunities

The concerns of parents provoked considerable institutional change at Cerro Vista High School. All of these changes resulted in greater support for Generation 1.5 students, although the potential of these supports was not always maximized. The change in scheduling and introduction of a tutorial period provided Generation 1.5 students with more opportunities to seek help if they needed assistance with some aspect of the project. Since many Generation 1.5 students were in the AVID program, they could approach either their caseloadteacher or their AVID teacher for help during tutorial periods.

Writing their American dream essays the prior year gave them the opportunity to familiarize themselves with their strengths and weaknesses related to research and writing, and they could choose a senior exhibition mentor who would be best equipped to help them with those identified weaknesses. In fact, of the five bilingual focal students, four chose teachers as their senior exhibition mentors, and three chose Cerro Vista teachers. These students had at least two, and possibly three, adults within the school who were familiar with the details of their senior exhibition projects and could provide ongoing guidance and feedback. Belinda felt that her greatest struggle was with "structure" or organization, so she chose her former English teacher as a mentor. Brenda felt that finding good research sources was her problem, so she chose her physics teacher to help her with her essay on nuclear power. Leesa knew that her greatest struggle was to stay engaged and meet deadlines, so she chose her AVID teacher, who was already a general "academic" mentor for AVID students.

Although these supports helped Generation 1.5 students throughout their senior exhibition projects, their school-wide implementation also introduced some constraints. For example, the institutionalized tutorial periods for all students school-wide resulted in senior exhibition teachers who were constantly responding to requests for guidance and feedback from a variety of students with myriad needs. There was no system in place to allocate tutorial time according to the degree or type of student need, and teachers were overwhelmed with the constant requests for help. Most of the focal students felt that more individual time from the teacher would have helped them to write a better senior exhibition paper, but the teacher simply did not have more time to give.

The mentor role also had potential that was under-explored by Generation 1.5 students. Almost all seniors used the mentor as an editor and/or writing tutor. A much smaller percentage of students sought mentors who were experts in the topic of their senior exhibition essay. Such a mentor could enrich the content of an essay, help to find sources from multiple perspectives, and introduce the student to new experiences and discourses related to a personal interest—the interest they were exploring in their project. For students whose parents were not highly educated professionals, however, it was difficult to find such a mentor within their social network; they would need someone within the school to facilitate such connections, and this did not happen often.

Cohort-Based Microsystems

Three cohort-based microsystems were part of the senior exhibition experience of many Generation 1.5 students. The senior exhibition itself made the senior year more of a cohort experience, since every senior knew that every other senior had this project in common. The Social Action Academy was also a cohort-based program, with students participating for two years, beginning in their junior year. This resulted in a spiraling of the writing curriculum, since seniors revisited writing strategies and techniques when they were introduced to the entering juniors in the academy. Seniors were expected to show greater mastery, but had opportunities to work on writing difficulties that they had discovered the prior year. AVID was also a cohort-based program with mechanisms to support the growing academic demands faced by students from year to year.

Impact of Cohort-Based Programs on Writing Opportunities

For Generation 1.5 students, cohort-based programs provided opportunities to develop their writing in ways that non-cohort programs could not. Having aspects and demands of the senior exhibition present in the everyday discourse of schooling may, in itself, have helped some Generation 1.5 students to identify some of their strengths and challenges and seek assistance when needed. Generation 1.5 students in the Social Action Academy had the added benefit of sharing English and social studies classes with seniors the year prior to their own senior exhibition experience. These students watched their classmates engage in every step of the senior exhibition process, and had the opportunity to experience a level of peer-modeling that was likely to help them the following year. The same was true of the AVID program, which involved cross-age tutoring that allowed younger students to learn from older students when they entered the program, followed by seniors taking on the role of expert as they became tutors later on.

In sum, macrosystemic influences, internal mesosystemic influences, external mesosystemic influences, and cohort-based microsystems all shaped writing instruction at Cerro Vista High School in a variety of ways. As school-wide and program-based policies made particular types of instructional practices more likely, the possibility for development and practice of academic writing by Generation 1.5 students became enabled in some ways and constrained in others.

Conclusions and Implications

In many ways, the senior exhibition at Cerro Vista High School had the potential to be an ideal context for the development of academic writing. First, the possibility for individual personalization of the project, with students selecting a topic of interest to them, seemed promising and could allow culturally diverse students to incorporate experiences and knowledge that are often neglected in school settings. The long-term engagement and multiple opportunities for feedback and revision suggested the potential for significant attention to inquiry and writing processes, rather than an exclusive focus on product. The school's attention to institutional change to support students through the project indicated a commitment not only to maintaining high standards, but also to supporting students to meet those standards. Finally, the convictions towards social justice of school leaders in the faculty and administration suggested responsiveness to the needs of students who often are neglected amidst school reform efforts. Many of the possibilities suggested by this unique context were not realized, however. Instead, they were subverted by efforts to meet minimally defined school-wide standards so that the senior exhibition would not become a gatekeeper that prevented bilingual writers from graduating.[2]

By considering how factors beyond the classroom subverted the project's purpose or otherwise interfered with teaching and learning, it is possible to suggest practical implications and directions for future research. Recommendations for practice include framing the senior exhibition as a personalized component of a larger group project, and enabling students to extend their learning beyond school. One suggestion for future research is to explore how institutions operationalize their commitment to language minority students in designing and implementing reform efforts.

Personalization within Group Membership

As noted in the previous section, cohort-based programs such as AVID and the Social Action Academy supported students as they shared experiences, purposes, and expectations. In spite of these cohort experiences, most students worked in isolation as they engaged in their senior exhibition projects, talking to other students about their projects only with regard to deadlines and the amount of work they had left to do. One student, Leesa, combated this isolation by using her senior exhibition to extend and deepen the work of her social action group community service project. She was the only group member to connect the social sction project with the senior exhibition, so interactions and crossover between the two were not systematic. However, of all ten students (bilingual and monolingual) included in the greater study, Leesa's writing demonstrated the most well-developed arguments, strongest evidence, and most attention to multiple perspectives on the topic.

If long-term writing projects like the senior exhibition were to involve individual perspectives or contributions to a greater group project, students' papers would be strengthened in several ways. Work in youth-based organizations suggests that group membership with individual contributing roles facilitates advanced language development (Heath, 2000). Group interactions around texts and ideas would be likely to promote greater depth in the ideas and content of students' work as they share resources and explore topics together. Evidence for their papers' arguments would often be stronger as students learn to contradict or challenge each other. Overall coherence of perspective and argument would likely improve as students review and respond to each others' work, since writing for an imaginary audience or an audience of one (the teacher) can be more challenging than writing for an authentic audience. For Generation 1.5 students, in particular, acquiring and practicing academic discourse on their topic of inquiry in the oral mode might facilitate academic discourse in writing as well, as each language mode facilitates the development of the other.

Extending Learning Beyond the School

The Social Action Academy and the senior exhibition project both had great potential to extend learning beyond the classroom, into or beyond the young person's community. Both projects involved contacting strangers through a variety of media, sometimes to arrange an interview, other times to submit formal requests for official action in response to a perceived need. For example, one student's social action group sought to change the name of a local park, which required navigating the bureaucracy of city government, developing petitions, and writing letters. Although the social action groups and the senior exhibition provided students with opportunities to extend learning beyond school, there were no formal mechanisms to guide that process. The degree of community involvement for social action projects varied. Many teachers hoped that students would use the senior exhibition as a chance to expand their realm of experience, but aside from interviewing two "experts" as sources for the paper, there was no requirement or built in support for extending the senior exhibition beyond the school.

The mentor component of the senior exhibition was the most promising aspect of the project to extend learning beyond the classroom. Students might use the mentor relationship as an opportunity to explore career interests, developing a senior exhibition project around future aspirations, and connecting with an adult in that field. Conversely, students with less commitment to a particular topic might connect with an adult role model and develop a line of inquiry together, as the adult mentors the student through the process. These possibilities were not realized among any of the students interviewed for this study. Instead, almost all "mentors" proved to be little more than editors of paper drafts. This was probably due in part to the timeline of the senior exhibition and sequencing of required activities. According to the calendar in the Senior Exhibition Guidelines handbook, students were required to submit their mentor data sheet in October. However, they were not required to conduct a preliminary interview with an expert in their topic until December—when their mentors were already established.

Beyond the institutionalized timeline, which limited the range of mentors that a student was likely to consider, the school had no mechanisms in place to help match students with mentors. Students with parents from professional backgrounds and an academic legacy were likely to have a range of mentor possibilities through family connections. It is not surprising, then, that four of the five Generation 1.5 students in Mr. Quinn's class chose teachers as their mentors. While it might be unreasonable to expect the school to help match every senior with a strong mentor, students with few professional connections, including many Generation 1.5 students, would benefit from having an effort coordinated by someone at the school or a community organization. For such students, the mentor relationship could be extremely powerful to socialize them into academic norms for inquiry and writing, particularly if mentors were given specific suggestions and were guided through the process as well. This would also free teachers to provide extra writing support to those who need it.

In sum, the policies and programs at Cerro Vista High School seemed to be ideal for the writing development of second language writers. Students experienced long-term engagement around a topic of personal interest, an adapted schedule, a variety of supports, and involvement in a variety of programs that seemed likely to move their writing forward. However, the ways in which national and state politics impacted local practices subverted or limited the success of these reforms. At this reform-oriented school, teachers had a great deal of input into school-wide practices, and did help Generation 1.5 students perform at the "competent" level according to school-wide writing standards. However, "competence" neglected advanced skills in argument, evidence, and global organization of their papers, instead prioritizing paragraph-level coherence and heuristics that were more appropriate for short essays.

As each of the school's reforms was developed, the unique strengths and challenges of second language writers were neglected. Second language writers, including those in mainstream classrooms, are not likely to develop advanced levels of academic writing unless standards of excellence can be locally defined with their experience, strengths and needs in mind. This requires explicit acknowledgement of various levels of systemic influence on local practices, and thoughtful informed responses to these influences so that local practices truly incorporate students' funds of knowledge (Moll, Amanti, Neff, & Gonzalez, 1992), practitioners' expertise, and the constraints and affordances of the institution.

Directions for Future Research

At the conceptual level, there is a need to more fully articulate the range of writing skills and abilities the young people must master in order to be effective academic writers of English. This represents an ongoing dilemma regarding the framing of academic English both for native and nonnative speakers of English (Valdés, 2004; Villalva, 2006). Perhaps teachers at Cerro Vista had the tendency to reduce instruction to minimal standards because those standards were the most clearly articulated and easiest to engage.

In the professional discourse at Cerro Vista High School, high standards and availability of supports were both seen by teachers as integral to the success of bilingual students. In practice, however, it appeared that faculty saw these as competing ideologies, rather than complementary aspects of an instructional program. More research is needed to understand the social, political, and institutional mechanisms that subvert efforts in schools when they attempt to integrate high standards and academic supports for language minority students. In particular, research is needed to understand how these mechanisms impact the writing opportunities and development of second language writers over the course of several years of schooling in a variety of instructional contexts, both traditional and reform.

NOTES

[1] Names of the school and study participants have been changed.

[2] This concern was borne out by the fact that one of the five bilingual focal students, Hilda, was unable to complete her senior exhibition project and did not graduate with her classmates.

REFERENCES

AVID Center (2006). *AVID: Decades of college dreams.* Retrieved from http://www.avidonline.org

Barton, D. (1994). *Literacy: An introduction to the ecology of written language.* Malden, MA: Blackwell Publishing.

Barton, D., & Hamilton, M. (2000). Literacy practices. In D. Barton, M. Hamilton & R. Ivanic (Eds.), *Situated literacies: Reading and writing in context* (pp. 7–15). New York: Routledge.

Bronfenbrenner, U. (1993). The ecology of cognitive development: Research models and fugitive findings. In R. H. Wozniak & K. W. Fischer (Eds.), *Development in context: Acting and thinking in specific environments* (pp. 3–44). Hillsdale, NJ: Lawrence Erlbaum Associates.

Bronfenbrenner, U. (1995). Developmental ecology through space and time: A future perspective. In P. Moen & J. G H. Elder (Eds.), *Examining lives in context: Perspectives on the ecology of human development* (pp. 619–647). Washington, DC: American Psychological Association.

Fettes, M. (2002). Critical realism, ecological psychology, and imagined communities: Foundations for a naturalist theory of language acquisition. In J. Leather & J. van Dam (Eds.), *Ecology of language acquisition* (pp. 31–47). Netherlands: Kluwer Academic Publishers.

Harklau, L. (1994). ESL versus mainstream classes: Contrasting L2 learning environments. *TESOL Quarterly, 28,* 241–272.

Harklau, L. (2002). The role of writing in classroom second language acquisition. *Journal of Second Language Writing, 11,* 329–350.

Heath, S. B. (1983). *Ways with words: Language, life, and work in communities and classrooms.* New York: Cambridge University Press.

Heath, S. B. (2000). Risks, rules, and roles: Youth perspectives on the work of learning for community development. *Zeitschrift für Erziehungswissenschaft, 1,* 51–80.

Kramsch, C. (Ed.). (2002). *Language acquisition and language socialization: Ecological perspectives.* New York: Continuum.

Leather, J., & van Dam, J. (2002a). Towards an ecology of language acquisition. In J. Leather & J. van Dam (Eds.), *Ecology of language acquisition* (pp. 1–30). Netherlands: Kluwer Academic Publishers.

Leather, J., & van Dam, J. (Eds.). (2002b). *Ecology of language acquisition* (Vol. 1). Dordrecht: Kluwer Academic Publishers.

Meier, D. (1995). *The power of their ideas: Lessons for America from a small school in Harlem.* Boston: Beacon Press.

Moll, L. C., Amanti, C., Neff, D., & Gonzalez, N. (1992). Funds of knowledge for teaching: Using a qualitative approach to connect homes and classrooms. *Theory into Practice, 31*(2), 132–141.

Sizer, T. R. (1996). *Horace's hope: What works for the American high school.* Boston: Houghton Mifflin.

Valdés, G. (1999). Incipient bilingualism and the development of English language writing abilities in the secondary school. In C. J. Faltis & P. M. Wolfe (Eds.), *So much to say: Adolescents, bilingualism, and ESL in the secondary school* (pp. 138-175). New York: Teachers College Press.

Valdés, G. (2004). The teaching of academic language to minority second language learners. In A. F. Ball & S. W. Freedman (Eds.), *Bakhtinian perspectives on language, literacy, and learning* (pp. 66–98). New York: Cambridge University Press.

van Lier, L. (2000). From input to affordance: Social-interaction learning from an ecological perspective. In J. P. Lantolf (Ed.), *Sociocultural theory and second language learning* (pp. 245–259). Oxford: Oxford University Press.

van Lier, L. (2002). An ecological-semiotic perspective on language and linguistics. In C. Kramsch (Ed.), *Language acquisition and language socialization: Ecological perspectives* (pp. 140–164). New York: Continuum.

Villalva, K. E. (2006). Hidden literacies and inquiry approaches of bilingual high school writers. *Written Communication, 23*(1), 91-129.

Waggoner, D. (1999). Who are secondary newcomer and linguistically different youth? In C. Faltis & P. Wolfe (Eds.), *So much to say: Adolescents, bilingualism, & ESL in the secondary school* (pp. 13–41). New York: Teachers College Press.

Appendix A

ESLR: Effective Communicator of Written Language

Presentation
Students understand and convey significant, creative, and well-developed ideas in a logical manner.

> **Exemplary Achievement**
> Thesis is insightful, specific, and unique.
> Thesis is developed in a compelling and logical manner.
> Relevant, credible, and persuasive evidence from a wide variety of sources is integrated.
> Detailed and insightful analysis of evidence is demonstrated.
> Alternative perspectives on the issue are carefully explored.
>
> **Competent Achievement**
> Thesis clearly answers the question or prompt.
> Thesis is developed in a logical manner.
> Evidence is reliable and fairly detailed. A reasonable number of resources are utilized.
> Analysis is logical and generally based on reliable evidence.
> Alternative perspectives on the issue are explored.
>
> **Evidence of Progress Exists**
> Thesis answers the question at a basic level.
> Thesis is addressed, but inconsistently and, at times, illogically.
> Evidence is sometimes of questionable reliability and depth; more sources should be used.
> Insufficient analysis, which may be based on opinion or questionable sources, is presented.
> Alternative perspectives are rarely examined.
>
> **Initial Stages of Achievement**
> Thesis is not apparent (paper is a report).
> Thesis is not logically supported by content.
> Little or questionable evidence, from few sources, is presented to support assertions.
> Analysis is largely missing.
> Issue is addressed from one point of view.

Content
Students write logically structured and coherent documents with grammatical correctness and support for opinion.

> **Exemplary Achievement**
> Information is communicated with eloquent, persuasive, and concise language.
> Paragraph structure is excellent throughout.

Extreme care is taken in spelling, punctuation, and grammar.
Meticulous source citation and credit given to others' ideas and words.

Competent Achievement

Language used is clear, organized, and appropriate.
Paragraphs consistently use topic sentences stemming from the thesis, followed by evidence and analysis tied back to the thesis.
Few errors in spelling, punctuation, and grammar.
Careful source citation and use of quotation marks.

Evidence of Progress Exists

Language is understandable, but lacks clarity and precision.
Paragraphs are sometimes poorly structured; may be lacking topic sentences, sufficient evidence, and analysis and/or tie-back to thesis.
Errors in more complex spelling, punctuation, and grammar.
Inconsistent or questionable source citations or use of quotation marks.

Initial Stages of Achievement

Language is often unclear and forces the reader to work to distinguish meaning.
Paragraphs may be lacking or are often poorly structured.
Errors in basic spelling, punctuation, and grammar.
Plagiarism or source citation/bibliography format is a problem.

Senior Exhibition

Exemplary Achievement

Answers an important question in a sophisticated manner.
Interview with expert is integrated effectively.
Complete paper turned in on time.

Competent Achievement

Answers a significant question competently.
Interview is used to bolster argument.
Complete paper is turned in on time.

Evidence of Progress Exists

Answers the question but is lacking originality and depth.
Evidence from interview is present but poorly integrated in paper.
Complete paper turned in on Friday.

Initial Stages of Achievement

Essential question is not answered.
Evidence from interview is missing or only minimally used.
Complete paper is turned in on Monday following Saturday review.

The Politics of L2 Writing Support Programs

3 The Legacy of First-Year Composition

Ilona Leki

At the Conference on College Composition and Communication some years ago, Silva (1999) argued that institutions of higher education doom first-year composition programs to fail by making writing courses compulsory, by making English departments responsible for first-year composition, by providing so little funding for the courses that they have to be staffed by indentured servants (TAs and instructors) with the least clout and, for TAs, the least experienced, by packing as many students as possible into the class, and by assuming writing gets learned in a year of first-year composition.

All these problems with the institution of first-year writing and more are part of the negative legacy that second language (L2) English writing students and practitioners have inherited and typically must live with. This is not to disparage the devoted and imaginative work done by first-year composition teachers, program directors, or L1 composition researchers. The issue is first-year composition as a (nearly) universally sanctioned institution in the U.S. As an institution, first-year composition comes complete with its sets of values and assumptions and an ability to impose those values and assumptions to some degree on the educational establishment as a whole and on units within it (Murphy, 2000, p. 30). If nothing else, as an institution within the university, first-year composition is seen by many faculty members as the repository of language correctness (Zhu, 2004) and writing teachers as even intimidating. If administrators and others at the university decline to *pay* first-year composition teachers, they certainly do not want these English teachers to catch them in spelling or grammar errors.

The existence and acceptance of first-year composition as a course required of all students and placed where it is in the curriculum has several consequences for L2 and other language minority students. The first one is a good one: that L2 writing courses exist for credit at all in universities. It is in part because first-year English courses exist and are accepted as a normal feature of the college curriculum that those who work with L2 English learners have been able to argue that there should also be courses, given for credit, to help those who are working and learning in a language that is not yet fully their own. Thanks to the existence of first-year composition, L2 writing professionals in many institutions of higher education have managed to squeeze out of universities separate sections of first-year composition for L2 students and give them credit for the courses—many institutions, but not all. In some institutions L2 students are required to take first-year composition in classes with native English speaking (NES) students, sometimes under teachers with no real awareness of L2 writing issues. The argument for this requirement rests on the notion of upholding standards; L2 students need to be held to the *same* standard as L1 students, the argument goes. Nevertheless, more fortunate programs provide at least the option of separate credit-bearing sections. But the gift of credit-bearing writing courses comes with price tags, the analysis of which forms the body of this discussion.

Writing vs. Communication

The focus of university attention in credit courses devoted to L2 English language development is relentlessly on writing rather than on any other language skill. This focus again reflects and follows the history of first-year writing in the U.S., which broke with the broader concerns of communication studies (including speaking and reading) in the 1940s, hence the vestigial bow to "communication" in the title of first-year writing's flagship professional conference, the Conference on College Composition and Communication (Crowley, 1993). The focus is also especially ironic for L2 writing since, in the modern history of language instruction in the U.S., writing was the least attended of the language skills, as it still is in much foreign language instruction (Leki, 2000). Yet now, insofar as the university is concerned, English L2 writing has become by far the most important of L2 language skills.

First-year composition cleared the way for granting credit for L2 writing but typically not for course work in any other language skills, not even in other standard literacy skills like reading or academic vocabulary building. Yet depending on their majors and their ultimate uses for English, L2 students may want and need to develop other areas of language proficiency more than they need or want to develop writing skill. The result of this one language skill becoming creditable has, thus, been the relative neglect in North American higher education of other language domains, such as speaking in particular, but also listening and even reading across the curriculum, that may be equally important in L2 students' college lives. Clearly much more than writing goes on in bilingual students' educational lives across the curriculum and interacts with literacy experiences in significant ways. Yet writing courses are required and credit courses for any language skills besides writing are nearly universally unavailable to L2 students.[1]

With writing typically the one creditable language skill, providing courses for credit that would meet L2 students' other language needs lacks institutional urgency, as illustrated in the following case from my own research. Yang, an undergraduate from China, had no trouble with the required L2 writing courses she was assigned to and in fact did quite well in all her general education courses, including history and philosophy, where she produced several short papers and essay exams. But as a student nurse, she was required to work with patients at a hospital, and her spoken English was difficult to understand, especially for sick patients at the hospital who had little experience with Chinese accents. Twice she was called into the dean's office and threatened with dismissal from the program if she did not improve her spoken English. But my institution has no credit course specifically focused on oral skill development in English, although of course it does offer credit bearing pronunciation, conversation, and grammar classes to students in, for example, French, Spanish, Italian, and Portuguese, and at a much more elementary level than Yang was capable of in English.

In response to the institutional threats against her, Yang tried to piece together what she could from non-credit classes and community classes. In the non-credit course, she learned the International Phonetic Alphabet (IPA) and repeated the professor's pronunciations in chorus with the rest of the students. But on a few occasions when she worked one-on-one on her pronunciation, she realized that what she thought were her perfect choral imitations of the professor continued to be considered quite flawed by NESs. Then she attended a community English conversation class, but because it enrolled some 15 or 20 people per class and focused on quite elementary, nonacademic language, it proved unuseful. Finally, although Yang had no interest whatsoever in Christianity or any other religion, when, as one L2 student described it, "they [proselytizers] come knocking at your door," and offered language classes, Yang attended English classes run by a local evangelizing church, although, as can be imagined, the Bible study they did there was not particularly helpful. All her attempts to improve her oral English had to be done on her own time and some required off campus transportation. Her program of study in nursing was quite time consuming, sometimes with 8–12 hour days spent at the hospital followed by hours of work at night preparing for clinicals and academic courses. Thus, not only did the university offer Yang nothing to help with her oral language development but the nursing program was set up so tightly she really had no time to pursue this improvement anyway. In the broad scheme of things, the year of first-year writing would have been better spent on oral work. But because first-year composition exists, the institution's obligation to the L2 students they admit was perceived as met with the offer of L2 writing classes.

First-Year Writing, English Departments, and Genre

Even if L2 students can, in fact, benefit from developing writing skills, they may not need to develop them along the same lines that first-year writing courses purport to develop writers. The focus in first-year writing classes is on English department genres, and L2 writing classes are often required to more or less duplicate the basic agenda of the L1 writing program. That means students typically write essays or term papers, often on topics they know little about because they are not actually studying those topics in their writing classes and are not expected to learn about them in any meaningful way beyond using them as a topic to write on. Because English department genres are privileged in these courses, even though the courses are required of students from many different majors, the institutional notion of what abilities define and undergird good writing shrinks to meet current standards of the first-year composition program, be that self-expression or rhetorical patterning or critical thinking often instantiated through analysis of pop culture or of current social issues.

In many institutions these courses are taught by former or current English majors who may well be under the impression that the narrow English department genres they are teaching are in fact universal. The arrogance that this engenders is exemplified in Atkinson and Ramanathan's (1995) exploration of the differences between writing as conceived and taught at an English language institute and in the first-year composition program at the same university. After successful completion of the ELI program, in the institution Atkinson and Ramanathan studied L2 students were then required to take and pass the first-year writing course, in principle under the same conditions as the L1 students. At the ELI the L2 students were given work in essay organization (in anticipation of their requirement to write this quintessential English department genre once they got into first-year writing) and were taught about thesis statements, topic sentences, and the five-paragraph theme, itself an artifact of previously preferred and enforced English genre requirements, however much it is currently disdained. The five-paragraph theme was in fact so disdained that teachers being trained to teach these first-year composition courses were told that students submitting a five-paragraph theme could be assumed to not have thought seriously about the topic. Thus, anyone submitting a five-paragraph theme could expect to get no better than a C-, without anyone even having read the paper. Obviously this advice or rule put the L2 students at something of a disadvantage, since the five-paragraph theme is precisely what they had been carefully instructed to create for their English writing assignments.

I would argue that English department genres have always been taught as though they defined writing, writing as self-expression, then writing as problem-solving, then writing as argument, changing from decade to decade but always serving to evaluate students by the prevailing scale at the time. Russell (2001, p. 272) notes that all disciplines behave as though their writing forms were universal. Whether or not this is true, since only first-year composition has an impact on virtually *all* students, its hegemonic bid is much more serious. Such power also elicits a certain elitist high handedness detectable in a writing assignment described in Atkinson and Ramanathan (1995). The assignment was distributed to students, carefully written out on a page or two, and included a stipulated purpose for the writing assignment, readings, background information, and instructions to select an ad and analyze the appeal the ad was attempting to make to the public. The students' writing task was described and then in the last paragraph the final commentary was:

> The cogency of your writing will depend upon your ability to identify and articulate an insightful claim as to how advertising functions. For this reason, do your best to go beyond obvious or commonplace kinds of appeals and seek instead to add something new and pertinent to our understanding of advertising. Similarly, do not focus on Virginia Slims or Marlboro ads unless you are confident you can contribute something innovative to what is a very long history of analysis. (Atkinson & Ramanathan, 1995, p. 567)

Why would L2 students (or others for that matter) be in a position to add something new and pertinent, how would they be able to tell if they were adding something new and pertinent or not, how would they know what the long history of Virginia Slims or Marlboro ads has been? More importantly, why would they care? Placed in an advertising, marketing, or journalism course an assignment like this might have some reason for being, might ask students to draw on a body of knowledge being contextualized by the course lectures and readings from the very first day of class, might be motivated by the need to learn about advertising, but this assignment appears to be motivated by the imperative of practicing a certain form of writing as an end in itself. The point of this example is not so much to criticize this particular assignment nor the program in which this writing took place but to draw attention to the sense of unreflective self-confidence evident in the writing stipulations and which, I maintain, reflect the assumption of the power to define writing.[2]

Another feature of English department genres, despite relatively recent, more skeptical accounts (Howard, 1995; Woodmansee & Janzi, 1995), is fetishizing plagiarism. It seems students are readily drawn to plagiarize in courses, such as first-year writing, in which they are asked to write on topics where they have little background information to draw on and where they have little interest in developing their knowledge on the subject—in other words, for example, arbitrary topics in compulsory writing courses. In response, a whole anti-plagiarism industry has arisen on the Internet. But there are entirely different ways of thinking about using previously written text that do not subscribe to hysteria about plagiarism. First, as many writing researchers have noted, in work environments, as opposed to school environments, texts are not typically seen as the personal creation of a single writer who has authorial say over what will be written (Dias, Freedman, Medway, & Pare, 1999). Often executive reports and technical reports are group efforts that not only include work by current employees but also draw on company archives to pilfer information or ways of saying at will. There may not even be authors' names listed; they are unimportant. What is important is that the information get to where it needs to go, into the distributed cognition of the worksite (Blakeslee, 1997; Dias, Freedman, Medway, & Pare, 1999).

Second, even in academia not all units share the first-year writing program's perennial problems with plagiarism. For example, in creating reports for her nursing courses, Yang frequently copied directly from previous reports, from the phrasing in the writing guidelines, or from the course textbook. This presented no special concern for the faculty at all. As long as the necessary material was correctly gathered, combined, and applied accurately to the analysis of the particular patient's condition, using this communal knowledge and phrasing was considered a part of enculturation into the way nurses must think and do. Nor is such an attitude limited to the nursing program at Yang's institution. Carson at Georgia State University (Carson, 2000) describes at least one psychology professor who felt that it was perfectly acceptable for students to reproduce her lecture words verbatim in their writing; she commented that after all she herself had said it best anyway.

Exams

Another legacy of the institution of first-year writing is entrance, progression, and exit exams. When they are instituted for domestic students, they are usually also required of L2 students, in a kind of misplaced sense of democracy. Although some of these exams are area exams, most of them are specifically writing exams. As such, they automatically disadvantage anyone who is still in the process of acquiring written academic English. Every flaw in the student's writing is exposed, lying on the paper for examiners to view, making the student inordinately vulnerable. Since the evaluators typically do not know the writer, they are in no position to contextualize the effort. The fear and depression that these exams engender in L2 students surfaces in resurgent threads throughout accounts by Mlynarczyk (1998) and Sternglass (1997), but in the name of standards, the tests go on; given current federal administration attitudes, the climate for this kind of testing has become even more favorable.

But why should the university studies or the degree of an L2 learner be held ransom because the student's writing is considered not up to some standard? Why is writing so privileged? We do not force this type of conformity on people's ability to give oral presentations or PowerPoint presentations or make websites, to name a few skills that could also be conceived of as part of a college education. Few, if any, institutions prevent students from graduating with a college degree because they never passed a public speaking course.

But in what way is first-year composition to blame for entrance, exit, and progression exams? The answer lies in the realization that these exams are intimately intertwined with first-year writing courses. The exams focusing on writing and the courses focusing on writing work together to index the singular importance of writing. In a conundrum like a mobius loop, we view writing as so important that we must devote a year of first-year composition to studying it and since all students devote a year to studying writing, writing must be very important.

First-Year Writing in the Freshman Year

A further ironic legacy of first-year composition lies in the conflict between the institutionally perceived importance of writing alongside its relegation to the freshman year. Yet if writing can do all that first-year composition claims for it—all the claims that have served to maintain first-year composition as an institution (such as promoting analytical and rhetorical thinking so that students not only recognize rhetorical manipulation but can use it for their own purposes, for example)—it would seem to make more sense to give writers support throughout their academic careers. It makes little sense to assign students to writing classes only during their first year when, as research repeatedly shows (Carson, Chase, & Gibson, 1993; Carson, Chase, Gibson, & Hargrove, 1992; Leki, 2003), most of the other courses students take simultaneously do not require writing. Thus students are learning something about writing at a time when they cannot even put that learning into practice outside the writing course. The placement of first-year writing in the curriculum, and even the legitimacy of the existence of first-year composition, is an old argument that L1 writing professionals have been battling over for more than a hundred years and in terms surprisingly similar to modern arguments (Connors, 2003; Roemer, Schultz, & Durst, 1999). But the first-year writing requirement remains essentially the same.

The development of writing centers was one attempt to answer the complaint that students need to be able to get help with writing beyond the first-year composition course. But unfortunately we do not really know much about how well L2 writers are served by writing centers. The research on L2 writers in the writing center is sketchy, directed mostly at writing center tutors working with L2 students, not focused on the L2 students' work. We have relatively little research on what L2 students come away with from writing center sessions and what they do with it. (See, however, the special issue of the *Journal of Second Language Writing*, 2004, on Second Language Writers in the Writing Center.) Still, excellent features of writing centers include that they are not compulsory and that they can be accessed when needed, ideally supporting students but without bogging them down with additional writing courses. Yet, beyond whatever help L2 students can get in writing centers, because first-year composition ends in a year, so does academic support for L2 writing at many universities.

THE PURPOSE OF FIRST-YEAR COMPOSITION

The final legacy of first-year composition to L2 writing is confusion about what that course should or can do. The defense of this universal writing requirement that may be the most convincing makes claims about writing's potential to enhance learning. But the claim that writing *can* enhance learning has been conflated with the claim that writing *does* enhance learning, which suggests that this is true for all students. In looking at the results of naturalistic studies of L1 students, Russell (2001) reasonably concludes that *some* L1 students will be able to use *some* writing assignments in *some* disciplines to enhance their learning given the right motivation, support for identity needs, tools, and processes. These stipulations are even more pertinent for L2 students but find no resonance in the universal requirement for first-year composition.

I come away from reading the L1 literature with the impression that many L1 writing professionals see the first-year composition course as losing legitimacy unless it can claim to be an end in itself, like other disciplinary courses. L1 writing professionals thus work hard to resist the notion that what happens in first-year composition is merely preparation for other writing tasks in the academy or the workplace because if writing courses are seen as only preparatory, first-year composition would slide into the category of the dreaded "mere service course." For a variety of essentially (legitimate) economic reasons, first-year composition must not be seen as a service course, with service apparently assumed to be service to other academic units at the university (rather than to students). In the literature on this issue the claim is that first-year composition has a great deal to offer intellectually in and of itself, ways of thinking, ways of reading, and obviously ways of structuring writing to have the effect that the writer seeks.[3]

Yet my sense of L2 writing suggests that many if not most L2 writing professionals are more pragmatic about credit bearing writing courses and justify required writing courses and exams in their own minds because they believe these courses will in fact serve as preparation for other future writing tasks, at least at the university if not in the work place. L2 students in these courses almost certainly believe and hope the same. If such is the case, then L2 writing professionals are relying crucially on the notion that what is taught in the L2 writing class can transfer from the writing class to other writing contexts. Leaving aside the significant objection that students are not doing much other writing in their other courses at the time they take writing classes and that by the time they are doing writing in their majors two years down the road whatever might have transferred has evaporated, the question becomes what, if anything, transfers from writing classes to other classes?

Psychologists of learning recognize two types of transfer, specific, near transfer and general, far transfer (Detterman & Sternberg, 1993). Despite the fervent wish that general, far transfer of overarching principles learned in one setting can be applied to other settings that are dissimilar, endless numbers of lab studies have shown that transfer of learning does not occur. What does occur more readily is specific, near transfer, that is, the transfer of specific, limited, narrow information, facts, processes from one situation to another one fairly similar to the first. In my own research with L2 students they repeatedly asserted that what they learned in their L2 first-year courses and then used in their writing for courses across the curriculum were features of punctuation, grammar, transition words, introductions—features of writing that are specific and narrow and can be transferred to locally similar contexts at the micro level. It may be that L2 writing teachers can be happy enough to think that they spent a year teaching writing and that these limited micro-level skills are what the students were able to transfer, that is, that any use L2 students can make of any language-related feature is a benefit. But we should not be under the illusion that we are preparing these students for writing across the curriculum except in the most minimalist ways.

We cannot, in fact, expect transfer of broader principles because new writing contexts, for engineering, computer science, business, or agriculture, are simply too dissimilar from what we can do in first-year writing. Writing in those contexts is a part of an entire activity system with dimensions altogether different from those of a generic writing class (Blakeslee, 1997; Dias, et al., 1999; Russell, 1997). So while L1 writing people may justify first-year writing in their own ways, in L2 writing we seem to look for justification for the course that includes transfer to other courses of important general principles and macro features of writing, and such an expectation can probably not be met, leaving in confusion the overall reason for the course's being.

Conclusion

L1 compositionists have long chafed under the rule of literature faculty in English departments (Silva & Leki, 2004). There is a sense in which the needs of L2 composition have been subordinated to the interests and concerns of L1 composition, a domination the L1 writing literature displays little awareness of. Still, in L2 writing we are fortunate that our L1 colleagues, creative and savvy as they are, continually come up with interesting ways of attempting to think through their own inheritance of the institution of first-year composition.

Thus, also a legacy of first-year composition is these scholars' remarkably imaginative thinking about alternatives to the traditional one year of writing courses still required by most institutions. Some advocate eliminating first-year composition, or making it optional, and substituting a whole array of possible approaches to intervening more helpfully in developing students' writing proficiency. Crowley (1993) describes one example of what life might look like for writing studies without the existence of required first-year composition courses, though supporting this elimination is definitely a minority position. Many of those who believe first-year writing should be an elective are advocates of writing across the curriculum (WAC) and writing in the disciplines (WID). As a result of the constant reflecting, organizing, and planning work of L1 compositionists some places have instituted WAC and WID programs, first-year writing seminars, such as the writing program at Cornell, Great Books courses taught by faculty from across the disciplines but emphasizing writing (see, for example, the description in Carroll, 2002), writing fellows programs, such as those at the University of Wisconsin and the University of Iowa. Still others propose that housing writing in a separate department, independent of its dominant sibling, literature, would allow the writing department to reach out more effectively to other units within the university which need help teaching disciplinary writing and to focus more sharply on WAC and WID, calling this aid "support" rather than "service" (O'Neill, Crow, & Burton, 2002). The writing program at the university analyzed in the Atkinson and Ramanathan (1995) study discussed above has itself undergone a complete overhaul to WAC.[4] In some instances scholars with L2 expertise have been at the center of innovations to writing programs, for example, Ann Johns's work with the Freshman Success Program at San Diego State University (Johns, 2001). As writing center director at the University of Iowa, Carol Severino operates their "enrollment program" with rolling enrollment for half to full hour writing tutorials, which allow students to move in and out of the program at any time during the semester, a system appealing to L2 students, especially graduate students (personal communication). They also have a full-time email tutor.

As the minority member of the L1/L2 compositionist pairing, we in L2 writing need to remain alert to shifts in thinking about first-year composition not only because so much of this thinking is perceptive and helpful but more importantly because, given university structures and the relative sizes of L1 and L2 populations in most places in English speaking North America, we often have little choice but to follow. At a major non-border state institution like mine, L2 students and their needs count for rather little. Their voices are lost in the roar as we and they more or less follow what is put in place for L1 students. When minority voices are just too small and, crucially, coming from students who are doing well academically across the curriculum, and so not making trouble for anyone, the need to provide better support for their writing—and their language development generally—is not experienced institutionally. Whatever we might be able to do, given a free hand, to foster intellectual development and academic success for L2 students is, like everything else in life, embedded in the institutions and institutional structures that surround us, entangled in other people's lives, desires, and histories.

Notes

[1] It is true that some universities offer and perhaps sometimes even require communications or public speaking courses. However, these courses are not nearly as wide-spread as first year writing courses and rarely, if ever, offer separate credit bearing sections for L2 students. Furthermore, public speaking is not the only kind of oral skill that would be useful to L2 students. A credit bearing communications course for L2 students might include help with the oral language skills needed to ask questions in a large lecture hall, to participate in class discussions, to work on group projects, to talk to domestic peers, to interact with faculty, and a host of others that would be unlikely in a course mixing English L1 and L2 students.

[2] To give another example: At a writing conference, when Carroll (2002) shared samples of university student science writing, "samples that had been judged as very successful by the student writers and their professors, some writing teachers dismissed the science writing as lacking a sense of audience and voice . . ." (p. 5). Not fronting qualities favored in English department genres, the writing was deemed crippled.

[3] One reviewer of an earlier draft of this manuscript suggested that the youth of the composition discipline is also a factor in this fear of being seen as providing a service. But, in fact, composition is not such a young field and composition research is not particularly new, as histories by Berlin (1987) and Russell (1991) make clear. On the other hand, without going into the whole argument, in Crowley's (1993) analysis, it is the fact that first-year composition is required that put the "mere" into service course, a designation that will continue to be an albatross around the neck of the discipline until the course as currently configured disappears.

And after 100 years of debate, why doesn't it disappear? It might be noted that, despite the broadening of research focuses among compositionists to, for example, workplace writing, many a career has been built on the captives in first-year composition. Clearly, compositionists have a vested interest in its continuation. For some, it's a job, not a great one maybe but they work hard to make it a better one. For others, it constitutes a program to become the director of. And for others, it is a wonderful site for research and thinking, leading to enhancement of professional careers through publications. In fact this is exactly one of the justifications for instituting writing courses (soon to be mandatory) at the University of Warwick in the UK, where traditionally no such writing courses existed (Ganobcsik-Williams, 2003). As Ganobscik-Williams straightforwardly notes:

> One effect of the general writing course is that it has greatly influenced American Composition scholarship. First-year writing classrooms have enabled pedagogical techniques (such as the teaching of writing as a process), as well as pedagogical theories (such as current traditional, expressivist, and social epistemic) to be tested through empirical, case, and ethnographic studies. Thus, for American Compositionists, general writing courses have served as an important site for controlled research.

A golden egg.

[4] Although I personally applaud shifts toward WAC and WID programs, I admit alarm bells go off as I note yet another mutation in the ongoing saga of writing instruction at the university. One website I consulted admonished WAC/WID teachers not to pass student papers that merely had excellent content.

REFERENCES

Atkinson, D., & Ramanathan, V. (1995). Cultures of writing: An ethnographic comparison of L1 and L2 university writing/language programs. *TESOL Quarterly, 29,* 539–568.

Berlin, J. (1987). *Rhetoric and reality: Writing instruction in American colleges 1890–1985.* Carbondale, IL: Southern Illinois University Press.

Blakeslee, A. (1997). Activity, context, interactions, and authority. *Journal of Business and Technical Communication, 11,* 125–169.

Carroll, L. (2002). *Rehearsing new roles: How college students develop as writers.* Carbondale, IL: Southern Illinois University Press.

Carson, J. (2000). Reading and writing for academic purposes. In M. Pally (Ed.), *Sustained content teaching in academic ESL/EFL* (pp. 19–34). Boston: Houghton Mifflin.

Carson, J., Chase, N., & Gibson, S. (1993). *Academic demands of the undergraduate curriculum: What students need.* Final Report to the Fund for the Improvement of Post-Secondary Education. Atlanta: Center for the Study of Adult Literacy, Georgia State University.

Carson, J., Chase, N., Gibson, S., & Hargrove, M. (1992). Literacy demands of the undergraduate curriculum. *Reading Research and Instruction, 31,* 25–50.

Connors, R. (2003). The abolition debate in composition: A short history. In L. Ede & A. Lunsford (Eds.), *Selected essays of Robert J. Connors* (pp. 279–294). Boston: Bedford/St. Martin's.

Crowley, S. (1993). *Composition in the university.* Pittsburgh, PA: University of Pittsburgh Press.

Detterman, D., & Sternberg, R. (Eds.). (1993). *Transfer on trial: Intelligence, cognition, and instruction.* Norwood, NJ: Ablex.

Dias, P., Freedman, A., Medway, P., & Pare, A. (Eds.). (1999). *Worlds apart: Acting and writing in academic and workplace contexts.* Mahwah, NJ: Lawrence Erlbaum.

Ganobcsik-Williams, L. (2003, June). *Is this freshman composition? Teaching general studies writing in Europe.* Paper presented at the Second Conference of the European Association for the Teaching of Academic Writing, Budapest.

Howard, R. (1995). Plagiarisms, authorships, and the academic death penalty. *College English, 57,* 788–806.

Johns, A. (2001). An interdisciplinary, interinstitutional, learning communities program: Student involvement and student success. In I. Leki (Ed.) *Academic writing programs* (pp. 61–72). Alexandria, VA: TESOL.

Leki, I. (2000). Writing, literacy, and applied linguistics. *Annual Review of Applied Linguistics, 20,* 99–115.

Leki, I. (2003). Living through college literacy: Nursing in a second language. *Written Communication, 20,* 81–98.

Mlynarczyk, R. (1998). *Conversations of the mind.* Mahwah, NJ: Lawrence Erlbaum.

Murphy, M. (2000). New faculty for a new university: Toward a full-time teaching-intensive faculty track in composition. *College Composition and Communication, 52,* 14–42.

O'Neill, P., Crow, A., & Burton, L. (Ed.). (2002). *A field of dreams: Independent writing programs and the future of composition studies.* Logan: Utah State University Press.

Roemer, M., Schultz, L., & Durst, R. (1999). Reframing the great debate on first-year writing. *College Composition and Communication, 50,* 377–392.

Russell, D. (1997). Rethinking genre in school and society: An activity theory analysis. *Written Communication, 14,* 504–554.

Russell, D. (2001). Where do the naturalistic studies of WAC/WID point? A research review. In S. McLeod, E. Miraglia, M. Soven, & C. Thaiss (Eds.), *WAC for the new millennium* (pp. 259–298). Urbana, IL: NCTE.

Severino, C., & Trachsel, M. (in press). Starting a writing fellows program: crossing disciplines or crossing pedagogies? *International Journal of Learning, 11.*

Silva, T. (1999, March). *First year writing at the big state university: Planned failure on a grand scale.* Paper presented at the Conference on College Composition and Communication, Atlanta, GA.

Silva, T., & Leki, I. (2004). Family matters: The influence of applied linguistics and composition studies on second language writing studies—past, present, and future. *Modern Language Journal, 88,* 1–13.

Sternglass, M. (1997). *Time to know them.* Mahwah, NJ: Lawrence Erlbaum Associates.

Williams, J., & Severino, C. (Eds.). (2004). Special issue on second language writers in the writing center. *Journal of Second Language Writing.*

Woodmansee, M., & Janzi, P. (1995). The law of texts: Copyright in the academy. *College English, 57,* 769–787.

Zhu, W. (2004). Faculty views on the importance of writing, the nature of academic writing, and teaching and responding to writing in the disciplines. *Journal of Second Language Writing, 13,* 29–48.

4 Improving Institutional ESL/EAP Support for International Students: Seeking the Promised Land

Ryuko Kubota and Kimberly Abels

Never doubt that a small group of thoughtful, committed citizens can change the world; indeed, it's the only thing that ever has.

—Margaret Mead

The amount of support for English language development offered by a university for international and Generation 1.5 students indicates its level of institutional commitment to provide all students with equal access to quality education. It also reflects how the institution views English language instruction—either as a quick-fix remedial service or as an educational activity with academic integrity. The 2004 Symposium on Second Language Writing revealed an insufficient amount of English language support at various institutions of higher education across the U.S. The situation at our university is no exception. In fact, only two specialized courses for international students are available through the English department. Furthermore, no courses or programs exist for academic and professional training for teaching college-level ESL or EAP. Although these conditions have persisted for many years, it may be possible to address the problems and try to make a change through faculty collaboration.

This chapter describes the collaborative efforts made over a period of two years by a small group of faculty who have worked together to make recommendations to the university for enhancing English language instruction and support for international students and scholars. In the process of making recommendations, it became apparent to us that providing English language support is closely connected to the institutional commitment to taking ethical responsibility in both local and international communities. We also became aware that the rationale for different program or service models stems from specific assumptions and philosophies about the role of English language support at an institution, which are further related to larger discourses on second language teaching and learning as well as diversity. In the following sections, we will describe the work that the ESL committee has done and discuss in detail our final recommendations to the university, which are still a work in progress. We hope that this chapter will provide insight for other institutions that share a similar situation.

Background

The University of North Carolina at Chapel Hill (UNC-CH) is a flagship, state-funded university with a student population of approximately 26,000, which is divided into 61 percent undergraduate, 30 percent graduate, and 9 percent professional school students (i.e., business, education, dentistry, journalism, law, library science, medicine, nursing, pharmacy, public health, and social work). According to The Top American Research Universities, published in 2002, UNC-CH ranked in the top five of public research universities nationwide. North Carolina state policy stipulates that 82 percent of first-year undergraduate students have to have in-state status. Such restriction does not apply for graduate admissions.

The international population on our campus as of Fall 2004 includes approximately 1,180 degree-seeking students (960 graduate and 220 undergraduate), 300 professional school students, 140 non-degree-seeking exchange students (mostly undergraduate but some graduate), 1,000 visiting scholars (e.g., visiting faculty, post-docs, and researchers), and the spouses of these individuals. Compared to some campuses in other parts of the country, the number of U.S. domestic students who need ESL support is not very large. However, the number of Generation 1.5 students may increase in the future, given the fact that North Carolina has a large growth rate in its Latino population—394 percent growth between 1990 and 2000 (North Carolina Rural Economic Development Center, 2004). Of course, a significant proportion of the international students on our campus does not require English language support because of native language or educational background. However, anecdotal evidence provided by some faculty members and administrators suggests that a large number of international students and scholars needs specialized language instruction and support but not all needs are met due to restricted resources, funding, and services. As described later, the university does offer language support through various programs, but it is neither sufficient nor coordinated. In many institutions, ESL/EAP instruction is supported by or affiliated with an academic program in TESOL and/or applied linguistics. However, our university offers no such academic program; the only training available in teaching ESL is through the K-12 ESL teacher education program offered by the school of education.

Although the number of international undergraduate students is small due to the state-mandated policy mentioned above, there are a larger number of graduate students from abroad. Interestingly, the university has not made a significant effort to increase the number of international students, despite the recent thrust for internationalization. In UNC-CH's Academic Plan, issued in 2003, which will guide the University in the next five years, internationalization is one of the six priorities. The university has launched several initiatives including the appointment of the Associate Provost of International Affairs and groundbreaking for a new Global Education Center, a building that will house the university's international academic and service activities. According to the recent data released by the Institute of International Education (2004), UNC-CH ranked seventh among all major research universities in the number of undergraduate students going abroad to study during the academic year of 2002–2003. However, this accomplishment does not match the level of effort to invite international students. According to the data, eight of the top ten research universities with a large number of U.S. students going abroad ranked between 4th and 29th in the total number of international students. However, UNC-CH was one of two universities that fell below the 40th in ranking, indicating an imbalance in the international exchanges and a disparity in educational investment between domestic and international students.

Independent of such international initiatives, the UNC-CH ESL committee was informally and voluntarily created in the fall of 2002 on the initiative of two faculty members in order to explore how to meet the needs for English language instruction and support among international students on campus. This group, including representatives from the study abroad office, the international center, the English department, the school of education, the center for teaching and learning, the writing center, and the business school, joined together out of mutual concerns and frustrations to learn more about one another's programs and problem-solve. Over the course of two years, the committee expanded its membership and played an active role in making concrete proposals for improving the situation.

The ESL Committee: From Birth to Evolution

In the fall of 2002, the director of the study abroad program and one of us met informally to explore ways to improve English support for international students. One of the issues we shared was a concern about the recent study abroad office decision to increase the minimum TOEFL score from 550 to 600 for international non-degree-seeking exchange students. The decision was made to compensate for the academic difficulties that exchange students were experiencing on our campus caused by their lack of English proficiency and no availability for specialized English language instruction through course work. We worried that the higher TOEFL standard might reduce the number of incoming international exchange students, which limits the number of exchanges, resulting in fewer opportunities for study abroad offered to UNC-CH students.

This was not the first time the lack of ESL support was discussed at UNC-CH. The two English courses currently offered in the English Department—the only EAP courses available with enrollment limited to graduate international students—were created through faculty's grassroots effort to address international students' needs. However, past efforts to increase English support did not result in any coordinated or increased academic service for this population. This time, the initial stage of our effort was exploratory in nature with a focus on identifying faculty members who might be interested in this project and inviting them into a dialogue. The group eventually included several key members: the lecturer of the EAP courses from the English department, the director of the writing center, the director of the international center, two faculty members from the business school, the assistant provost for international programs, and the coordinator of the Duke-UNC Rotary Center for International Studies. The committee also involved at one time other members such as the instructors of the newly created Preparing International Teaching Assistants Program and other training courses offered by the Graduate School.

During the academic year of 2002–2003, the committee gathered the following information: (1) the ESL services offered at our peer institutions (through a Web search); (2) the needs for ESL instructional support among international non-degree-seeking exchange students; and (3) the needs in the composition program. First, it was found that all our peer institutions (i.e., top research universities across the nation) offer clearly identifiable ESL support programs or services to various degrees. Second, a survey was sent by email to undergraduate exchange students. Although the returned responses were small in number (a total of seventeen), about three quarters of the respondents said that specialized English language instruction, particularly in the area of writing and speaking, would be beneficial for them. Their reported TOEFL computer-based scores ranged from 159 to 293. These results indicated that some level of English language instruction would be necessary for them, especially because the EAP courses offered by the English department have no slots available for undergraduate students. Third, an interview with a graduate instructor in the composition program in the English department suggested that a lack of instructional resources and support for Generation 1.5 students was becoming a serious issue, causing a great deal of frustration among instructors. However, the committee agreed that because the size of this population is still small, the need for ESL-type support (mainly grammar and mechanics) could be provided within the composition program or in the writing center.

Committee's Report on the State of English Language Support on Campus

During the following academic year of 2003–2004, the committee increased its membership. The larger representation allowed the committee to identify what types of English language support were available on our campus. In May 2004, the committee compiled a report on the status of English language instruction and support and submitted it to the associate provost of international affairs. The following is a summary of the report:

Academic Support

- Two English courses—ENGL101X (mainly academic writing) and 103X (mainly oral communication): A full-time lecturer and a TA in the English department teach four sections of ENGL101X and three sections of ENGL103X per year. Due to the limited number of sections, graduate students receive priority for enrollment. A total of approximately 100 students are enrolled each year. All incoming international graduate students who are nonnative speakers of English take a placement test for grammar, vocabulary, reading, listening, and writing. Those who did not meet the minimum requirement are required to take 101X. 103X is elective. Variable credit hours are available for both courses to accommodate students' needs.
- Preparing International Teaching Assistants Program (PITAP) offered through the graduate school: This program was created in 2003 to respond to persistent complaints from the parents of undergraduate students about international TAs' communication skills. Six sections of GRAD310 aim to improve pronunciation, cross-cultural communication, and teaching skills and one section of GRAD 311 is a continuation of 310. Approximately 80 students are enrolled per year. All international graduate students who plan to be teaching assistants are evaluated for their communication skills. Those students whose skills fall below the passing level will be automatically registered in a PITAP course.
- The Business School ESL course: the business school has the largest number of international students of all academic units on campus. America 101 aims to prepare students for global business, the academic culture at the school, participating in study groups, and job hunting. This course is offered mostly in the summer as incoming students attend pre-MBA analytic skills workshops. The business school also offers a short-term executive education program with intensive English instruction and on-on-one help through the business communications center.
- The Writing Center: The center is funded by the college of arts and sciences (rather than the graduate school) and it primarily serves undergraduate students. It also serves a smaller number of graduate students, staff and faculty members. Although as-

sisting nonnative English speakers is not the writing center's primary mission, approximately 25 percent of its clientele are nonnative English speakers, many of whom are graduate students. Due to a lack of staff, students are turned away 1,000–1,500 times each year. The center keeps a list of local copyeditors who provide service with fees and makes the list available for students who seek copyediting help.

- The Learning Center: Like the writing center, the learning center is funded by the college of arts and sciences and its primary clientele are undergraduate students, but graduate students receive its service as well. The center sees nonnative English speakers primarily through the reading program, in which ESL materials are made available. The reading program allows these students to work on reading skills, study strategies, and conversational English by using self-teaching workbooks and by frequent meetings with one of the instructional staff.

Non-Academic Support

- The International Center: The center coordinates the Conversation Partners Program, which provides international students and their spouses with once-a-week, one-on-one conversation with a volunteer American friend from the university or local community. The International Women's English Conversation group provides a two-hour-per-week opportunity for the spouses of international students and scholars. Participants learn about local activities for themselves and their children, and have informal English conversation lessons. The center also maintains a directory of ESL tutors and programs in the local community.
- ESL class in the Training and Development Department in the Office of Human Resources: This ESL program was created in 2001 for UNC employees (staff, housekeepers, and faculty) to improve their listening, speaking, reading, and writing skills in English. If space is available, spouses and retirees may enroll. The class is offered twice a year for 6 weeks each. It meets twice a week for 1.5 hours each and is taught by an instructor from Durham Technical Community College.

Soon after this report was submitted, the associate provost of international affairs requested that the committee develop specific recommendations for improved service by December 2004.

Developing the Final Recommendations

During the fall of 2004, the ESL committee formed a subcommittee to develop concrete recommendations for increasing English language instruction, support, and EAP instructor training. The subcommittee developed several draft proposals, each of which was reviewed by the large committee for further clarification and refinement. The committee decided to propose three models and specific recommendations with estimated budgets. The final document included an executive summary, an overview and rationale for each model, recommendations for the model and budget, detailed descriptions of each model, a summary of university members who seek support at present, and proposed new EAP courses. In the process of developing this document, it became clear to us that each model reflected underlying assumptions about the role of ESL support in the university community and the status of non-native English-speaking international students on campus. We also renewed our awareness that to increase English language support would be to recognize the university's academic and social responsibility in the local and global communities.

We quickly became aware that gathering data and imagining possible programmatic and institutional solutions would not be persuasive alone. Accordingly, the committee began to strategize possible rhetorical frames for communicating our findings to decision-makers. With both scholars and practitioners assembled on the committee, we were drawn to represent both the real, practical immediate needs of our students, but also to represent the larger ethical and intellectual pressures inherent in the situation. Recognizing an audience who might also respond to these combined pressures, we chose to include ethical, practical, historical, and community dimensions as we developed our arguments and shaped our proposal. We chose to motivate the report not just with facts, but also with appeals that directly linked the problem to the stated mission the university espouses and the complete array of constituents it serves.

The Rationale for Increasing English Language Support

The committee recognized that the insufficient and uncoordinated language support for international members limits the university's ability to internationalize the campus. Internationalization involves taking responsibility to provide both domestic and international students with educational opportunities and resources. We listed the following four ethical points that motivated our proposals:

1. The responsibility to provide appropriate English language learning opportunities: When international students come to our university to participate in academic programs, they must demonstrate their academic preparedness in English by submitting their TOEFL scores. Most institutions recognize this preparation as minimal and accept, *as standard,* the responsibility to provide continuous education for these students' linguistic and cultural development through coursework and language support services. UNC-CH should become academically accountable and develop a program to meet the ongoing language needs of its international students.

2. The university's responsibility to respect local community needs: Because UNC-CH offers so little English language support to its internationals, a significant number take ESL classes offered free of charge by a local community college. However, their ESL program is funded by the state and designed as local literacy education for academically and economically disadvantaged students. UNC-CH international students, scholars and their spouses take spaces provided for these local residents. Due to limited resources, the community college will discontinue advanced level ESL courses in 2006, courses in which many UNC-CH students, scholars, and their spouses are currently enrolled.

3. The university's responsibility for reciprocity with other exchange programs: UNC-CH has a number of student exchange agreements with foreign institutions. When UNC-CH students participate in study abroad programs, they usually receive a full range of target language support in programs specifically created for exchange students. Conversely, when international exchange students come to UNC-CH, they are *not* provided with equivalent services and are, instead, thrown into a sink-or-swim situation. UNC-CH should make a good-faith effort to correct this unfair access to language instruction.

4. The university's departments' responsibility to support language instruction: A number of departments bring international post-docs, researchers, and graduate students to campus on research grants and special projects funding knowing that they will need or could benefit from additional language instruction at UNC-CH. Departments hosting these students pressure the limited resources of the English department, writing center, learning center, international center, and graduate school as well as community college courses for English language support, although they do not contribute to the funding of these units. Creating a process by which departments or units which bring international students to campus might contribute, as part of the overhead on grants or through other measures, to funds to support English language instruction may offset some of the costs of developing appropriate levels of support.

These ethical points address the widespread ideologies and assumptions about second language learning and teaching at U.S. universities and in American society in general. The following critical reflections on ideologies informed our conceptualization of the ethical points. First, there is a prevalent assumption that takes for granted the use and acquisition of English as easy and natural for nonnative speakers of English. Crawford (2004), for example, lists several language ideologies and folk beliefs in the U.S. that shape everyday practices and policies. They include "family legends" ("My great-grandfather came to this country without a word of English and he succeeded . . ." and "conventional wisdom" ("The best way to teach English is 'total immersion" . . .) (p. 62). However, such ideologies have been critiqued as not only failing to corroborate research evidence but also reflecting persistent ideologies that champion monolingualism, assimilation, and Anglo-conformity, as well as individualism, which places the sole responsibility on individuals to correct perceived linguistic deficiencies, giving the dominant group an excuse for not providing educational services and, instead, blaming the victim (Crawford, 2004; Wiley, 2004; Wiley & Lukes, 1997).

The differential expectations for international students coming from abroad and American students going abroad parallels an elitist double standard as seen in the American attitudes toward bilingualism (Kubota, forthcoming; Lo Bianco , 2002; Ortega, 1999). Such a double standard celebrates bilingualism for socio-economically privileged monolingual English speakers, while viewing bilingualism among immigrant groups as a problem. In this ideology, providing UNC-CH students with opportunities for special second language instruction abroad is perceived as more valuable than offering instruction for English language development as a second language for international students. Combined with the ideologies of individualism and assimilation, international students are expected to know English on their own, while American students studying abroad are to learn another language and culture in an environment equipped with specialized instruction and resources.

This elitist double standard relates to what counts as a "diversity" experience. As we mentioned earlier, the university takes pride in promoting "internationalization" by sending a large number of U.S. domestic students abroad, while not inviting an equal number of international students to its campus. The university champions the amount of study abroad experience among American students as an indication of internationalization, but it makes little effort to expand and enrich the intercultural experience that they could have with international students here at home. This view demonstrates that going abroad equals internationalization and thus equals multi/intercultural experience. However, a lack of support for international diversity on campus signifies a view that devalues domestic diversity, reinforcing monolingualism and monoculturalism at home as the norm. This normative thinking alienates the existing linguistically and culturally diverse people in the U.S., assigning them the label of *foreignness* (Osborn, 2000; Reagan & Osborn 2002). Just like the double standard of bilingualism, the concept of *foreignness* has a double meaning: *foreignness* abroad is more sophisticated than *foreignness* at home. Internationalization of a university should involve not only a vision looking outward to seek experience abroad but also an aspiration moving inward to promote intercultural exchange at home.

Another prevalent attitude held by many research universities views learning English as a second language as remedial rather than developmental. Some assumed that a research university is not responsible for correcting nonnative speakers' English deficiencies—community colleges or other adult education programs would be a more appropriate place for students to get help. However, the lack of English language support stemming from this attitude creates great frustration among teachers at the community college and students who cannot find a program or a course that meets their needs. It is important to point out that when American students learn a foreign language, it is rarely viewed as remedial. The differential expectation given to domestic students and international students is once again manifested in this remedial-developmental dichotomy.

Furthermore, the view of ESL as remedial reflects an institutional lack of understanding of the importance of the professionalism in the teaching of college-level ESL ("Anyone who can speak English can teach English") or the academic legitimacy of applied linguistics research ("No one does such a thing in our university"). For instance, UNC-CH has no academic program in TESOL or applied linguistics and that the departments that could logically house this program— namely, education, English, and linguistics—all expressed disinterest in getting involved in developing a program. These perspectives informed our thinking process in developing the three models, which will be described in the next section.

The Three Models

The committee proposed a choice of three models: (1) a TESOL graduate certificate program model, (2) a distributed resources model, and (3) an ESL Center model. Briefly, the TESOL graduate certificate program model envisions increased English language instructional services, especially EAP courses and tutorials in the writing center, which are supported by a graduate program. The distributed resources model maintains the distribution of various services currently available but simultaneously increases the amount of service and the level of coordination. The ESL center model merges all the services into a single center. Each model responds to the existing wide range of needs from degree-seeking undergraduate and graduate students, non-degree seeking exchange students, visiting faculty, and post-docs. The models also address the needs of the spouses of these students and scholars to some degree.

After carefully examining the advantages and disadvantages of the three models, the committee recommended that the university (1) take immediate action to increase the amount of English language support described in the distributed resources model, while developing an interdisciplinary TESOL graduate certificate program; (2) develop a longitudinal plan for creating an interdisciplinary TESOL graduate certificate (and degree) program, which works in combination with the services described in the distributed resources model; and (3) treat the ESL center model as a less desirable option than the other two in light of the academic mission of UNC-CH.

This decision was made based on our recognition that how we solve the problem of designing English language support depends upon how we define the problem and who we prioritize for support within the university community. The continuum of solutions, as described in Figure 1, runs between viewing English language support as an intellectual and developmental activity best situated and supervised by an academic unit and viewing English language support as a remedial problem that requires student services. We also situated the models on a cost continuum and according to which constituents we prioritize for support within the institution. In order to show in more detail the reasoning behind our recommendation, we will summarize each model briefly and presents pros and cons in the next sections.

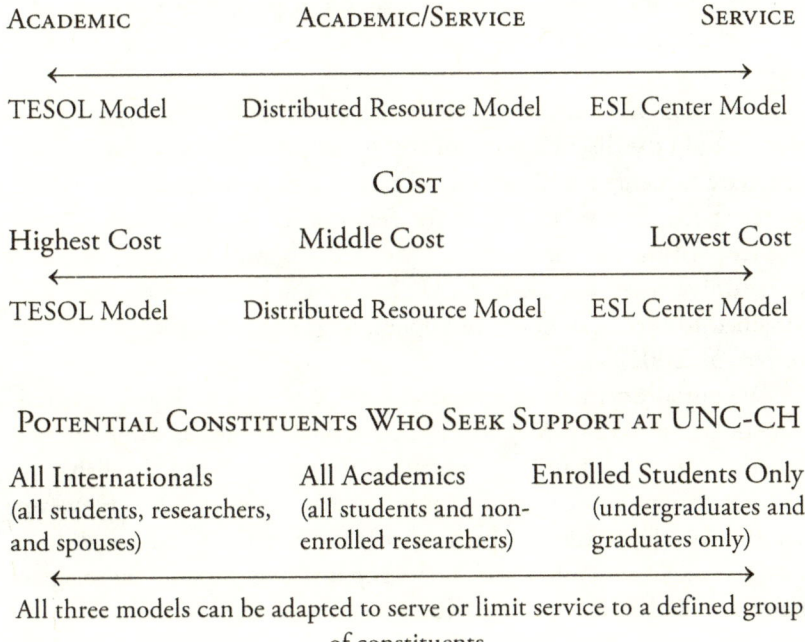

Figure 1. Comparison of the three models.

(1) TESOL Graduate Certificate Program Model

We agreed that establishing an interdisciplinary graduate certificate program, and later a graduate degree program, in TESOL and applied linguistics would provide an integrated, intellectual, visible home for English language support for students throughout the university. A graduate program would create a cadre of ESL professionals on campus who could teach international students, lead others to develop appropriate, informed support programs, and provide an academic nexus for research and learning around English language learning issues. Especially because very few graduate TESOL programs exist and no program is available at the Ph.D. level in our state, UNC-CH could take the lead in this arena.

Moreover, a TESOL graduate program directly supports UNC-CH's international initiative. Because English language teaching is an educational activity conducted in almost every society in the world, the field of TESOL and applied linguistics directly responds to one of the recommendations in the UNC-CH academic plan issued in 2003; namely, the integration of global issues and perspectives into graduate and professional experiences and the university's overall research enterprise.

The TESOL model works in combination with existing resources described in the distributed resource model below. TESOL faculty and graduate students training in the TESOL program would be available to teach the courses and staff the services for internationals already in place within the institution. This model is widely implemented in other universities. For instance, UCLA has the ESL service course unit attached to the department of applied linguistics and TESL (Brinton & Jensen, 2002).

We initially wanted to propose a TESOL/Applied Linguistics graduate degree program (MA and Ph.D.) model. However, after contacting three academic units—education, linguistics, and English—we learned that none of them was willing to pursue the idea. However, the English department, which currently offers EAP courses, did not mind hiring faculty in TESOL to support and expand the English language instruction and a graduate certificate program. Thus, we decided to propose that UNC-CH create a graduate certificate program first and eventually work toward developing an interdisciplinary degree program. We also decided to delete the word, applied linguistics from our document because it might foster the impression with the administration that the program should belong to the linguistics department, which already indicated that such an academic focus would not be embraced by the department faculty.

There are many advantages for a TESOL graduate program model. Perhaps the most important point is that the program provides an intellectual locus for language instruction rather than viewing the service as troubleshooting or problem solving. In doing so, the program creates needed academic and research leadership in TESOL/applied linguistics in the state and sends a strong message to the university and beyond concerning internationalization. It offers specific training in teaching second languages for TAs and tutors who teach in the English department or in the writing center. The courses would also support undergraduate and graduate students who want to learn to teach English abroad. All advantages listed under the distributed resources model below are applicable as well. Disadvantages would include the cost of creating tenure-line position(s) to sustain the program and the need for long-term planning. However, advantages listed above seem to overpower these disadvantages.

(2) Distributed Resources Model

This model builds upon the existing, nascent structure of English language support and funds and staffs it at appropriate levels, especially by increasing tutorial services in the writing center and EAP course offerings in the English department. We were led to imagine this model because, while currently inadequate, our existing structures do appropriately address the variety of needs and constituents that seek support. This model also combines an academic program with a service model. With additional funding and coordination this model would better meet existing needs. This model takes what currently exists and adds resources to current units plus a new ESL coordinator who serves as a resource to and liaison between various services. This model is likely the least expensive as it builds on existing structures, services, and allocated space. It mainly requires hiring additional faculty and staff and creating a budget and office for an ESL coordinator.

The greatest advantage is that this model utilizes existing intellectual resources, particularly the expertise in the writing center, ensuring academic quality of tutorial services, which constitute a large component of current needs. In addition, the model integrates internationals into the services and units offered to other students, avoiding the creation of a separate island of internationals on campus. Moreover, it is consistent with a decentralized education philosophy and distributes responsibilities to various units and offices. Because this model builds on what already exists and funds it at appropriate levels, it is relatively easy to develop through utilizing available resources and offers a mix of academic and non-academic, credit and non-credit services. However, there are disadvantages. Although the creation of an ESL coordinator would facilitate coordination, the programs and services remain distributed and they could be fragmented. Various units and offices are currently cooperative in the effort of providing English language support, but there is no guarantee that they will remain so. Nonetheless, this model overall seems to be better than the next model.

(3) ESL Center Model

This model creates one central office that provides all English language support except for English courses. In other words, all the existing services, other than English courses, are taken out of existing units and taken over by the ESL center. On the continuum, this model falls at the opposite extreme of the academic model and focuses efforts primarily in a service mode. In an ESL center, constituents from various parts of the university come to the center for individualized instruction, remediation, and tailored workshops as needed. Under this model, existing offices would no longer serve ESL students and would, instead, redirect them to the new ESL center. A new ESL director assumes responsibilities for the center activities. This service model may be the most expensive model as it requires new positions, operating budgets, and space. This model requires additional tutors for the center, multiple office spaces, and a separate budget.

There are a few advantages to this model. It centralizes coordination and reporting would become less complicated. It would create a strong identity for ESL service and a physical space to which international students could go to for not only academic but also social purposes. The model provides services for a wide range of proficiency levels and individualized instruction in various forms.

However, the committee identified a number of disadvantages. Most importantly, the model provides remedial services only; it does not acknowledge the academic, intellectual work of the ESL field that undergirds it. Furthermore, it is a segregated model which can lead to marginalization of the students and services and imposition of all responsibilities on the ESL center. The problem of student stigmatization and the unshared burden of serving ESL student population is observed in the K-12 setting as well. Educators often recommend an integrated model such as the two-way immersion program over segregated model for such reasons (see Ovando, Collier, & Combs, 2003). Another great disadvantage is that the quality of service is highly dependent on the expertise of the director and tutors, requiring close monitoring. This arrangement is a serious concern in a state where there is no advanced degree program that provides training in teaching EAP, which limits the pool of candidates for these positions. Other disadvantages include the need for more new physical space and the time to establish the program.

Conclusion

University faculty who are concerned about the education of international and Generation 1.5 students often struggle to find ways to increase linguistic and academic support for them. It is difficult to make changes especially when the institution is large and has a long history of paying little attention to this population. However, as this chapter shows, it is possible to form a small advocacy group to take initiative and collaborate in an effort to improve the situation. The work we have invested in has been quite challenging because it required a significant amount of time to solve complex issues. In the process, we realized how complicated it is to navigate through the institutional history and bureaucracy related to issues of course offerings, faculty evaluation, reporting, budget allocation, and so forth in order to establish a sensible arrangement for coordinating various instructional and support services. Nevertheless, this experience has been fulfilling because there is a hope that the document that we produced can bring about a dramatic change, creating a roadmap to the "Promised Land" (Kroll, 2004).

In our effort, it became clear that certain assumptions and ideologies in the institution and wider society are hidden behind many obstacles. In preparing the committee's recommendations, we tried to expose them, argue against them, and incorporate the counter arguments in our rationale for the recommendations. We also found it necessary to know what other institutions offer and incorporate the information in our proposal. It would be useful for our field to begin sharing information about what services and programs each institution offers and what kind of institutional ideologies are hindering or enhancing better education for international and Generation 1.5 students. Such information sharing and dialogue would facilitate the process of making policy recommendations that are sound and convincing.

The ESL committee is still uncertain what kind of action the university would take upon receiving our recommendations. A large part of the decision would depend on the financial resources available and what kind of philosophy the administration adopts. We sincerely hope that the university will take proactive steps to improve the current situation and provide equal and sufficient educational opportunities to all students on campus. Such an initiative would make the university a truly responsible and respected member of the local and global community.

REFERENCES

Brinton, D. M., & Jensen, L. (2002). Appropriating the adjunct model: English for academic purposes at the university level. In J. Crandall & D. Kaufman (Eds.), *Content-Based instruction in higher education settings* (pp. 125–137). Alexandria, VA: TESOL.

Crawford, J. (2004). *Educating English learners: Language diversity in the classroom* (5th ed.). Los Angeles, CA: Bilingual Educational Services.

Institute of International Education. (2004). Study abroad surging among American students: After Sept 11, interest in study abroad continues to grow rapidly. Retrieved December 11, 2004, from http://opendoors.iienetwork.org/?p=50138

Kroll, B. (2004, October). Complicating factors in addressing the English language needs of international visa students. Paper presented at The 4th Symposium on Second Language Writing, West Lafayette, IN: Purdue University.

Kubota, R. (forthcoming). Second language teaching for multilingualism and multiculturalism: Politics, challenges, and possibilities. In R. Hoosain & F. Salili (Eds.), *Language and multicultural education*. Greenwich, CT: Information Age Publishing.

Lo Bianco, J. (2002). Uncle Sam & Mister Unz. *Australian Language Matters, 10,* 8–10.

North Carolina Rural Economic Development Center. (2004). North Carolina experienced rapid growth in rural and urban areas in the 1990s. Retrieved December 11, 2004, from http://www.ncruralcenter.org/databank/trendpage_Population.asp

Ortega, L. (1999). Rethinking foreign language education: Political dimensions of the profession. In K. A. Davis (Ed.), *Foreign language teaching*

& *language minority education* (pp. 21–39). Honolulu, HI: Second Language Teaching & Curriculum Center, University of Hawaii.

Osborn, T. A. (2000). *Critical reflection and the foreign language classroom.* Westport, CT: Bergin & Garvey.

Ovando, C. J., Collier, V. P., & Combs, M. C. (2003). *Bilingual and ESL classrooms: Teaching in multicultural contexts* (3rd ed.). Boston: McGraw Hill.

Reagan, T. G., & Osborn, T. A. (2002). *The foreign language educator in society: Toward a critical pedagogy.* Mahwah, NJ: Lawrence Erlbaum Associates.

Wiley, T. G. (2004). Language planning, language policy, and the English-only movement. In E. Finegan & J. R. Rickford (Eds.), *Language in the USA: Themes for the twenty-first century* (pp. 319–338). Cambridge: Cambridge University Press.

Wiley, T. G., & Lukes, M. (1996). English-only and standard English ideologies in the U.S. *TESOL Quarterly, 30,* 511–535.

5 No ESL Allowed: A Case Exploring University and College Writing Program Practices

Angela M. Dadak

Our commitment to becoming the premier global university in the United States remains firm.

—American University President in a speech to the AU community, 2001

. . . we have decided to phase out the English Institute and to withdraw from the area of remedial language preparation.

—American University Provost in a memorandum to the AU community, 2002

The American University (AU) in Washington, DC, finds itself in a rather intriguing position at the moment in regards to nonnative English speaking students and, in particular, second language writers. In October 2001, the university president outlined fifteen guiding principles for the university. Among them was a reaffirmation to become a "premier global university" (Ladner, 2001). Objectives toward achieving this goal include expanding the number of AU students studying abroad, revising and improving the current study abroad programs, and increasing the presence of international students at the university. Specifically, the university would like to double the 15.9 percent of the student body that consists of students from outside the U.S. (Project Team, 2003).

In a seemingly paradoxical move, less than a year after the president first presented the fifteen points the university community received a memorandum from the provost that announced the closing of its English Language Institute (ELI), which for many years had served both as an IEP and EAP for the university. The provost stated that AU would no longer be in the business of "remedial language preparation."

The ELI faculty was unionized, which can enhance a faculty's position and department's identity on campus in beneficial ways (Vandrick, this volume), but the results at AU were less positive and the union could not protect the faculty from dissolution of the entire unit. However, because they were unionized, there was a negotiated "Memorandum of Understanding" regarding the closing of the ELI between its faculty and the administration. Part of that agreement states that

> after the university closes ELI on May 15, 2003 and if within four years thereafter it re-opens the ELI in whole or in part (under the name ELI or some other name), or establishes any comparable program with graduate students from other countries, teaching positions created in connection with the re-opening or the establishment of a comparable program shall be awarded to former ELI faculty teachers in seniority order.... Through May 15, 2005, the university shall not contract with any outside contractor(s), graduate students, or persons other than university employees to provide teaching services the same or similar to those the university offers through the ELI. (Memorandum of Understanding)

As a result, there is a practical moratorium on fully integrated ESOL instruction at AU for four years. This includes no ESL sections of first-year composition courses, specialized second language writing courses, or indeed most any support beyond the individual level.

While this top-down razing of language support services caused considerable shock to units that worked with—or would now have to work with—nonnative English speakers and writers, it also cleared the ground for some interesting new growth. This chapter will outline the essentials of the plan that was developed for this four-year moratorium, illustrate how this plan was executed in the first year, show how our undergraduate writing program has and has not changed, and outline some challenges and possibilities for the future. I'd like to suggest that this time may be used as a period not only of challenge, struggle, and complaint, but also of learning, experimentation, and reflection on not only the place of second language writers in our writing program but, perhaps even a forced examination of the goals and assumptions of this program. What happens at AU under its current restrictions may serve as an example to other institutions and programs in an era of shrinking resources and diversifying student populations.

The Plan and Implementation

A year before the ELI was to disappear, a new university committee brought together ESOL specialists and nonspecialists from across the university—international student services, academic support center, school of international studies, Kogod School of Business, TESOL, college of arts and sciences, college writing program and writing center—and even from the ELI itself. This first Academic Support Working Group (ASWG) "was convened to propose a comprehensive approach for offering services to international students with varying degrees of English competence. The abolishment of the ELI as well as changes in immigration regulations and AU admissions requirements, were all factors that shaped [its] recommendations" (Academic Support Working Group, 2003, p. 1). John Hyman, director of the college writing program and a member of the committee, anecdotally commented on the first days of the ASWG: "The dean told us this was an opportunity—but we spent our first few meetings complaining about how it was really a nightmare. We finally realized—'hey, this is really going to happen here, and we have to have a plan!' So to do this we decided to pretend the dean was right" (personal communication, September 2004). The plan the group developed had four main parts: language assessment, a course on U.S. academic discourse and cultural adaptation, an international student coordinating committee and the creation of three staff support positions.

Language Assessment

The ASWG recommended that all incoming international undergraduate students (with some exceptions) and certain graduate students (at the recommendation of their advisors) undergo language assessment during orientation week (Academic Support Working Group, 2003). The assessment focuses on academic tasks, such as listening to lectures, taking notes, and responding to questions based on those notes; and reading and providing short-answers, including paraphrases. The test has low stakes: Results are used to make recommendations for courses and to introduce students to campus services they may need, such as the writing center or tutors. It is not used for admissions decisions or any required actions. For example, based on the assessment an undergraduate student may be advised to delay starting the college writing courses for one semester, yet he or she may still choose to do so.

Over the first academic year of the plan, 58 students were assessed and advised based on their results. Experience showed that the initial advising was not the only boon for those who were assessed: it was a good way to initiate personal contact with a student and introduce them to other resources. On the other hand, students are not officially required to take the test, and awareness of the opportunity to take it is still limited; thus, several students who needed support were not detected until later in the year. Recommendations for future years include expanding awareness of the assessment and of the number of students who would be recommended to take it (Academic Support Working Group, 2004).

Course on U.S. Academic Discourse and Cultural Adaptation

Many academic IEP or EAP courses in the U.S. not only teach language skills but also serve as a cultural introduction to the U.S. academic community. Without the language courses, this resource also disappeared. The introduction of a course that would focus on U.S. academic discourse and culture was planned to fill that gap. The ASWG envisioned this as a required one-credit course in students' first and second semesters taught by adjunct instructors. The course topics spread across an ambitious array, including:
- ways of demonstrating knowledge across educational cultures
- learning and teaching styles
- collegial relations
- administrative concerns and resources
- personal study skills
- successful classroom participation
- research and critical thinking skills

- reporting research and the university's academic integrity policy (Academic Support Working Group, 2003).

In its first year, the course evolved considerably, moving from a transmission model, necessitated in part by the large number of topics addressed in a course with less than 20 hours of instruction, to a more learner-centered format, which included the negotiation with the students of a select number of topics to be addressed as well as individualized learning contracts. Class sizes averaged between ten and twenty students, mostly Asian students from AU's dual degree programs in Japan and Korea and athletes from Europe and South America.

International Student Coordination Committee

The original ASWG further recommended the creation of a more permanent committee that would consist of a core of three new staff positions (detailed below), academic advisors from each unit, and other campus staff as consultants to the group. In essence, this became an extension of the original ASWG and retained the same name. Since its creation, the group has met monthly to coordinate services and programs for international students such as improved language assessment and connecting the assessment results with academic advising.

Integrating Campus-Wide Expertise

The first ASWG also recommended the creation of three new full-time staff positions in areas that would be most affected by the dissolution of the ELI. In international student services, a senior advisor would chair the coordinating committee, direct language assessment, advise students on course selection in consultation with relevant AU staff, and program orientation events (Academic Support Working Group, 2003). In the first year, the senior advisor also took part in numerous activities related to new visa regulations, taught sections of the one-credit course, and oversaw advising of international students who were at academic risk indicated by low GPAs (Academic Support Working Group, 2004).

A second position was placed in the academic support center. This international student counselor offered individual academic counseling and transition assistance, created and led specialized workshops on topics of particular use to international students, provided oversight of language tutor referrals, and performed outreach activities to the AU community. The counselor also hired, trained, and oversaw the writing lab staff in the center (Academic Support Working Group, 2003). Due to acute need, in the first year the counselor created an ongoing workshop focused on classroom participation and was able to increase the number of writing lab tutors, and thus hours, available to work with international students.

The final position was the international student coordinator for the college writing program in the department of literature. Responsibilities associated with this position included advising the director of the writing program on individual students' readiness to take the required writing courses based on their initial language assessment, conduct workshops and ongoing support for the writing program faculty, provide training for writing center consultants, and teach a section of the one-credit course. In addition to these tasks, the coordinator also met individually with students enrolled in college writing courses and began to undertake research activities related to second language writers in the program, including undertaking a language use survey to learn more about the linguistic characteristics of students in college writing courses and begin to roughly ascertain the presence and size of its "generation 1.5" population.

The College Writing Program at American University

The college writing program (CWP) is considered one of the areas most affected by the dissolution of the ELI for several reasons. Passing the two-course sequences is a graduation requirement for all undergraduate students. Under the previous system, second language writers could elect to take equivalent writing courses in the ELI to satisfy the requirement, but as of the 2003–2004 academic year, all the nonnative English speakers were mainstreamed into the CWP. In addition, because of the Memorandum of Understanding, it was not possible to offer specialized ESL sections of college writing courses, so all sections across the program were potentially affected. Finally, without an ELI, it was expected that second language writers would increase their use of other writing supports, such as AU's writing center, which is located in the same department as and has a close relationship with the CWP.

The CWP and the writing center are, like many such programs at other universities, both located in the department of literature. (AU does not have an English department, per se, but the literature department includes all the English literature courses.) Students typically take the two-course writing requirement the fall and spring of their first year. Students are initially placed into college writing courses by their advisors. There are three choices for placement: honors sections for those in the honors program, a section for students with identified learning disabilities, and regular composition sections. Each section of regular composition is capped at twenty students, and roughly sixty sections are offered each semester. Consistency across the sections is held through the program's curriculum and grading criteria developed by the faculty and director that is made available to all writing instructors and also published online (http://www.american.edu/cas/lit/college_writing.cfm).

In terms of faculty, there are typically 15 full-time composition instructors and twenty adjunct instructors, including a small number of "gradjuncts" (graduate-student instructors) who have finished both the department's teaching of writing course as well as a semester-long internship with one of the full-time instructors. Almost all of the instructors have an MFA or MA in Literature, many of which were earned at AU, and are practically universally monolingual and monocultural.

The program is quite professional, with writing instructors holding full voting membership in the department of literature council and its committees. The full-time instructors hold one- or multi-year contracts, and the latter is considered tenure analogous. They also create and hold three professional development workshops and discussions each semester on topics such as writing course descriptions, commenting on student papers, crafting assignments that encourage students to get off campus, and other topics of interest or concern. These meetings are open and often attended by literature faculty in addition to the writing instructors themselves. Each year the department provides support for writing instructors to travel and present at national conventions such as CCCC, to which the instructors regularly contribute.

In terms of working with second language writers, the writing instructors, monolingual and monocultural, have little to no ESL training aside from some experience with nonnative English speakers in their courses previously at AU or elsewhere. Thus, they were to a large degree unprepared for, and resistant to, "having to deal" with the new second language writers coming into their courses. When asked what their main concerns were regarding these new students, the instructors commented "we're not trained to deal with this," "I don't teach grammar," and, most often, "they just don't speak English."

The resistance was certainly fostered to some degree by the administrative top-down placement of all ESL students into college writing courses without consulting the instructors. However, in handing down this decision, the administration also gave the program a full-time resource in the form of the international student coordinator. The dean insisted on this steady support instead of short-term training or a series of workshops, intending for the person in the position not only to foster longer-term faculty development and awareness and serve as a more permanent and ready resource, but also to help facilitate the creation of ties between the writing instructors and ESL experts across the campus.

The position in the CWP was created with several components: support writing faculty, second language writers, and writing center consultants; participate in campus-wide activities regarding international students; and teach one section of the cross-cultural course.

Faculty Development

As stated in the job description, one of the primary responsibilities of the international student coordinator is to provide support and development regarding second language writers for college writing faculty. One of the first requests from the faculty was that the coordinator lead one of their professional development workshops. The resulting session on contrastive rhetoric successfully challenged the instructors' ideas of "good writing," introducing it as a cultural concept instead of a worldwide universal. Through participation in the program's administrative meetings, the coordinator is also able to introduce cultural considerations into such areas as prompts for the writing placement test for transfer students and the choice of texts for summer freshman reading.

However, faculty support and development largely relies on a less formal, more individualized basis. The coordinator frequently meets individually with writing instructors to discuss individual students' performances and papers. Through these consultations, she is able to offer insights into cultural assumptions and practices that might be interfering with international students' integration into courses. She is also able to provide information and advice related to language acquisition, cultural-rhetorical choices and moves, and sentence-level issues.

A final evolution in this part of the position has been in collaborating with writing instructors on research and conference presentations. This type of collaboration fosters increased integration and understanding among L1 and L2 composition specialists (Stanley, Wald, & Winn, 2004).

Student Support

Support for second language writers taking college writing courses also falls into both group and individual activities. Over the first semester, the coordinator met with over half of the nonnative English speaking students in the writing program in over 100 hours of individualized instruction. Topics of the meetings included not only consultations on writing assignments, but also advice on discussion skills and peer-editing sessions, putting readings into cultural context, developing self-editing skills, and consultation on general cultural adjustment.

As a result of common themes apparent in the individual meetings, the coordinator developed a new series of informal sessions for international students new to the college writing program. On several evenings in the first half of every semester, the coordinator invites students new to the CWP and students who have successfully passed the writing courses to meet and discuss topics such as participating in discussions, handling peer workshops with native speakers, and the academic integrity code. The format for these meetings is generally a brief activity led by the coordinator, followed by breaking up into smaller groups so that new students can ask questions and veteran students can give advice. These discussions not only benefit the students; they often offer the coordinator further insights into students' concerns and strategies.

Writing Center

The coordinator also provides support as a second language specialist to the writing center, a service not unusual to many such centers (Williams, this volume). At the beginning of each semester, the coordinator is involved with the training of new writing center consultants. In addition, a group of consultants each semester sign up for further training on working with second language writers. In these sessions, the coordinator focuses on a balance of topics ranging from cross-cultural communication to English grammar. The vast majority of the consultants are graduate students in the department of literature, and only a few have experience living and communicating in non-English-speaking cultures. However, many of them are considering teaching as a career (in fact, several writing program faculty were once consultants themselves when they were students). Training and advice to the consultants opens their eyes to second language writing issues that they will face in the future.

On an individual level, when the consultants and/or their director are struggling in their support of a particular client, the coordinator also offers advice, and in some cases, even intervention or serves as a consultant for several sessions with a particular client.

Changes in the College Writing Program

One year into the moratorium on ESL instruction at AU, small changes can be detected within the writing program. For example, the level of resistance toward working with second language writers has decreased. No one is quite dancing in the halls, although a few faculty have admitted that they prefer their more diverse classes to the all-American, 18-year-old freshman ones. But the fear and resistance to nonnative speakers in their classes is less. One instructor mentioned that as a result of working with the International Student Coordinator, "I don't feel like I'm just baby-sitting my ESL students anymore. I feel like I can actually help them and teach more effectively."

Faculty are also beginning to develop more awareness of second language writing issues and question some of their practices. Evidence for this comes from individual meetings with instructors in which comments have moved from "I don't know what to do with these students" or "My Japanese student has a really hard time with this assignment"—an assignment based on U.S. K-12 school experiences—to "I was thinking about doing an assignment based on American myths, but wanted to talk to you about whether this could work for the international students in my class or not."

Second language issues have a stronger place in the training of the writing center consultants, and that may have not only present but also future effects since some of the peer consultants go on to teach writing—some even in the AU program.

One administrative change that has occurred is that class sizes have been reduced somewhat, due in part to the increased presence of second language writers in the classes. Regular composition classes are to be capped at 19 students in the fall, and off-sequence classes (those in which students start the writing sequence in the spring instead of the fall), which tend to be more diverse in terms of language and education backgrounds, will be capped at 15 students. This change came about not only through support from the dean, but also through testimonies of college writing faculty who taught these courses and recommendations from the CCCC Statement on Second Language Writing and Writers (2001).

Challenges Remaining

Among the numerous challenges to second language writers in the CWP, two are particularly prominent. One is the persistent deficit view of these writers within the program. Although most, if not all, of the instructors will express admiration for students who have accomplished various degrees of academic fluency in different languages, often such expressions are part of a conversation about what these students lack in writing, such as not stating a direct thesis, missing articles, and putting awkward phrases together. As Jane Stanley of the University of California at Berkley stated at the 4th Symposium on Second Language Writing, "Change in the hearts and minds of instructors is slow and I'm learning patience" (Stanley, Wald and Winn, 2004). There are still instructors who baldly state, "Their [second language writers] writing is just bad," and when pressed to describe how it is bad reply "in everything." However, the mantra from the first days of this experiment has changed from "They don't speak English" to "They don't speak English as a native language." A small evolution, but one that shows the beginning of change in hearts and minds.

A second major challenge for second language writers is the lack of choice in writing courses, which is the result of two administrative policies. Obviously, one is that no ESL sections can be held for a four-year period. A second cause is that there is, for all practical purposes, only one level of required writing class for undergraduate students. Mainstreaming second language writers into these classes has the advantages of not having to create new courses and of increased interaction between native-speaking and nonnative-speaking students; however, it can also disadvantage these writers in terms of the curriculum not being appropriate for their needs and skills, and instead of increasing interaction these courses may actually increase feelings of alienation and loss of self-confidence (Braine, 1996; Silva, 1994, 2004). These negatives can be enhanced in situations where the nonnative speaker is in the vast minority, and although less than 10 percent of all college writing courses at AU have only monolingual English-speakers in them, in the remaining courses the number of multilingual students range from one to eight, roughly 5 to 40 percent of the class. Hurdles to increasing choice in writing classes, whether the choice be for ESL writing classes or cross-cultural composition classes (Matsuda & Silva, 1999), stem not from the lack of sufficient numbers of ESL students, but mainly from logistical issues: as mentioned before, ESL sections cannot be offered, and, additionally, all students are placed into the first of the two writing courses (a practice resulting from an administrative decree following years of logistical problems resulting from over 800 incoming students choosing and switching their writing course sections).

A third challenge, not only for the CWP, but for support for international students campus-wide, is lack of specific policies from the university in terms of support for international students. What does it mean to be a "global university"? How will increasing the numbers of international students affect academic and campus life? How will we support these students to provide a welcome environment and foster their integration?

This lack of clear policies regarding the support of international students is hardly new in U.S. institutions of higher education. In the early 1980s, the American Council on Education and the Institute of International Education examined U.S. university and college policies toward international students and concluded that, overall, institutes of higher learning tended toward ad hoc or ambiguous policies or even "nonpolicy" (Rawley, 1997). Despite increasing numbers of foreign students coming to the U.S. throughout the 1990s, this policy practice remained. In a study of four IEP directors at U.S. schools of varied size and location, Rawley found that "nonpolicy remains the norm. Neither increased international student enrollments nor the ... focus on curricular globalization has brought about carefully drafted policies to address the needs of international students" (Rawley, 1997, p. 95). Decades after her study and despite the decisive dissolution of the ELI, a similar situation toward international students is still found at American University.

Conclusion

Overall, the AU administrative policy toward international students and ESL instruction in the first years of this century have affected our practices in the following ways:

Support for international students is more individualized. For example, in terms of writing support specifically for second language writers, a student can meet individually with a writing center consultant, a writing lab tutor, the international student counselor in the academic support center, or, if he or she is an undergraduate, with the international student coordinator in the CWP. Some students also hire tutors or proofreaders from the academic support center. While some group support exists, there are no second language writing or other language support courses.

There is increased integration and cross-campus cooperation between international and second language specialists to develop and provide this support and to increase knowledge and awareness of cross-cultural and language acquisition issues among faculty and staff. The continued existence of the ASWG means that issues such as graduate student support and outreach to faculty on international student issues is coordinated and available across campus. In addition, the three core members of the group continually reach out to specialists and non-specialists to increase awareness of cross-cultural issues and language acquisition. For example, the group brings together cross-cultural specialists from different divisions on campus to present on issues relating to working with international students at AU's annual conference on teaching excellence. This kind of increased collaboration in an environment of lacking institutional support can also be observed at other U.S. institutions (Kubota & Abels, this volume).

Within the CWP and writing center there is greater awareness of second language writer concerns and cross-cultural communication. Just like Barbara, a character in Kubota's (2003) article about a composition teacher learning to recognize cultural differences in writing and then progressing to an understanding beyond cultural relativism, writing instructors in the CWP at AU are just at the beginning of a potentially longer journey toward greater understanding of second language writers. With increased experience, experimentation, and input from second language writing specialists, this awareness can begin to transform the CWP in ways more sensitive to an increasingly diverse student body. The college writing faculty are already professionally reflective in their practice and concerned with the success of all their students. In the spirit of improving writing support for second language learners, grass-roots support at this level may eventually address some of the major challenges these students face in the writing program.

In conclusion, recent administrative policies and changes at American University have resulted in a situation in which the number of international students is encouraged to increase while support for these students—particularly language support—is non-existent. While this context at a university with a significant international focus and population is rare, the policies and ways in which they are formed in regards toward international students remains virtually unchanged from decades-old trends. However, AU's situation created an environment in which support for international students is more individualized, cross-campus expertise in terms of cultural and language issues is more fully integrated than it has been before, and, particularly in the college writing program, faculty are beginning to re-examine some of their assumptions and practices as they progress toward further inclusion of their second language students into their courses. As a result, what happens at AU under its current restrictions may serve as an example to other institutions and programs in an era of shrinking resources yet diversifying student populations.

References

Academic Support Working Group (2003). *Final report.* Washington, DC: The American University

Academic Support Working Group.(2004). *Final report.* Washington, DC: The American University.

Braine, G. (1996). ESL students in first-year writing courses: ESL versus mainstream classes. *Journal of Second Language Writing,* 5(2), 91–107.

Conference on College Composition and Communication. (2001). CCCC Statement on second language writing and writers. Retrieved on August 25, 2004, from http://www.ncte.org/cccc/resources/positions/123794.htm.

Kubota, R. (2003). Unfinished knowledge: The story of Barbara. *College ESL,* 10(1–2), 11–21.

Ladner, B. (2001, October 3). 15 points: Ideas into action, action into service. Retrieved September 20, 2003, from http://www.american.edu/15pointplan/speech.html

Matsuda, P. K., & Silva, T. (1999). Cross-cultural composition: Mediated integration of U.S. and international students. *Composition Studies, 27,* 15–30.

Project Team. (2003). *Transforming American University into the "premier global university" phase I.* Washington, DC: The American University. Retrieved on November 5, 2004, from http://www.american.edu/internationalaffairs/pdfs/premier_global_university_phase1.pdf

Rawley, L. A. (1997). The language program administrator and policy formation at institutions of higher learning. In M. A. Christison & F. L. Stohler (Eds.), *A handbook for language program administrators* (pp. 91–103). Burlingame, CA: Alta Book Center.

Silva, T. (1994). An examination of options for the placement of ESL students in first year writing classes. *Writing Program Administration, 18,* 37–43.

Silva, T. (2004, March). Where do we place them? *Working with second language writers: Demographics, assessment, placement, and instruction.* Workshop presented at the Conference on College Composition and Communication, San Antonio, TX.

Stanley, J., Wald, M., & Winn, M. (2004, October). *Impractical distinctions between NS and NNS: One program's attempts to re-vision the responsibilities of composition specialists.* Paper presented at the 4th Symposium on Second Language Writing. West Lafayette, IN: Purdue University.

6 The Role(s) of Writing Centers in Second Language Writing Instruction

Jessica Williams

Writing centers (WCs) or labs have been established at many if not most major universities in the United States and Canada to provide assistance and support for writers across the institution. Second language (L2) writers come to WCs for many reasons and with a range of goals. Some come hoping to work on drafts of papers they are writing; some have wider aims—to improve their writing skills. Some come because their professors have suggested that they come to the WC, often for "help with grammar." Other L2 writers come when their instructors simply do not know what else do with them. In part, this may be due to the fact that, at many institutions, composition instructors receive little preparation in how to work with L2 writers and still fewer, any theoretical background in second language acquisition (Williams, 1995). In addition, some faculty may assume that, since L2 writers are in college, their language proficiency is—or should be—no longer an issue, and that their language problems have somehow been taken care of prior to matriculation.

In spite of their visibility at WCs, L2 writers have received relatively little attention in WC research. In contrast, the literature on WCs in general, and on peer tutoring in particular, is extensive (e.g., Bouquet, 1999; Gillespie, Gillam, Brown & Stay, 2002; Kinkead & Harris, 1993; Murphy & Law, 1995 and two dedicated journals: *Writing Lab Newsletter* and *Writing Center Journal*). Until recently there had only been a handful of articles on the topic (e.g., Cogie, Strain & Lorinksas, 1999; Gadbow, 1992; Harris & Silva, 1993; Kennedy, 1993; Moser, 1993; Powers, 1993; Ronesi, 1995; Shin, 2002; Thonus,

1993), many of them limited to cautious advice or do's and don'ts for tutors working with L2 writers. In the past five years or so, however, more in-depth and empirically-based work has begun to emerge (e.g., Blau & Hall, 2002; Ritter, 2000, 2002a; Thonus 1999a, 1999b, 2002, 2004; Williams, 2004, 2005).

In the L2 writing literature as well, research that explicitly focuses on one-to-one tutoring has not been a major area of focus. Several studies have addressed expert-novice interaction in writing more generally (e.g., Aljaafreh & Lantolf, 1994; Cumming & So, 1996; Goldstein & Conrad, 1990; Haneda, 2004), and there is a vast body of work on interaction in peer groups or pairs (e.g., Berg, 1999; Connor & Asenavage, 1994; De Guerrero & Villamil, 2000; Liu & Hansen, 2002; Mendonça, & Johnson, 1994; Paulus, 1999; Storch, 2002; Swain, Brooks, & Tocalli-Beller, 2002; Tsui, & Ng 2000).

In spite of the absence of broad research findings, it has been suggested that the WC is an ideal place to address the problems and challenges of L2 writing (Ronesi 1995; Myers, 2003; Williams, 2004). The extra time and attention that L2 writers need are often not available in class or from their teachers, and since WCs are, by their very nature, focused on the individual, they may indeed be a perfect place for L2 writers. Muriel Harris, in a study of L2 writers in the WC, reported that they perceived tutors to be "immediately more helpful, more approachable, more practical and more personal than teachers" (1997, p. 223). Recent thinking points to a central role for WCs in writing instruction, one that suggests a reciprocal relationship between writing instructors and the WC staff (Tassoni, 1998). In other words, the WC does not simply provide supplementary or remedial instruction; rather, it is often a site of primary learning. In the WC, writers can work in a more focused manner on their writing and in some cases, on language development in ways that are perhaps not possible on their own or in classes with a greater student-to-teacher ratio (Myers, 2003).

Regardless of whether the WC is the *best* place for L2 writers, they are an inevitable and significant part of the WC clientele. According to many in the field, L2 writers are coming in increasing numbers and there is no indication that this trend is on the wane (Carter-Tod, 1996; Powers, 1993; Ronesi, 1995). All of the WC directors and tutors who participated in this study reported an increase in this population in recent years, in some cases, quite a sharp one. The center with the lowest L2 figures reported that about 20 percent of all sessions were with L2 writers; for others, the figure went as high as 80 percent. It should be noted that none of the institutions that participated was a community college; they were all major state or private four-year colleges or universities. It is likely that at two-year especially urban institutions the number would be even higher.

There are many factors that impact the performance of a WC. Certainly one of the most important is the place it has in the larger institution, how it is supported and staffed, and the lines of communication and reporting between it and other units in the institution. Because there was little information on the institutional role of WCs as regards L2 writers available in published sources, I began with the most basic form of research: interviewing those who run WCs and the people who work with L2 writers. I conducted a series of interviews with directors and tutors. This was not a large or scientific sampling; rather, I contacted institutions with well-known WCs and ones that I knew served a large number of L2 writers. I interviewed staff at twelve WCs, located in both private and public institutions in a variety of locations and settings (large, small, urban, land grant, east, west, south, and Midwest). The remainder of this article will pull together themes about institutional issues addressed in those discussions, from my own experience and the literature. This process has necessarily led to generalizations—perhaps overgeneralizations—and the result may not always faithfully represent the points of view of the individuals who generously agreed to share their knowledge and ideas.[1]

WRITING CENTER STAFF AND CLIENTS

Some of the most important issues in how, and perhaps how well, the L2 writer population is served are embedded in institutional relationships. For WCs, these relationships may determine who uses the WC, who is running the center, who is staffing it, how staff are trained, and how they view their mission, particularly as regards L2 writers. The first and perhaps most obvious thing to note is that no two WCs are the same, in their institutional relationships, their design, training, philosophy, or population that they serve. There are many different models for setting up WCs, but there is one basic defining feature: whether professional or peer tutors are the primary staff. Though some of the centers I spoke with have a limited number of permanent professional tutors, the majority had a mix of a few graduate student/TA "master" tutors and a much larger cadre of peer, mostly undergraduate peer tutors. The ethos of the peer-tutoring model, pioneered by Bruffee (1984), runs deep in many WCs. It is based on the notion that well-trained peers have the greatest potential to engage writers in authentic conversations about writing. Teachers can *teach* about many aspects of writing, but in WCs, the idea is to *talk* about writing in a supportive context. Indeed, only peers can truly engage in collaboration among equals, in contrast to academic professionals and even other graduate students, who may inevitably tip the balance of power as they take on the role of expert. This brief description presents the ideal of peer tutoring (Trimbur, 1987), which, as I will suggest later, is one often more fraught with conflict than the term suggests, especially in contexts that involve L2 writers.

As regards the L2 writers themselves, there are also important differences, the most important of which are twofold: First, some universities, most often urban ones, serve primarily resident populations, the so-called Generation 1.5, at least at the undergraduate level (Harklau, Losey & Siegal, 1999; Matsuda, 2003; Thonus, 2003). At others, the L2 population is largely international. The second major distinction is between graduate or undergraduate students. These two issues are closely linked since most graduate L2 writers are international students at any institution whereas undergraduate populations vary more widely from one institution to another. Clearly, the backgrounds and needs of international and resident students are likely to be quite different, and the needs of graduates and undergraduates diverge considerably as well.

At some institutions, even if it is not always clear what L2 learners need in the WC, at least it is clear who they are. At other institutions, however, this identification is not so easy, especially among undergraduates, and especially on urban campuses with large immigrant populations. Those who are labeled L2 writers may run the gamut from international students to students who were born in the United States but have spent their lives in bilingual communities. Evidence of the difficulty of pinpointing exactly who is an L2 writer is seen in many placement procedures (especially those that are limited to the results of a one-shot timed essay), which every year produce some anomalous results: African-American and white Anglo students ending up in classes for L2 writers, or L2 students identified as developmental because of the oral style, not necessarily the L2 features, of their placement essays.

These issues of identification are also important in the WC. Should writers, when they sign up or make an appointment, be identified or identify themselves as L2 writers? The answer is not always clear. On the one hand, doing so may get them the specialized help that they (may) need. On the other hand, it may also lead to labeling that may ultimately be unproductive. One possibility for getting around this problem is self-identification, but this option is as fraught as any other procedure with problems that may have little do with the influence of another language on their writing in English. At least one institution where the labels for international, immigrant, bilingual, 1.5, 1.25, etc. had become increasingly confusing and unhelpful, the staff decided simply to stop attempting to identify students in this way. It was assumed that each tutor would deal with the shadings of L2 as, and if, they become an issue.

The Place of the Writing Center in the Larger Institution

There are other institutional issues to consider. Most WCs have some institutional relationship with an English, composition, or rhetoric department or program. Beyond this generalization, there is variation in the extent to which they are integrated into these departments and programs. One major issue is whether the WC director is a tenured/tenure track faculty member in that department. If this is not the case, this will have significant impact on the clout that the WC can wield when resources are allotted. A second issue is the extent to which the rest of the staff of the WC is integrated with the department. Do WC tutors also work as teaching assistants in composition or literature courses? Or, do tutors work exclusively in the WC with relatively little to do with other programs in the department? In other words, are responsibilities and knowledge shared between the department and the WC?

What emerged as perhaps the most important issue, based on my interviews, is the relationships among the people: Programs differed in whether they could be characterized by what sociolinguist Leslie Milroy (1987) has called a *dense and multiplex network* among department and WC faculty, and particularly those who serve L2 writers. Network *density* refers to whether all parties, in composition, literature, the WC, and even applied linguistics, are connected independently, in this case, through institutional links. *Plexity* refers to whether individuals are connected in more than one way: in their research interests, their institutional roles, and even, in many cases, their social relationships. Interestingly, but perhaps not surprisingly, the intersection of professional and social relationships seemed to be the most prevalent in institutions in smaller cities and towns in which the university community is the primary source of social relationships and thus, also the nexus of social interaction. It is in institutions where faculty and staff report such networks that they also report satisfaction at the job they are doing generally and often, in how well they are serving the L2 population. In other words, where faculty and staff get together for lunch and for seminars, and not just departmental meetings, operations run more smoothly and students' needs are more likely to be met.

Although many WCs in this sample reported ongoing and institutional relationships with English departments; in contrast, none reported a primary relationship with an applied linguistics program, although some reported more informal ties. This is consistent with the history of writing centers (Bouquet, 1999; Carino, 2002); although all WCs are set up to help students become better writers, few consider it their primary mission to facilitate L2 acquisition (see also Matsuda, 1999). Yet for those WCs with a significant L2 client population, an important step is to acknowledge openly that L2 writers are not only learning to write in an L2, but that they are still learning that L2 (Harris & Silva, 1993; Kroll, 1990; Myers, 2003; Ritter, 2002; Williams, 2002). And, although these are intertwined in practice, in fact, they are quite different processes.

In some institutions, this separation between language and academic literacy acquisition plays out in composition programs as well, with L2 writers and NS writers in separate courses, or in some cases, taught by different faculty. Introductory English as a second language (ESL) composition classes may be taught by teaching assistants in the linguistics program and composition classes for native speakers of English, by teaching assistants in the literature, composition, and creative writing programs (Matsuda, 2003; Williams, 1995). This division in staffing is also seen at many WCs. The ESL specialist often comes from the applied linguistics program and the other tutors come from many other backgrounds, but primarily from English. Yet, at all of the institutions, whether or not there is a separate composition track for L2 writers, L2 writers inevitably show up in "regular" composition sections and from there, often make their way to the WC. Most WC directors reported that a large percentage of their undergraduate L2 clients come for assistance with their composition class assignments, though many reported a considerable number of other classes as well.

Preparing Tutors to Work with L2 Writers

There seem to be two basic options that have been taken in ensuring that there is expertise in L2 writing in the center.

The ESL Expert

Typically there is one or two individuals who are designated as an ESL specialist. This person's expertise may come as the result of hands-on experience with L2 writers or having completed relevant coursework or a degree in applied linguistics or related field. At WCs in universities that also house TESOL/applied linguistics programs, this is where the connection between the two programs can often be found. For example, a teaching assistant from the applied linguistics program might be hired as the/an ESL tutor. Duties for this specialist beyond actual tutoring may include a guest appearance in the tutor training course, workshops, or other forms of professional development for other tutors. How these specialists are viewed by others in the WC varies. For some, this person becomes the ESL oracle, in charge of dealing with all L2 issues. This expert often comes to embody the hope that there is some magic bullet, some secret that has been withheld from other tutors, which will finally be revealed.

Interestingly however, ESL specialists may also be viewed with some skepticism. One director maintained that expertise, be it in ESL or any other area, may not always be an asset within the peer tutoring model. Experts, in this case ESL specialists, may immediately see L2 writers as an "ESL writers," making assumptions about what their needs and problems are. Peers without specialized expertise are more likely to work as *peers,* to see L2 writers as individuals with unpredictable needs and problems that may include, but may also be independent of, their L2 status. In this director's view, peer tutors should take a learning stance as their teaching stance, and because of their special knowledge, it is harder for ESL specialists to do this.

Spread It Around

A second common approach for preparing tutors to work with L2 writers is to provide some limited training to all of the tutors. This generally comes as part of a one-semester course that students must take prior to becoming staff tutors at most WCs. Within this course, some attention is usually given to L2 issues. This typically consists of setting aside one unit or module of the course for this purpose. This may include one to several readings on the topic, perhaps some workshopping of papers, and a general discussion of the issues, often led by the resident ESL specialist if there is one, or a visitor from the ESL program. There was considerable overlap in the recommended readings about L2 writers (see Appendix). Whether this is because these are indeed the best sources or because they are the most readily available is not clear.

The Writing Center Mission and L2 Writers

There was considerable variation in how centers view their mission as regards L2 writers. Most centers include as part of their mission helping L2 writers of all proficiency levels to become better writers, at least in theory. Yet, this public stance was often tempered by private doubts about how realistic such a goal might be, especially in institutions that admit students with very low levels of language proficiency. Some WC staff members maintained that the WC is not really the place to work on developing language proficiency. Indeed, writers with very low language proficiency often leave sessions frustrated, as do their tutors. Expectations may be high, and tutor training for working with this population may be inadequate. Myers (2003), on the other hand, maintains that assisting L2 learners toward target language proficiency is precisely what tutors ought to be doing during their sessions with L2 writers. She argues that,

> it is both possible and desirable for writing center staff to fill the role of "foreign/second language teachers" as well as writing instructors. In fact, writing tutors are perfectly positioned to facilitate the language learning these students need in order to develop their ability to write in English. The central insight in foreign language pedagogy in the last thirty years is that, in fact, language acquisition emerges from learners wrestling with meaning in acts of communicating or trying to communicate. That is exactly what ESL students are doing in writing centers, person to person. (p. 64)

This is a debate that perhaps many WCs need to have. What obligations do university WCs have in assisting L2 students toward target language proficiency? Again, there is both a public and private face on this issue. Naturally, most centers maintain that they wish to assist L2 students to become better writers. Yet, L2 writers are widely seen as resource hogs by WC directors. Some L2 writers make as many appointments per week as is permitted; some may make appointments at different centers (in universities that have multiple centers) in an effort to get around appointment limitations. Indeed L2 writers are such enthusiastic users of the WC that some centers have had to set limits on their services directly in response to massive L2 writer demand. A center may place a limit on the number of hours or the number of appointments. Another method of controlling this limited resource is setting a floor on the kinds of services the WC is willing to offer. One center has set a policy that L2 students still enrolled in ESL classes are expected to refer to their ESL teachers for additional support rather than the WC. Several WC directors specifically stated their wish for more assistance from in-house intensive English programs or other programs expressly designed for L2 instruction. Indeed, some directors privately expressed the opinion that intensive programs were not shouldering as much responsibility as they might in supporting L2 students at the university, particularly those at lower levels of proficiency, whom WC staff sometimes feel ill prepared to assist.[2] Although this view of L2 writers as taking a disproportionate share of resources was widespread, at least in private reflection, almost the opposite view was also voiced: a perhaps grudging admiration for the L2 students who had learned so ably and efficiently to work the system to their advantage. One director mentioned that he had come to see L2 writers as active *agents* rather than the passive users he had previously assumed them to be. He saw them as optimal users of the system.

Writing Centers as a Site for Research

WCs are not often the site of formal outcomes evaluation (Bell, 2000; Jones, 2001; Thonus, 2002). There are a number of difficulties in carrying out such evaluations and indeed, some directors find the suggestion at cross purposes with the very idea of the WC, which they maintain is all about process (Yancey, 2002). In addition, the WC is a place where staff frequently reflect on their own learning, on their mission, and how well they are fulfilling it. In fact, WC research could be done in a variety of ways. I begin with the most immediately practical proposal of action research. Action research is generally considered some sort of inquiry that is conducted in an effort to improve the quality of an institution and its performance. It is typically designed and conducted by members of that institution, that is, practitioners. They analyze the information they collect and use their analysis to improve their own practice and the institution more broadly. This already goes on in WCs on a small scale: for example, as part of their preparation, individual tutors often analyze transcripts of their interaction, hoping to gain insight into their practice and improve their performance (e.g., Gilewicz & Thonus, 2003). What is lacking is action research at the more institutional level. For example, in most other L2 settings, there is an assumption that the instruction we provide is based on some knowledge of learners' needs, ideally developed through a formal needs analysis. As obvious as this may seem, such analysis has been largely absent from work with L2 writers in WCs. Only one formal needs analysis of L2 writers in the WC has been published (Powers & Nelson, 1995), and this is limited to graduate students.

Similarly, we have little idea of the outcomes of tutoring sessions beyond anecdotal evidence and generalizations about client satisfaction. An annotated bibliography of articles published in *Writing Center Journal* through 2000 (DeShaw, Mullin, & DeCiccio, 2000) offers no articles on the topic. We can look at outcomes in several ways: for individuals and for populations, in the near term (on individual papers) and in the long term (as writers). This kind of research is exceptionally hard to do for a variety of reasons. There is often resistance on the part of WC professionals to any program evaluation of this type, emphasizing as it does, the products over the process. Some would argue that the very notion of quantifying success flies in the face of the WC's mission and philosophy, the development of better writers through conversation and collaboration. Above all, it is almost impossible to establish the controlled conditions of a traditional experimental design. There are multiple factors that are important in the development of student writing such that it would be foolhardy to attribute improvement directly or exclusively to their WC experiences.

Difficulties notwithstanding, it is both possible and essential to establish whether what happens in WC sessions makes a difference. It may be that more qualitative approaches are appropriate, but these still need to go beyond the descriptive studies that have been offered in the literature. The results of descriptive studies have been valuable; however, given the current fiscal health of both public and private institutions across the nation, it is imperative that WC administrators, in concert with their colleagues in other programs and departments, be able to demonstrate in terms that central university administrators can understand, the value and success of the services they offer.

Aside from the very practical importance of this kind of research, the WC is also a potential rich site for more basic research in applied linguistics. Carol Severino made a call for such research more than ten years ago (1994). Thankfully, this research has started to trickle in, with an increasing number of articles and a steady supply of dissertations investigating a variety of questions. Most of the research on L2 writers in the center has focused on "the conversation," that is, the nature of the interaction between tutor and writer, and much of that, on the tutors and their role in the interaction. The role of the peer tutor can be an ambiguous and delicate one, combining as it does a status that is equal, yet somehow unequal to the writer-client (Blalock, 1997; Dyehouse, 1999; Thonus, 1999a, 1999b, 2001; Williams, 2005). By-now-traditional WC theory and practice suggest a nondirective, collaborative approach to tutoring (see Clark, 2001), with questioning a primary method for encouraging writers to discover their own meaning. Tutors are generally instructed not to tell writers how to change their texts; rather, they are often taught to use leading questions to help writers formulate their own plan for effective revision. The very premise of this model of the WC is predicated on negotiation between peers. Yet most literature on peer tutoring, much of it among children, assumes that the two participants do not have equal status in their instructional relationship (e.g., Damon & Phelps, 1989; Storch, 2002). Furthermore, this notion of peerness, however contentious it may be when applied to tutors of native speakers, becomes even more problematic in interaction with L2 writers. It is an open question whether native speaking tutors, who bear the inherent authority of their native speaker status, and L2 writers, can really be said to operate on an equal footing. One may wonder further whether this equality is absolutely necessary for a successful tutoring relationship.

The results of several studies suggest that in fact, tutors of L2 writers do not behave as equal collaborators. Their interactional contributions are marked by many features that indicate authority and dominance. Tutors of L2 writers take longer turns, more frequently interrupt their

L2 tutees, give more bald, on-record directives and suggestions than they do to native English speaking tutees (Thonus, 1999a, Williams, 2005). Recent work has also pointed to the differences in the interactional structure of sessions with L2 writers, compared to that of sessions with native speakers, again suggesting a more dominant role for tutors than is often described or at least advocated in the WC literature (Thonus, 2004; Williams, 2005). These are issues that have potential impact beyond the WC and could have implications for all interaction in which native speakers and L2 learners find themselves collaborating or simply conversing.

Several WC researchers have claimed that the WC is an important potential venue for learning the L2 as well as learning to write in the L2 (Myers, 2003; Ritter, 2002), yet we have little empirical support for this one way or the other. The lack of institutional connections between WCs and applied linguistics programs may explain why there is so little research linking L2 learning and learning to write. In spite of this lack of institutional connection, the link between the WC research and L2 learning is already apparent in findings of recent studies. Thonus (1999a) and Williams (2005) point to the tendency of tutors to try to make their interaction more useful by checking for comprehension and by using more direct language and less hedging, even if it means violating pragmatic norms. However, Ritter (2002) suggests that the opposite is often the case as well, in that the institutionally prescribed dominant status of tutors may actually curtail writer participation, thus limiting opportunities for learning the L2 and academic literacy.

There are other common findings. Several studies suggest that, as in the acquisition of an L2, active participation in negotiation of meaning may facilitate acquisition of literacy skills. Goldstein & Conrad (1990) and Williams (2004) both find that greater student participation leads to more significant revision. Conversely, Ritter suggests that the structure of the WC conversation with L2 writers can often block such participation, though she does not explicitly describe any impact on writing. Williams (2004) demonstrates clear connections between what goes on in WC sessions and the revisions that follow those sessions. Although it is difficult to make generalizations from the small sample in that study, the results point to a close relationship between both the nature and content of sessions and the nature and extent of the revisions that followed. This did not always end with a positive result; often the drafts students wrote following the WC session were rated worse or at least no better than the drafts they wrote before the session. This brings us right back to the issue of evaluation. What does it mean in terms of the success and effectiveness of the work at the WC if we cannot measure results in terms of direct improvement in a student's writing? Is such improvement part of the idea of the writing center (North, 1984)? I think most WC directors would agree: It's not about the papers; it's about the writers. That kind of change is a great deal harder to measure and harder to frame in terms that are acceptable to the larger institution. It is nevertheless important that WCs attempt to do so because, if history is any guide, WCs and their staff are more visible and vulnerable to university budget cuts than tenured faculty and programs housed safely in departments. Empirical research, effectively communicated, is a WC's best defense.

Notes

[1] Because the IRB approval of this study specified that the identity of the participating individuals and institutions would be kept confidential, I have not included names of any of the participating institutions or individuals.

[2] It should be acknowledged that intensive programs are often separate budget or even profit centers, and as such, may have rather different agendas than the WC.

References

Aljaafreh, A., & Lantolf, J. (1994). Negative feedback as regulation and second language learning in the zone of proximal development. *Modern Language Journal, 78,* 465–83.

Bell, J. (2000). When hard questions are asked: Evaluating writing centers. *Writing Center Journal, 21,* 7–28.

Berg, C. (1999). The effect of trained peer response on ESL students' revision types and writing quality. *Journal of Second Language Writing, 8,* 215–241.

Blalock, S. (1997). Negotiating authority through one-to-one collaboration in the multicultural writing center. In C. Severino, J. Guerra, & J. Butler (Eds.), *Writing in multicultural settings* (pp. 79–93). New York: Modern Language Association.

Blau, S., & Hall, J. (2002). Guilt-free tutoring: Rethinking how we tutor non-native-English-speaking students. *Writing Center Journal, 23,* 23–44.

Bouquet, E. (1999). "Our little secret:" A history of writing centers, pre- to post-open admissions. *College Composition and Communication, 50,* 462–483.

Bruffee, K. (1984). Peer tutoring and the conversation of mankind. In G. Olsen (Ed.), *Writing centers: Theory and administration* (pp. 3–14). Urbana, IL: NCTE.

Carino, P. (2002). Reading our own words: Rhetorical analysis and the institutional discourse of writing centers. In P. Gillespie, A. Gillam, L.F. Brown, & B. Stay (Eds.), *Writing center research: Extending the conversation* (pp. 91–110). Mahwah, NJ: Erlbaum.

Carter-Tod, S. (1996). The role of the writing center in the writing practices of L2 students. (Doctoral dissertation, Virginia Polytechnic Institute. 1995). *Dissertation Abstracts International, 56*(11A), 4262.

Clark, I. (2001). Perspectives on the directive/non-directive continuum in the writing center. *Writing Center Journal, 22,* 33–57.

Cogie, J., Strain, K., & Lorinskas, S. (1999). Avoiding the proofreading trap: the value of error correction strategies. *Writing Center Journal, 19,* 19–39.

Connor, U., & Asenavage, K. (1994). Peer response groups in ESL writing class: How much impact on revision? *Journal of Second Language Writing, 3,* 257–276.

Cumming, A., & So, S. (1996). Tutoring second language text revision: Does the approach to instruction and the language of communication make a difference? *Journal of Second Language Writing, 5,* 197–225.

Damon, W., & Phelps, E. (1989). Critical distinctions among three approaches to peer education. *International Journal of Educational Research, 58,* 9–19.

De Guerrero, M., & Villamil, O. (2000). Activating the ZPD. Scaffolding in L2 peer revision. *Modern Language Journal, 84,* 484–496.

DeShaw, D., Mullin, J., & DeCiccio, A. (2000). Twenty years of *Writing Center Journal* research. *Writing Center Journal, 20,* 39–72.

Dyehouse, J. (1999). Peer tutors and institutional authority. In L. Podis & J Podis (Eds.), *Working with student writers* (pp. 53–57). New York: Peter Lang.

Gadbow, K. (1992). Foreign students in the writing lab: Some ethical and practical considerations. *Writing Lab Newsletter, 17,* 1–5.

Gilewicz, M. & Thonus, T. (2003). Close vertical transcription in writing center training and research. *Writing Center Journal, 24,* 25–49.

Gillespie, P., Gillam, A., Brown, L. F., & Stay, B. (Eds.). (2002). *Writing center research: Extending the conversation.* Mahwah, NJ: Erlbaum.

Goldstein, L., & Conrad, S. (1990). Student input and negotiation of meaning in ESL writing conferences. *TESOL Quarterly, 24,* 443–460.

Haneda, M. (2004). The joint construction of meaning in writing conferences. *Applied Linguistics, 25*, 178–219.

Harklau, L., Losey, K., & Siegal, M. (Eds.). (1999). *Generation 1.5 meets college composition*. Mahwah, NJ: Erlbaum.

Harris, M. (1997). Cultural conflicts in the writing center: Expectations and assumptions of ESL students. In C. Severino, J. Guerra & J. Butler (Eds.), *Writing in multicultural settings* (pp. 220–233). New York: Modern Language Association.

Harris, M., & Silva, T. (1993). Tutoring ESL students: Issues and options. *College Composition and Communication, 44*, 525–537.

Jones, C. (2001). The relationship between writing centers and improvement in writing ability. An assessment of the literature. *Education, 122*, 3–20.

Kennedy, B. (1993). Non-native speakers as students in first-year composition classes with native speakers: Can writing tutors help? *Writing Center Journal, 13*, 27–38.

Kinkead, J., & Harris, J. (Eds.). (1993). *Writing centers in context*. Urbana, IL: NCTE.

Kroll, B. (1990). The rhetoric and syntax split: Designing a curriculum for ESL students. *Journal of Basic Writing, 9*, 40–45.

Liu, J., & Hansen, J. (2002). *Peer response in second language writing classrooms*. Mahwah, NJ: Erlbaum.

Matsuda, P. K. (1999). Composition studies and ESL writing: A disciplinary division of labor. *College Composition and Communication, 50*, 691–721.

Matsuda, P. K. (2003). Basic writing and second language writers: Toward an inclusive definition. *Journal of Basic Writing, 22*, 67–89

Mendonça, C., & Johnson, K (1994). Peer review negotiations: Revision activities in ESL writing instruction. *TESOL Quarterly, 28*, 745–69.

Milroy, L. (1987) *Language and social networks* (2nd ed.). Oxford: Blackwell.

Moser, J. (1993). Crossed currents: ESL students and their peer tutors. *Research and Teaching in Developmental Education, 9*, 37–43.

Murphy, S., & Law, J. (Eds.). (1995). *Landmark essays on writing centers*. Mahwah, NJ: Erlbaum.

Myers, S. (2003). Reassessing the "Proofreading Trap": ESL tutoring and writing instruction. *Writing Center Journal, 24*, 51–70.

North, S. (1984). The idea of a writing center. *College English, 46*, 433–446.

Paulus, T. (1999). The effect of peer and teacher feedback on student writing. *Journal of Second Language Writing, 8*, 265–289.

Powers, J. (1993). Rethinking writing center conferencing strategies for the ESL writer. *Writing Center Journal, 13*, 39–47.

Powers, J., & Nelson, J. (1995). L2 writers and the writing center: A national survey of writing center conferencing at graduate institutions. *Journal of Second Language Writing, 4,* 113–138.

Ritter, J. (2002a). Negotiating the center: An analysis of writing center tutorial interactions between ESL learners and native-English speaking writing center tutors. (Doctoral dissertation, Indiana University of Pennsylvania, 2000). *Dissertation Abstracts International, 63*(06), 2224A.

Ritter, J. (2002b). Recent developments in assisting ESL writers. In. B. Rafoth (Ed.), *A tutor's guide: Helping writers one to one* (pp. 102–110). Portsmouth, NH: Heinemann.

Ronesi, L. (1995). Meeting in the writing center: The field of ESL. *TESL-EJ, 1,* 3. Retrieved June 14, 2001 from http://www-writing.berkeley.edu/TESL-EJ/ej03/a1.html

Severino, C. (1994). The writing center as a site for cross-language research. *Writing Center Journal, 15,* 51–61.

Shin, S. (2002). Ten techniques for successful writing tutorials. *TESOL Journal, 11,* 25–31.

Storch, N. (2002). Patterns of interaction in ESL pair work. *Language Learning, 52,* 119–158.

Swain, M., Brooks, L., & Tocalli-Beller, A. (2002). Peer-peer dialogue as a means of second language learning. *Annual Review of Applied Linguistics, 22,* 171–185.

Tassoni, J. (1998). The liberatory composition teacher's obligation to writing centers at two-year colleges. *Teaching English in the Two-Year College, 25,* 34–43.

Thonus, T. (1993). Tutors as teachers: Assisting ESL/EFL students in the writing center. *Writing Center Journal, 13,* 102–114.

Thonus, T. (1999a). Dominance in academic writing tutorials: Gender, language proficiency and the offering of suggestions. *Discourse and Society, 10,* 225–248.

Thonus, T. (1999b). How to communicate politely and be a tutor, too: NS-NNS interaction and writing center practice. *Text, 19,* 253–279.

Thonus, T. (2001). Triangulation in the writing center: Tutor, tutee, and instructor perception of the tutor's role. *Writing Center Journal, 22,* 59–81.

Thonus, T. (2002). Tutor and student assessments of academic writing tutorials: What is "success?" *Assessing Writing, 8,* 110–134.

Thonus, T. (2003). Serving generation 1.5 students in the university writing center. *TESOL Journal, 12,* 17–24.

Thonus, T. (2004). What are the differences? Tutor interactions with first- and second-language writers. *Journal of Second Language Writing, 13,* 227–242.

Trimbur, J. (1987). "Peer tutoring": A contradiction in terms? *Writing Center Journal, 7,* 21–28.

Tsui, A., & Ng, M. (2000). Do secondary L2 writers benefit from peer comments? *Journal of Second Language Writing, 9,* 147–170.

Williams, J. (1995). ESL composition program administration in the United States. *Journal of Second Language Writing, 4,* 157–179.

Williams, J. (2002) Undergraduate second language writers in the writing center. *Journal of Basic Writing, 21,* 16–34.

Williams, J. (2004). Tutoring and revision: Second language writers in the writing center. *Journal of Second Language Writing, 13,* 173–201.

Williams, J. (2005). Writing center interaction: Institutional discourse and the role of peer tutors. In K. Bardovi-Harlig & B. Hartford (Eds.), *Interlanguage pragmatics: Exploring institutional* (pp. 37-65). Mahwah, NJ: Erlbaum.

Yancey, K. (2002). Seeing practice through their eyes: Reflection as teacher. In P. Gillespie, A. Gillam, L. Brown, & B. Stay (Eds.), *Writing center research: Extending the conversation* (pp. 189–201). Mahwah, NJ: Erlbaum.

APPENDIX

A RESOURCE LIST FOR FACULTY AND TUTORS AT WRITING CENTERS THAT SERVE L2 WRITERS

Aljaafreh, A., & Lantolf, J. (1994). Negative feedback as regulation and second language learning in the zone of proximal development. *Modern Language Journal, 78,* 465–83.

*Blau, S., & Hall, J. (2002). Guilt-free tutoring: Rethinking how we tutor non-native-English-speaking students. *Writing Center Journal, 23,* 23–44.

Blau, S., Hall, J., & Strauss, T. (1998). Exploring the tutor-client conversation: A linguistic analysis. *Writing Center Journal, 19,* 19–48.

*Cogie, J. Strain, K., & Lorinskas, S. (1999). Avoiding the proofreading trap: The value of error correction strategies. *Writing Center Journal 19,* 19–39.

Currie, P. (1998). Staying out of trouble: Apparent plagiarism and academic survival. *Journal of Second Language Writing, 7,* 1–18.

Ferris, D. (2002). *Treatment of error in second language student writing.* Mahwah, NJ: Erlbaum.

*Fox, H. (1994). *Listening to the world: Cultural issues in academic writing.* Urbana, IL: NCTE.

*Harris, M. (1997). Cultural conflicts in the writing center: Expectations and assumptions of ESL students. In C. Severino, J. Guerra, & J. Butler (Eds.), *Writing in multicultural settings* (pp. 220–233). New York: Modern Language Association.

*Harris, M., & Silva. T. (1993). Tutoring ESL students: Issues and options. *College Composition and Communication, 44,* 525–537.

Kennedy, B. (1993). Non-native speakers as students in first-year composition classes with native speakers: Can writing tutors help? *Writing Center Journal, 13,* 27–38.

Moser, J. (1993). Crossed currents: ESL students and their peer tutors. *Research and Teaching in Developmental Education, 9,* 37–43.

Myers, S. (2003). Reassessing the "Proofreading Trap": ESL tutoring and writing instruction. *Writing Center Journal, 24,* 51–70.

*Powers, J. (1993). Rethinking writing center conferencing strategies for the ESL writer. *Writing Center Journal, 13,* 39–47.

Reid, J. (1995). Which non-native speaker? Differences between international students and U.S. resident students. *New Directions in Teaching and Learning, 7,* 17–27.

*Ritter, J. (2000). Recent developments in assisting ESL writers. In B. Rafoth (Ed.). *Helping writers one to one.* Portsmouth, NH: Heinemann.

Ronesi, L. (1995). Meeting in the writing center: The field of ESL. *TESL-EJ 1,* 3.

Silva, T., Leki, I., & Carson, J. (1997). Broadening the perspective of mainstream composition studies. *Written Communication, 14,* 398–428.

*Shin, S. (2002). Ten techniques for successful writing tutorials. *TESOL Journal, 11,* 25–31.

Spack, R. (1997). The acquisition of academic literacy in a second language. *Written Communication, 14,* 3–62.

Thonus, T. (1999). How to communicate politely and be a tutor, too: NS-NNS interaction and writing center practice. *Text, 19,* 253–279.

Thonus, T. (2001). Triangulation in the writing center: Tutor, tutee, and instructor perception of the tutor's role. *Writing Center Journal, 22,* 59–81.

Thonus, T. (2003). Serving generation 1.5 learners in the university writing center. *TESOL Journal, 12,* 17–24.

Thonus, T. (2004). What are the differences? Tutor interactions with first- and second-language writers. *Journal of Second Language Writing, 13,* 227–242.

Weigle, S., & Nelson, G. (2004). Novice tutors and their ESL tutees: Three case studies of tutor roles and perceptions of tutorial success. *Journal of Second Language Writing, 13,* 203–225.

Williams, J. (2002). Undergraduate second language writers in the writing center. *Journal of Basic Writing, 21,* 16–34.

Williams, J. (2004). Tutoring and revision: Second language writers in the writing center. *Journal of Second Language Writing, 13,* 173–201.

Williams, J., & Evans, J. (2002). How useful are handbooks for second language writers? *Writing Program Administration, 10,* 59–75.

* Articles mentioned as a useful resource by multiple WC directors and/or staff.

The Politics of English Writing for Academic and Professional Purposes

7 Understanding Context for Writing in University Content Classrooms

Wei Zhu

An important goal of second language writing instruction in English for Academic Purposes (EAP) programs is to help second language students develop skills and strategies to cope with academic writing tasks in university content classrooms. To achieve this goal, it is critical for EAP writing researchers and practitioners to understand the nature of writing tasks required of students and the context for writing in university content classrooms. Writing task analysis has deepened our understanding of writing in university content classrooms (e.g., Carson, 2001; Hale, et al., 1996); however, more needs to be known about the context for writing and about the influences of the institutional, disciplinary, and rhetorical contexts on writing in university content classrooms. This chapter addresses the politics of second language writing by exploring questions concerning the influences of the context on writing in university content classrooms, which many second language writers will enter.

Context has been defined and redefined as a construct in writing research (Brandt, 1986; Chin, 1994; Piazza, 1987). Piazza (1987) provides a useful analysis of different theoretical perspectives on context. The cognitive perspective focuses on information processing, decision making, and strategy deployment involved in performing the writing task. Context from this perspective consists of the writer, the task, and the text. The sociological perspective sees writing as a social activity and pays particular attention to how social roles, status, norms and interactions in specific social and communicative events or situations support or constrain the functions and uses of writing. The focus is on how various social forces and factors influence writing, and how writing reflects or serves to establish or maintain social relationships and norms. Context from this perspective is defined as setting and interaction. The cultural perspective sees writing as a cultural process and "emphasizes the importance of society and culture in defining the role of context in writing" (Piazza, 1987, p. 120). More specifically, it focuses on goals and norms of literacy in different communities, on values and beliefs concerning literacy in different communities, as well as on the socialization of learners into literacy practices. This emphasis contributes to a definition of context as a literacy event. Piazza (1987) argues for combining the different perspectives and creating a multiple-perspective framework for understanding the context for writing.

More recently, Samraj (2002) provides a useful framework for conceptualizing the context for writing in university content classrooms. Samraj's framework consists of five layers of contextual variables: academic institution, discipline, course, task, and student. The "layers of context" (p. 165) are arranged with the most general element, academic institution, at the top, and four increasingly more specific contextual elements, namely, the academic discipline, the course, the task, and the student, form layers below it. Each layer is connected to and influenced by but does not completely overlap with the layer(s) above it. Depicting the complexity of the context and the relationship among the various contextual elements, Samraj's framework offers insight for understanding writing in university content classrooms.

Academic writing research has explored how various layers of context influence student writing in university classrooms. A particularly interesting line of research has examined how context influences features of writing tasks required of students and students' written texts. Much of the research on academic writing task analysis indicates that disciplinary context exerts an important influence on the writing tasks required of students (Braine, 1989, 1995; Carson, 2001; Hale et al., 1996; Zhu, 2004). Carson (2001) analyzed student writing tasks at the graduate and undergraduate levels in three disciplines: biology, history, and psychology. The writing tasks analyzed exhibited both similarities and differences across disciplines and instructional levels, with the differences "more apparent across disciplines at the graduate level than at the undergraduate level" (p. 79). Zhu (2004) examined writing assignments in business and analyzed data from various sources, including course syllabi, handouts on writing assignments, and qualitative interviews with selected faculty members. Zhu found that several major types of assignments required of students in business courses were specifically connected to the business discipline because features of the tasks (e.g., the problem-solving and decision-making orientation of the tasks) and desired textual features in student texts reflected the goals and nature of the business field. Also, a main purpose of these assignments was to initiate students into the business world.

Academic writing research has also examined the influence of the writing context on features of student texts. Herrington (1985) examined writing in two chemical engineering classes, lab and design, and found that these two courses constituted two different discourse forums in which students assumed different social roles. The writing tasks served different purposes in the two courses, and students wrote for different audiences using different lines of reasoning and types of evidence. Samraj (2002) explored the relationship between layers of the writing context and examined the influence of the contextual layers, particularly the layers of course and task, on student writing in two graduate courses in a master's program in environmental science. Samraj found that "features of different contextual layers can be in dissonance" (p. 173) and that certain unsuccessful features in students' written texts could be explained by the dissonance among different contextual layers and by students' lack of consideration of certain contextual layers.

Academic writing research has tended to focus on context at the discipline, course, and task levels and the impact of context at these levels on features of writing tasks and student written texts in university content classrooms. Research on practices and policies in higher education, however, sheds light on the potential impact of context at the institution and discipline levels on other aspects of writing in university content classrooms. This body of research addresses how institutional and disciplinary contexts influence learning and teaching in the university setting and has examined a host of issues, including the epistemological orientations and knowledge validation of different disciplines (e.g., Donald, 1986, 1995), the relationship between institutional and departmental cultures across disciplines (e.g., Lee, 2004), disciplinary variation in teaching and learning and faculty involvement in teaching and research (Neumann, 2001; Neumann, Parry, & Becher, 2002; Smeby, 1996), students' epistemological beliefs (Schommer-Aikins, Duell, & Barker, 2002), and graduate students' access to academic research cultures (Deem & Brehony, 2000). Research concerning the epistemological orientations of different disciplines and disciplinary variation in teaching and research is particularly relevant to an understanding of writing in university content classrooms.

Referring to a set of variables developed by Kyvik (1991, cited in Smeby, 1996), Smeby (1996) points out that disciplines differ depending on the communication language used. Fields that are more codified are "characterized by a stringent symbol system and a heavy use of mathematics" (p. 71). In contrast, literary fields tend to rely on prose and "the codes are more implicit" (p. 71). Along this line, research that examines learning and teaching across disciplines suggests the different roles that writing may play as an instructional activity in different fields. Neumann, Parry, and Becher (2002) discuss various aspects of learning and teaching for undergraduate education in hard pure, hard applied, soft pure, and soft applied fields, including curriculum, assessment, and methods of teaching.[1] Their review of relevant research indicates that in soft pure and soft applied fields, essays, papers, and projects are preferred means of assessment, whereas in hard pure and hard applied fields, the preferred means of assessment are objective tests. Neumann, Parry, and Becher argue that the preferred means of assessment are related to the knowledge structure of the fields in which they are used.

Several studies have found that faculty conceptualization of and involvement in teaching and research differ across academic fields (Lueddeke, 2003; Smeby, 1996). For example, Smeby (1996) surveyed faculty members at the rank of assistant professor or higher in humanities, social sciences, natural sciences, medicine, and technology at four universities in Norway and found that the amount of time faculty spent on instruction differed across academic fields. The difference in faculty involvement in teaching has been explained in terms of not only "epistemological orientations" (Braxton & Hargens, 1996, cited in Lee, 2004) but also the "available resources" (Clark, 1987a, cited in Lee, 2004) in different academic fields. Further, research has examined faculty perception of the academic reward system and has revealed "a perception that teaching is undervalued" (Neumann, 2001, p. 135). Shulman (1993) addresses the value placed on teaching vs. research in higher education and argues that teaching is not valued as much as research at universities because teaching has not been accorded the status of "community property" and because teaching is often perceived and treated as "non-disciplinary," that is, "not part of the community that means so much to most faculty" (p. 6).

Although much of the research examining practices in higher education often does not directly focus on writing in the university setting, it nevertheless raises some questions about writing in university content classrooms. Research has suggested that writing serves as a major assessment tool in some disciplines, but what other purposes does writing serve in university classrooms? Research has also indicated that various institutional and disciplinary factors influence teaching and learning in university content classrooms. Given the potential role that writing can play in teaching and learning, it is important to examine how these factors influence writing in university classrooms. The study reported in this chapter examined questions concerning purposes of and factors influencing student writing in university content classrooms.

METHOD

Setting

The results reported below were part of a larger study designed to examine several aspects of writing across disciplines. Several sources of data were collected for the larger study, including faculty surveys, qualitative interviews with faculty members, and course materials. The study took place at a large, public research university in the southeast of the United States. The university offers a wide range of degree programs and enrolls about 35,000 students, among whom about one thousand are international students.

Procedure

The primary source of data analyzed to answer the questions posed above came from faculty surveys. Three hundred faculty members representing approximately 20 percent of the faculty at the university were invited to participate in the survey. The invited faculty members represented several academic areas: humanities, business, engineering, natural sciences, and education. Each academic area was represented by several specific disciplines, and "humanities" in this chapter served as an umbrella term covering the traditional humanities disciplines (e.g., history) as well as a few social science disciplines (e.g., sociology and anthropology). These academic areas were selected because they offer a significant portion of the undergraduate and graduate degree programs and thus are likely to enroll a large number of second language learners. The sampling procedure used for the survey was stratified random sampling (Leedy, 2001). The academic areas constituted the strata, and random sampling took place within each stratum. Once the academic areas and the specific disciplines were chosen, faculty members were randomly selected for the purpose of the survey.

In the Fall 1999 semester, an initial letter was sent to the 300 faculty members selected to participate in the study to inform them of the purpose of the study and of the survey that would be sent to them. Two weeks later, the survey was mailed to the faculty members. The 18-item survey, consisting of both selected responses and open-ended questions, was designed to elicit faculty responses to questions concerning several aspects of writing in undergraduate and graduate courses. The selected responses addressed a) the importance of writing; b) the types of writing tasks required of students; c) the nature and extent of guidance and instruction on academic writing available to students; and d) student writing difficulties. Because a goal of the survey was to capture a full picture of the use of writing in university content classrooms, faculty members were invited to respond to questions dealing with writing on tests or exams (i.e., essay responses to test questions) as well as questions dealing with writing assignments, defined as "papers, assignments, or projects requiring any type of writing on the part of the students." Two related open-ended questions elicited faculty responses concerning the rationale for assigning writing in university content courses and factors that may influence faculty decisions concerning student writing requirements in their courses.[2] Faculty responses to the open-ended questions in the survey constituted the primary source of data for the results reported below.

Eighty-nine faculty members returned the survey, representing a 30 percent overall response rate. Seventy-one faculty members chose to respond to the open-ended questions included in the survey: 18 from humanities, 14 from business, 16 from the sciences, 14 from engineering, and 9 from education. The returned surveys were grouped according to the academic areas represented by the respondents, and each survey was assigned a numerical code for purpose of reference. For example, a survey designated as "Business 3" refers to a returned survey from business that was assigned the numerical code 3.

A secondary source of data for the results reported below came from qualitative interviews (Rubin & Rubin, 1995) with 23 faculty members. The interview questions addressed a) the types of writing assignments required; b) faculty perception of student writing skills; c) the importance of writing; and d) the role of content course professors in helping students develop academic writing skills. The interviews were tape-recorded and transcribed. Similar to the surveys, the interviews were grouped according to academic areas, and each interview was assigned a numerical code.

Data Analysis

Faculty responses to the open-ended survey questions and interview questions were analyzed qualitatively. The approach to analysis was inductive and recursive. Faculty responses were coded based on the content of the responses, and all the codes were derived from the data. A response to the survey questions might consist of multiple segments addressing different issues, and each segment was coded to reflect its underlying theme. Comments with the same codes were then grouped. The interview transcripts were analyzed in the same inductive and recursive fashion. In the process of analysis, a few categories were modified, combined, or eliminated.

Results

Analysis of faculty responses to the open-ended survey questions and interview questions revealed several main purposes for writing in university content classrooms as well as factors which influence faculty decisions concerning student writing in content courses.

Major Purposes for Writing

Analysis of faculty responses to the open-ended survey questions indicated several purposes for writing in university content classrooms. The main purposes included a) to evaluate student learning; b) to prepare students for academic/disciplinary and career success; c) to address course goals; and d) to foster individual development.

To Evaluate Student Learning

Faculty members across academic fields indicated that an important purpose for writing in their classrooms was to evaluate student learning. Faculty members who gave evaluation of student learning as the main purpose for writing explained that, compared to "objective tests," written responses to exam questions and writing assignments constituted a more effective method for evaluating students' real understanding of course materials and for assessing students' ability to analyze and synthesize information and to apply their knowledge to solving real world problems. Responses such as the following were reflective of this purpose.

> Best way to assess their knowledge. (Business 15)

> Written answers show ability to synthesize information. (Sciences 3)

> Only essay responses can give a true picture of students' knowledge and skills. (Engineering 7)

> I use essay questions on exams and written responses on course projects, lab reports and assignments so that I can evaluate the depth and breath of students' understanding and application of knowledge and concepts. (Education 8)

To Prepare Students for Success in Their Disciplines and Careers

Some faculty members referred to the importance of writing for students' success in their disciplines and/or future careers as a reason for requiring writing assignments. For these professors, the writing assignments provided students with opportunities to develop the types of writing skills crucial for success in the students' disciplines and/or future careers. Faculty members from humanities and business, in particular, emphasized the importance of writing for student success in their disciplines, although a few engineering faculty members also mentioned the importance of writing for student career success.

> My field requires not only retention of facts, but also the ability to argue points and interpret material. Writing skills are essential. (Humanities 15)

> It is a major tool of high-level managers. Our students should be prepared for this responsibility. (Business 16)

> I use major writing assignments exclusively with my senior undergraduates. They are graduating seniors and the assignments are designed to allow them to show that they can analyze all aspects of a business to make decisions for its future. With the graduate students, the written assignments allow them to integrate what they have learned and think like a manager. (Business 8)

> My rationale is that in their career, students will have to work in problem-solving most of the time. Being able to communicate concepts and ideas is crucial in team environments. (Engineering 10)

To Address Course Goals and Content

Some faculty members indicated that writing assignments were required because of the specific nature of their courses. A few faculty members made it clear that writing was required because enhancing student written communication skills was an explicitly stated course goal.

> A major goal in my class is to improve written and oral communication skills. I have the students interview someone in a management position and write an 8-page paper based on the interview. They do this twice during the semester. The papers account for 50 percent of their grades. (Business 7)

> To teach writing in order that my students will become teachers of writing. (Education 14)

Other faculty members referred to the nature of the content of their courses when explaining why they required writing:

> Nature of the content and analysis required. (Education 3)

> The courses I teach are design type that include qualitative/quantitative reasoning that needs to be articulated. (Engineering 1)

To Foster Individual Development

A few faculty members mentioned another purpose for writing in university content classrooms: to foster individual development. According to these faculty members, writing provided opportunities for students to develop thinking skills that would help them grow as individuals.

> I feel that writing one's thought and ideas is not only essential to learning in academia and being successful in the work world, but that it helps us grow as individuals. (Humanities 4)

> Logical thinking requires writing. By trying to write, students learn how to think logically. The processes of thinking, critical thinking, are more important than just obtaining right answers. (Sciences 17)

The main purposes for writing expressed by faculty members in their responses to the open-ended survey questions echoed those mentioned by faculty members during the interviews.

Factors Influencing Faculty Decisions Concerning Writing in Content Classrooms

Analysis of faculty responses to the survey questions revealed several factors that influence faculty decisions on student writing requirement in university classrooms. Two main factors included a) class size and time needed to design and grade assignments; and b) the nature of the discipline and course.

Class Size/Time Needed to Design and Grade Assignments

The large size of some undergraduate classes and the demand on faculty time for designing and evaluating essay responses and writing assignments in large classes were perceived by the survey respondents to be major impediments for requiring writing in large classes. Large class size and lack of time needed for evaluating student writing posed difficulties for faculty members across academic fields, as indicated by the comments below.

> Students should learn how to express their thoughts in writing. It is a critical lifelong skill. I think it teaches students to think and not regurgitate material. I stress creativity and analysis of concepts, not details. But, as I am getting pushed to teach large classes, I will not have any more writing assignments. Students will lose immensely from this change. They learn so much more from writing and from me writing back to them. (Humanities 8)

> My "specialty" is mass lecture classes ranging from 70 to 390 students. I don't require writing assignments because of the time needed for grading. (Business 17)

> I can't use essays in classes with large enrollment. It takes too long to grade the exam. The same is true for written papers and reports. (Sciences 11)

> I typically teach 2 courses each with 60 or more students. My teaching assignment is 50 percent. I don't have time to grade writing assignments. (Engineering 9)

Nature of Discipline/Course

Some faculty members indicated that writing assignments would not be appropriate for their courses due to the highly technical nature of their disciplines or courses. The perceived lack of compatibility between the technical nature of the disciplines and/or courses and the use of written language to deal with the content was pointed out particularly by faculty members from the science and engineering fields.

> Much of our work is calculation and involves scientific notation—not long explanation and description. (Sciences 14)

> I do not require essay responses because I am asking technical questions using symbolic expressions. I want students to learn to read and respond using

> mathematical notation. The nature of the material I am teaching suggests that I rely on other disciplines to train students to write. (Engineering 4)

A few responses also indicated that the specific nature of a course was sometimes a more important factor in influencing faculty decisions on student writing requirement than the discipline. One engineering faculty member commented:

> For a technical course, such as dynamics and fluid mechanics, the ability to solve problems is more important than writing. However, for a project course, writing reports is definitely very essential. (Engineering 14).

Analysis of faculty responses to the survey questions also indicated a few other factors that seem to influence faculty decisions about student writing in their classes. These factors included a) instructional level; b) concern for scoring reliability; and c) student writing competence. These factors will not be detailed here because of limited space.

Analysis of faculty interviews suggested additional factors that could influence student writing in university classrooms. Two of the factors identified through analysis of faculty interviews concerned disciplinary specialization and the academic reward structure. These factors seem to influence faculty decisions concerning student writing requirements as well as the type and amount of guidance available to students on writing assignments. A few faculty members indicated that, due to disciplinary specialization, they did not have the expertise needed to teach or evaluate writing:

> I find myself doing things I think an English professor should do. I find myself teaching grammar and I am not qualified to teach grammar. (Sciences 2)

> Most engineering professors are not used to grading essays . . . most engineering professors don't assign that, they don't want to grade that, and I am not sure if they'll do a good job anyway. (Engineering 2)

> Most of us are not professional writers, and may not be able to articulate very well just what needs to be

> done to make this better. So we tend to focus on, well, are the thoughts organized? Are you demonstrating creativity? (Humanities 3)

During the interviews, several faculty members suggested that teaching writing lay outside of the specialization of their disciplines. This view was expressed by faculty members in different academic fields, as indicated in comments such as the following:

> There is an expectation that they've already picked that [writing] up somewhere. It's not my job. So, no, there is very little guidance. (Humanities 3)

> We should stick to the applied stuff we are experts at, and if there are other experts in the college, let's let those professionals do the teaching. It would be presumptuous for me to think that I can teach communication better than you. You had better be better at it than me. It's your Ph.D. It's your life, and your application of skills goes to that. (Business 2)

The view that writing lies outside of the disciplinary area of content course professors and that content course professors lack the expertise to teach writing, however, was not shared by all faculty members interviewed. In fact, some faculty members indicated that they had much to contribute to student writing development because of their expertise in writing in their disciplines.

Another factor mentioned by a few faculty members in the interviews concerned the academic reward structure, particularly the value placed on research vs. teaching in research universities. Faculty responses during the interviews suggested that faculty perception of the value placed on instruction vs. research could potentially influence faculty decisions on and involvement in student writing. One humanities faculty member explained this relationship:

> Not as much as I probably ought to. The system is set in such a way that the rewards from instructional activity are mighty few. Rewards for research and scholarly work drive the machine so the amount of time that is spent on reading and commenting on somebody's paper is time that is dropped. (Humanities 1)

This comment indicated how perception of the academic reward structure could influence faculty involvement in teaching and consequently faculty decisions to work with student writing in university content classrooms.

Discussion and Conclusion

This chapter addresses questions concerning purposes of writing and factors influencing faculty decisions about student writing in university content classrooms. Faculty responses to the survey and interview questions indicated that factors related to the context at the institution, discipline, and course levels influence both purposes of and student opportunities for writing in university content classrooms. At the institution level, factors influencing writing in the content classroom include class size and consequently faculty work load/time, institutional reward structure (value placed on teaching vs. research), and institutional organizational structure (the university's organization in terms of academic departments and disciplines with different specializations). At the discipline and course levels, the nature of the discipline, the communication language used in the discipline (Smeby, 1996), and course goals seem to exert influence on student writing in university content classrooms.

Of the factors that faculty perceived to influence their uses of and decisions concerning writing in university content classes, those related to the institutional context deserve our attention in particular because these factors have not been extensively investigated in EAP writing research and because examining these factors helps us understand how writing in the university classroom can be influenced by institutional policies. After all, institutional policies contribute to the creation of the institutional context for writing. Analysis of faculty responses indicated that many faculty members were interested in using writing as a tool to help students learn content and acquire appropriate ways of communication. This suggests potential opportunities for writing in university content classrooms. However, several factors related to the institutional context could potentially constrain opportunities for student writing, particularly for undergraduates, due to large class size and increased faculty work load for working with student writing. The impact of institutional policies concerning issues such as class size on student writing in university content classrooms should not be overlooked. The comments from faculty members that students would lose opportunities for writing which are crucial to learning due to increased class size may be particularly revealing of the potential influences of institutional polices on student writing in university content classrooms.

Faculty comments concerning class size and lack of time to create and evaluate writing assignments might also reflect the influence of the academic reward structure on student writing in university content classrooms. Research examining the academic reward system has indicated that faculty members are concerned about "the inadequate recognition that universities accord to teaching" (Neumann, 2001, p. 144). Faculty interview comments concerning the reward structure and time spent on student writing indicated how faculty perception of what is valued in the academic reward system could affect faculty involvement in teaching and in student writing. In fact, faculty concern about class size and time needed for working with student writing as expressed in faculty comments might indicate a concern about spending time on certain instructional activities that were perceived to be less valued and rewarded in the academic reward structure. Again, institutional policies such as those that deal with the academic reward structure could influence writing in the university content classroom.

In their responses to the survey and interview questions, faculty members identified several purposes for writing and factors influencing writing in university content classrooms. Underlying faculty comments were different views of academic writing. Some faculty members were aware that writing is situated in the specific disciplinary context in which it occurs and as such cannot be detached from the context. These faculty members perceived writing as a useful tool for students to acquire disciplinary knowledge and ways of thinking (e.g., Business 8). By contrast, other faculty members seemed to see writing largely in terms of a decontextualized language performance to which a set of universal rules and standards would apply. According to these faculty members, writing should be taught by those who specialize in writing instruction (e.g., Sciences 2, Engineering 2, Humanities 2). This view of writing is not compatible with our current understanding of the social and cultural nature of academic writing. This view, however, is not surprising as it is rooted in and reinforced by the established division of labor among different departments of universities. The widely observed tradition to house writing courses and train writing instructors in the English department may have contributed to the view that writing is largely a language ability which should be taught by specifically trained writing instructors. This view in fact reflects the influence of the institutional context on faculty members' perception of the nature of writing.

This study examined the purposes for writing and factors which influence writing in university content classrooms which many second language students will enter. Although the study did not specifically focus on second language writers, the information it provides concerning the context for content course writing is useful for EAP writing instructors and curriculum designers. The study also raises questions for further research which would be relevant for second language writing instruction in EAP programs. One research area addresses how factors related to context at the institutional level influence other contextual layers and student writing. Investigating questions about the institutional context for writing is particularly important at a time when many universities set goals to achieve increased enrollment, including increased international student enrollment, but face increasing challenges in terms of personnel and other resources. What institutional policies do universities implement to achieve their goals and address the challenges? How do these policies influence faculty views of and practices in teaching and classroom writing, and how do these policies influence learning and writing by second language learners? What kind of tension might exist between certain institutional policies that may constrain opportunities for student writing in university content classrooms and the recognized need to help students develop written communication skills essential for dealing with disciplinary content in some disciplines? Examining questions addressing the institutional context for writing may help us better understand many aspects of writing in university content classrooms, which will contribute to more effective preparation of EAP students.

NOTES

I would like to thank the Faculty Research Council of the University of South Florida for a faculty research grant that supported the study. I would also like to thank my research assistant, Lisana Mohamed, for her assistance with data collection and interview transcription.

[1] Classification of academic areas along multiple dimensions originated from Biglan's studies (1973a; 1973b). Examples of hard pure areas include chemistry and physics, and engineering and computer science are typical ex-

amples of hard applied fields. Academic areas which are soft pure are typified by history and philosophy, and business and education constitute examples of soft applied fields.

[2] The two open-ended questions were "What is your rationale for requiring/not requiring essay responses on exams and/or writing assignments in your classes? What factors influence decisions concerning whether or not to give essay questions and/or writing assignments in your classes?"

REFERENCES

Biglan, A. (1973a). The characteristics of subject matter in different academic areas. *Journal of Applied Psychology, 57*(3), 195–203.

Biglan, A. (1973b). Relationships between subject matter characteristics and the structure and output of university departments. *Journal of Applied Psychology, 57*(3), 204–213.

Braine, G. (1989). Writing in science and technology: An analysis of assignments from ten undergraduate courses. *English for Specific Purposes, 8*, 3–16.

Braine, G. (1995). Writing in the natural sciences and engineering. In D. Belcher & G. Braine (Eds.), *Academic writing in a second language* (pp. 113–134). Norwood, NJ: Ablex.

Brandt, D. (1986). Toward an understanding of context in composition. *Written Communication, 3*, 139–157.

Carson, J. (2001). A task analysis of reading and writing in academic contexts. In D. Belcher & A. Hirvela (Eds.), *Linking literacies: Perspectives on L2 reading-writing connections* (pp. 48–83). Ann Arbor: The University of Michigan Press.

Chin, E. (1994). Redefining "context" in research on writing. *Written Communication, 11*, 445–482.

Donald, J. (1986). Knowledge and the university curriculum. *Higher Education, 15*, 267-282.

Donald, J. (1995). Disciplinary differences in knowledge validation. In N. Hativa & M. Marincovich (Eds.), *Disciplinary differences in teaching and learning: Implications for practice* (pp. 7–17). San Francisco: Jossey-Bass.

Deem, R., & Brehony, K. (2000). Doctoral students' access to research cultures—Are some more unequal than others? *Studies in Higher Education, 25*(2), 149–165.

Hale, G., Taylor, C., Bridgeman, B., Carson, J., Kroll, B., & Kantor, R. (1996). *A study of writing tasks assigned in academic degree programs.* (TOEFL Research Report 54). Princeton, NJ: Educational Testing Service.

Herrington, A. (1985). Writing in academic settings: A study of the contexts for writing in two college chemical engineering courses. *Research in the Teaching of English, 19,* 331–358.

Lee, J. (2004). Comparing institutional relationships with academic departments: A study of five academic fields. *Research in Higher Education, 45,* 603–624.

Leedy, P. (2001). *Practical research: Planning and design.* Upper Saddle River, NJ: Merrill Prentice Hall.

Lueddeke, G. (2003). Professionalizing teaching practice in higher education: A study of disciplinary variation and "teaching-scholarship." *Studies in Higher Education, 28,* 213–228.

Neumann, R. (2001). Disciplinary differences and university teaching. *Studies in Higher Education, 26,* 135–146.

Neumann, R., Parry, S., & Becher, T. (2002). Teaching and learning in their disciplinary contexts: A conceptual analysis. *Studies in Higher Education, 27,* 405–417.

Piazza, C. (1987). Identifying context variables in research on writing. *Written Communication, 4,* 107–137.

Rubin, H., & Rubin, I. (1995). *Qualitative interviewing: The art of hearing data.* Thousand Oaks, CA: Sage Publications

Samraj, B. (2002). Texts and contextual layers: Academic writing in content courses. In A. Johns (Ed.), *Genre in the classroom* (pp. 163–176). Mahwah, NJ: Lawrence Erlbaum Associates.

Schommer-Aikins, M., Duell, O., & Barker, S. (2002). Epistemological beliefs across domains using Biglan's classification of academic disciplines. *Research in Higher Education, 44*(3), 347–366.

Shulman, L. (1993). Teaching as community property. *Change, 25*(6), 6–7.

Smeby, J. C. (1996). Disciplinary differences in university teaching. *Studies in Higher Education, 21*(1), 69–79.

Zhu, W. (2004). Writing in business courses: An analysis of assignment types, their characteristics, and required skills. *English for Specific Purposes, 23,* 111–135.

8 EAP and Technical Writing Without Borders: The Impact of Departmentalization on the Teaching and Learning of Academic Writing in a First and Second Language

Guillaume Gentil

According to historical accounts of the field (e.g., Matsuda, 2003), second language writing emerged as a sub-discipline of Teaching English as a Second Language (TESL) in the 1960s, in part in response to the growing population of ESL international students in U.S. higher education. It was felt at the time that these students were not adequately prepared for the demands of academic literacy at the university, neither by ESL classes, which emphasized oral skills in keeping with the then trendy audiolingual approach, nor by first-year composition courses, which were geared to L1 speakers of English. With the disengagement of college composition from ESL issues, language educators dealing with L2 writers began to develop their own methodologies and literature at the conjunction of L1 composition and L2 language studies. Second language writing gained maturity as a distinct field of practice and inquiry in the 1990s with the creation of specialized forums (e.g., the *Journal of Second Language Writing* in 1992 and the biennial Symposium on Second Language Writing in 1998), the development of specialized professional preparation programs (mostly within TESL), and the emergence of a metadisciplinary discourse on the nature and history of second language writing as a field (Matsuda, 2003). At the same time, the disciplinary status of second language writing remains somewhat precarious in that instruction and professional development in L2 writing are for the most part situated within broader departments and programs, such as composition studies, foreign languages, applied linguistics, and TESL. For lack of a proper institutional infrastructure, second language studies may thus be more adequately regarded as an "interdisciplinary field" rather than a discipline per se. This field both resulted from and contributed to the increasing "disciplinary division of labor" (Matsuda, 2003, p. 18) between composition studies and L2 studies.

Reflecting the conditions of its emergence, second language writing has focused mostly on international ESL students in U.S. higher education. Indeed, one of the main contributions of second language writing to language education might have been to generate professional knowledge and instruction tailored to the specific needs of that student population. Arguably, ESL university students struggling with academic writing assignments are better served with theoretically sound instruction by well-trained L2 writing specialists than if left to swim or drown in content courses and first-year composition courses. However, while recognizing the benefits of and rationale for L2 writing instruction for ESL university students, this chapter asks whether the current disciplinary divisions of labor between L2 writing and L1 composition also serve the needs of bilingual students (international as well as domestic) who wish to develop academic literacies in both their first and their second language. Reichelt (1999) has recently argued for a more comprehensive view of L2 writing that includes not only ESL composition but also foreign language writing in the U.S. Yet foreign language writing still assumes a specialization of writing instruction in either the L1 or the L2 rather than aiming for bilingual writing development in both the L1 and the L2.

Whereas L2 writing research has been growing over the last two decades, there remains scant research on academic and professional biliteracy (notable exceptions include Canagarajah, 2002, 2004; Casanave, 1998; Colombi & Schleppegrell, 2002; Curry & Lillis, 2004; Gentil, 2002, 2004, 2005a2; Parks & Maguire, 1999; Parks, 2001; Vignola, 1998). Academic and professional biliteracy can be defined as the social, individual, and intersubjective practices and competencies associated with the use and production of written texts in two languages within postsecondary and professional settings. The dearth of research in this area is surprising considering the growing number of students who come to the university with some command of more than one language and who might be expected to use more than one language at work upon graduation. According to the last Canadian census, nearly one worker out of seven uses more than one language at work (Statistics Canada, 2001). Yet little research has been conducted on the multilingual practices of the workplace and on the ways in which institutions of higher education might help prepare students for these demands. By means of an institutional case study of an English-speaking university in the predominantly French-speaking province of Québec, in Canada, this chapter investigates two main questions: 1) How do institutional policies, politics, and structures enable or constrain the teaching and learning of academic writing in both English and French, the two official languages of Canada? 2) What disciplinary divisions of labor and attendant institutional infrastructures may best facilitate students' development and use of bilingual writing competencies for the workplace and academia?

Theoretical Framework

To conceptualize how institutional learning contexts mediate individual biliteracy development, I draw on theories of situated and mediated activity (Lantolf, 2000; Vygotsky, 1978; Wertsch, 1991), as well as on Hornberger's (1989, 2003) continua model of biliteracy. First, I conceive of writing as a cluster of mediated and mediating activities involving the production of written texts. These activities can take very diverse forms, such as a Vai farmer writing a letter on a leaf (Scribner & Cole, 1981), a U.S. university student composing an essay on paper or on a computer screen, or a teenager sending a text message to a friend with a cell phone. Yet, despite such diversity, writing activities derive a certain "family resemblance" (Wittgenstein, 1953) from sharing an essential feature—they all revolve around the construction of written texts. Furthermore, writing is mediated in that it necessitates the use of mediational tools or sociocultural artifacts (Wertsch, 1991), such as quills, pens, and paper, and more recently, software, hardware, printers, and some form of computer-human interface, such as a monitor, an operating system, a mouse, and a keyboard. Importantly, it is also mediated by the semiotic resources of particular writing systems and languages. Thus, one way in which writing in a second language might differ from writing in a first language for some writers is that the degree of familiarity with the lexicogrammatical and semantic resources of one language system or another will constrain the writers' ability to construct meaning in that language system even though they might be able to apply genre and discourse knowledge and composition expertise across language systems (Cumming, 1994; Lefrançois, 2001; Silva, 1993; Whalen & Ménard, 1995). While essentially mediated by tools and agents (e.g., collaborators and superiors), writing is also fundamentally a mediating activity in that people typically write for a particular purpose and to carry out a higher order activity, such as playing, learning, working, exchanging news, socializing, etc. (Russell, 1997). In Leont'ev's (1981) three-tiered distinction among operation, action, and activity, writing involves more or less routinized operations at the service of goal-directed individual actions and interactions that, in turn, contribute to collective activities oriented toward more or less conscious objects and motives.

From the conception of writing as a family of mediated and mediating activities it logically follows that the appropriate unit of analysis for writing development research is the "individual-acting-with-mediational-means-and-mediational-agents-within-particular-contexts-of-possibilities-for-personal-and-interpersonal-engagement-in-the-world" (Wertsch, 1991; see also Maguire & Graves, 2001). The contexts of possibilities for individual biliteracy development can be conceived of as a series of concentric nested circles along a micro-macro continuum (Hornberger, 2003; Maguire, 1994). The inner, largely invisible contexts include the personal, subjective, and intersubjective perspectives or orientations, within which each individual evaluates and responds to the outer contexts of biliteracy. These outer contexts include the societal, political, historical, national, and international environment, including the status and use of particular languages on the regional, national, and international market of linguistic exchanges (Bourdieu, 1982). Thus, an individual's degree of investment in developing literacies in a particular language will depend in part on the symbolic and practical value of this language locally, nationally, and internationally. More generally, the more the contexts of language use encourage and allow individual learners to use two or more languages in a variety of oral and written, formal and informal situations and for a variety of communicative and expressive purposes, the greater their chances for full biliterate development (Hornberger, 1989; Gentil, 2005a).

The institutional contexts—including institutional policies, structures, and practices—play a key role in individuals' interpersonal negotiations of day-to-day activities as they mediate between the inner-subjective and intersubjective contexts of activity on the one hand and broader societal, geopolitical, and socio-historical influences on the other hand. Established and maintained for a given social purpose, such as higher education and research in the case of universities, institutions are bounded and somewhat autonomous discursive and physical spaces with more or less restricted access and within which special jurisdictions and rules of practice apply. Once established through some collective declaration of statute and mission, institutions take up a life of their own as internally regulated social structures that themselves regulate the individual and collective behaviour of its members. As partly self-enclosed and self-regulated social spaces, they constitute an important level of structuration of human activity. It is on this institutional level that this study focuses. Specifically, by means of a case study of an English-medium university within the predominantly French-speaking province of Québec, I aim to understand how the institutional contexts of postsecondary education, particularly the organization of the curriculum along disciplinary and administrative lines, can delimit a range of possibilities for the students' development of academic and professional biliteracy in English and French throughout their program of study. To this end, I first describe the particular university under study and then, by focusing on the learning and teaching experience of a selected group of instructors and students, examine how the institution mediates the biliteracy development of its members.

THE INSTITUTIONAL CONTEXT

The University[1] is a publicly funded Canadian institution of higher education and research serving a student population of over 25,000. While it shares many of the features and challenges of other major postsecondary institutions in North America, it is in a unique situation in that the language of instruction, English, is the majority language of the country and yet the minority language of the province. In fact, with 21 percent of French-mother tongue students and 53 percent of English-mother tongue students, the language demographics of the student population is strikingly similar to Canada's, though in sharp contrast to Québec's (where French-mother-tongue speakers make up

81 percent of the population and English-mother-tongue speakers only 8 percent; see Table 1). In an effort to serve the specific language needs of its student population, the university offers first-language and second-language instruction in English and French in three faculties (see Table 2).

Table 1. Demographic Contexts (Statistics Canada, 2001; University census, 2000)

	Francophones	Anglophones	Allophones
Canada	22.9% (6.8 million)	59.1% (17.5 million)	18% (5.3 million)
Province of Québec	81.4%	8.3%	10.3%
The University	21%	53%	26%

Table 2. Language and Writing Instruction at the University

Faculty	Language Instruction in English	Language Instruction in French	Instruction in Translation
Arts	**Language Center:** Courses in English for Academic Purposes (emphasis on academic writing; graduate and undergraduate sections)	**Language Center:** General oral and written FSL courses **Department of French:** Grammar & advanced composition courses reserved for students of French	**Department of French:** Translation courses (leading to a B.A. in French and translation)
Education	**Writing Center:** Discipline-specific and general first-year and advanced courses in written communication in the professions (a few graduate sections)	None	None
Continuing Education	Part-time and intensive ESL programs	Part-time and intensive FSL programs; French for the Workplace	Certificate and Graduate Diploma in Translation

The faculty of arts provides ESL and FSL instruction at the Language Center (LC), a special unit that was created in the 1970s when FSL courses were transferred from the department of French language and literature. Ten years later, the LC's mandate extended to ESL instruction as the department of English also delegated its second language courses. Currently, the LC offers comprehensive courses in both ESL and FSL at all levels to nearly 2,000 students yearly. The FSL syllabus encompasses both oral and written French and aims to help FSL students who are new to Québec gain access to the French-speaking environment and culture that surrounds the university. The ESL syllabus, on the other hand, aims to prepare ESL students for study in English at the university; hence, its focus is English for Academic Purposes (EAP), particularly academic writing in English as a second language. In addition to the second language courses offered at the LC, the faculty of arts also offers French language instruction within the department of French. However, language instruction in the department of French is normally restricted to students of French who need advanced courses in grammar, stylistics, and academic writing in preparation for their major or minor in French.

The faculty of education offers courses in written communication for students of Education as well as for students from other faculties, such as engineering, management, and social work. The unit within education responsible for the study and teaching of writing is the writing center (WC). It was first founded as a tutorial service in the early 1980s in response to the demand from other faculties for remedial writing. The WC quickly grew in the 1980s to offer over 70 sections of credit courses in effective written communication, in addition to maintaining a writing tutorial service. Many course sections are restricted to students from specific faculties and are therefore discipline-specific; other sections are open to students from all disciplines. The WC courses are offered in English and are aimed at students who possess a native-like command of English. However, students come to class with various repertoires and competencies in English and in one and sometimes two or three other languages. The normal policy of the WC is to screen out students with limited English proficiency prior to or early in the WC course they have registered for and to direct these students to ESL/EAP courses at the LC and the faculty of continuing education.

The faculty of continuing education also offers second-language instruction in French, English, and other languages, as well as courses in professional oral and written communication in English and French. In keeping with its mandate, the faculty of continuing education gears its certificate, non-degree programs toward professional development and academic preparation. It normally does not offer credit courses for students registered in degree programs in other faculties.

Access to the Institutional Site and Recruitment of the Participants

Two writing instructors, Peter and Katherine, and four students participated in the study (Table 3).[2] I first established contact with Peter and Katherine by means of a letter describing the purpose of my research. At the time of initial contact, I was a master's student of second language education and my primary interest for my thesis was the instructional strategies used by writing instructors with educational backgrounds in English literature and English language education for teaching writing to graduate students of other disciplines (Gentil, 1998). After completion of my master's thesis, I maintained contact with Katherine and Peter and re-approached them for participation in my doctoral research with a new focus on bilingual students' development of academic biliteracy (Gentil, 2002, 2005). The instructors let me present my research project in their classes and thus proved instrumental in the recruitment of students. Furthermore, we became colleagues when I was hired, after I earned my MA, as a sessional lecturer in the WC. My status within the institution afforded a particular vantage point from which to observe the participants in their institutional contexts; that is, it allowed for an insider's insight from a certain social position. The analyses and arguments that follow in this report are thus bounded within my particular interpretive perspective—and bias.

Table 3. Participants

Students	Discipline	Level	EAP Instructor	Written Communication Instructor
Pierre	engineering	Ph.D	Peter	Katherine
Katia	social science	Ph.D.	Peter	
François	chemistry	M. Sc.	Peter	
Philippe	engineering	B. Eng.		Researcher

At the time of research, Peter was a full-time instructor at the LC and taught advanced EAP courses for graduate and undergraduate students with a focus on academic writing. A native speaker of English from Canada and holder of a Ph.D. in English literature, he had over two decades of ESL teaching experience. He allowed me to observe all of the classes for one section of his graduate academic writing course. He also let me recruit students for participation in two research projects on the learning and teaching of academic writing in English and French. Among his students were Pierre, a doctoral student of engineering from France, Katia, a doctoral student of social science from Canada, and François, a master's student of chemistry, also from Canada.

Katherine was a full-time instructor at the WC. A native speaker of English born and raised in the U.S., she had over 20 years of experience teaching written communication, with a B.A. in English literature and an M.Ed. in English education as credentials. She let me observe all classes for one section of a graduate course in effective communication specifically designed for doctoral students in engineering. One particularity of this section was that all students were international students whose first language was not English. Pierre was one of them. The last participant was Philippe, an undergraduate student of engineering who took one section of a WC course I taught. That section targeted engineering students. All four participating students were native speakers of French and received all of their primary and secondary education in French. So did I.

Data Collection and Analysis

I collected the data as part of my master's and doctoral research over three years (Gentil, 1998, 2002). Data sets included 1) approximately 40 hours of interviews over three years with the students and instructors; 2) inventories and analyses of the participating students' academic writing in English and French; 3) participant observations of writing classes; and 4) documentary artifacts (course syllabi, course calendars, newspaper clippings from student press, teaching materials, documents about the history of particular curricular programs). I triangulated these data sets in order to situate the participants' teaching and learning experiences within the university's institutional space of constraints and possibilities for personal and professional development.

Main Findings

Through the interviews with the instructors and program administrators, it was apparent that the WC and the LC did little to coordinate their curricular efforts, despite or perhaps because of their overlapping mandates. Several factors might help explain such a lack of collaboration between the two units. For one, their physical location on opposite sides of the campus was certainly not conducive to fortuitous encounters or interfaculty communication. It is unclear, however, whether communication might have been improved had they been on the same floor. Perhaps because of their affiliations with two different faculties, the two units were at best ignoring each other, and at worst competing for resources and attention within the university. In many ways, the instructors of the two units were waging parallel struggles for academic recognition and remuneration on par with faculty members of other administrative units such as the department of French or the department of English. As in other universities where language instructors are seen as offering a service role ancillary to credit-bearing programs, many instructors at the WC and the LC were underpaid sessionals with few prospects of tenure and whose continued employment was contingent on fluctuating student enrolment. Somewhat understandably, then, instructors at the WC and LC were prone to envy each other when the word got out that some had advantages the others did not, such as an opportunity for tenure or sabbatical.

Competition between the WC and the LC was further heightened by the fact that, while distinct at first, the respective mandate of the two units had become overlapping over the years. Originally, the LC was devoted exclusively to second language instruction in English and French, and the English courses it offered were designed to prepare ESL students for academic study at the university. The WC's mandate, however, was to provide first-language instruction in written communication for the professions. Nevertheless, the separation of mandates blurred when the LC opened an advanced academic writing course for native speakers of English while the WC initiated a course to help ESL graduate students of engineering write research reports, including dissertations and theses. Furthermore, while the WC courses are in principle aimed at preparing students for professional communication in the workplace, they also cover the academic genres that first- or second-year students need to learn for study at the university because most students are advised to take and do take the WC courses early in their programs. Last but not least, the very distinction between L1 and L2 students upon which the curriculum is compartmentalized has become somewhat arbitrary and impractical in light of the sheer diversity of the literacies and language competencies that the students bring to class. Thus, in the WC classes I taught, monolingual English speakers were a small minority; some students had native-like oral proficiency in English, but their writing showed evidence of interlanguage influences; other students expressed themselves with greater ease and more idiomatically in written English than in spoken English. As elsewhere, the native vs. nonnative speakers' distinction collapsed in the face of linguistic realities and yet still informed much of the students' placement into distinct curricular streams.

One consequence of the lack of cooperation, or the outright competition, between the LC and the WC can be felt in lost opportunities for professional development. Instructors at the LC and WC were struggling with similar instructional challenges and yet did not share the local strategies and resources they were drawing upon in response to these challenges. One common challenge I witnessed at both the WC and the LC has been described by Spack (1988) and concerns the difficulty in initiating students into unfamiliar specialized disciplinary discourses. Katherine and Peter had devised creative strategies for dealing with students whose disciplines were remote from their own academic backgrounds in English literature and education. Katherine, for instance, asked her graduate students of engineering to write a popularized piece for a lay audience before they wrote a technical report for an expert audience. Peter, on the other hand, dealing with a multidisciplinary graduate class of social science and natural science students, chose an article of general interest, for instance, on epistemological or ethical issues, and had the whole class discuss it, summarize it, and critique it, in addition to having students write research reports directly related to their disciplines of study. While I interviewed Katherine and Peter and observed their classes, gaining unique insights into the cultures and practices of the WC and the LC, I was struck by how mutually beneficial sharing resources and strategies could be for both instructors and students within the two units. The lack of resource sharing was all the more surprising to me because I could clearly identify shared instructional goals between the two units—in the short term, to assist students in appropriating the written academic genres they need to master to complete their programs of study, and in the mid-term, to facilitate the students' transition from writing at the university to writing in the workplace. While there were mechanisms and resources in place within each unit for professional development—such as teacher handbooks, staff meetings, joint elaboration of teaching materials, and mentorship for new instructors—there were no mechanisms in place for resource sharing between the units.

The absence of collaboration between the WC and the LC affected students' opportunities for learning as well. Few students could benefit from instruction at both the WC and the LC, in part because of the limited number of credits that they could take in elective courses outside their majors, particularly in language courses. One participant in this study, Pierre, is one of the few students who took both a written communication course in the WC and an EAP graduate writing course at the LC, the former with Katherine and the latter with Peter. He explained during an interview how complementary the two courses had been for him. For instance, he appreciated Katherine's stylistic insights into sentence and paragraph effectiveness, while learning much from Peter's grammar lessons in article usage. My observations of Peter's and Katherine's classes as well as analyses of the course outlines confirmed Pierre's perception of the complementary orientation of each course. Using Swales and Feak (1994) and Simon & Schuster's *Handbook for Writers* (Troyka, Buckley, & Gates, 1996) as the course texts, Peter taught writing by raising students' awareness of the language and textual features associated with particular academic genres, focussing especially on the language points known to be problematic to second language users of English such as tense and article usage. Well versed in L1 composition theory and genre theory, Katherine focused instruction on the writing process, providing heuristics for drafting and revising texts in the context of genre-specific assignments. Undoubtedly, some of the students in the WC courses would have benefited from the kind of form-focused instruction in English grammar provided by Peter, while students in the LC courses would have benefited from Katherine's process approach. Yet, students were directed toward one course or the other mostly based on major and their home faculty rather than their learning needs.

The main reason students were not streamed according to their needs was the absence of a university-wide language placement test conducted collaboratively by the WC and the LC. Rather, each center independently assessed and placed the students that were directed to them by various faculties. Furthermore, even if, in principle, the WC catered to L1 students and the LC to L2 students, in actuality, each center had, over time, developed privileged relationships with particular faculties. The WC, for instance, had concluded agreements with the faculties of engineering, education, management, and social work to make its written communication courses part of the mandatory curriculum. Consequently, it catered to all students in these faculties. The LC, on the other hand, as a dependent of the faculty of arts, received students mostly from that faculty and the faculty of science. Hence, the streaming of students through the university's writing and language courses was not informed pedagogically but reflected various administrative arrangements and historical vicissitudes, not to mention turf wars.

Thus far, I have discussed the negative impact of curricular and departmental divisions on the learning and teaching of academic and professional writing in English. These divisions constrained possibilities for, but still permitted, development of literacy in English. More significant, perhaps, is the deleterious effect these divisions had on bilingual students' academic literacy development in both English and French, the two official languages of Canada. Katia's learning experiences offer a case in point. Katia was a doctoral student in cultural studies in Peter's class. A French-mother tongue student, she chose to study in an English-medium university in part to develop professional communication repertoires in English. At the same time, out of linguistic loyalty to her francophone community, she was also determined to further develop her academic and professional literacies in French. As a result, she decided to avail herself of the right guaranteed by the University's Charter of Students' Rights to submit assignments in either English or French. For the three comprehensive examination essays she had to write in partial fulfilment of her doctoral program, she chose to write two essays (the first and the third) in English and one essay (the second) in French. Each essay consisted of a critical bibliographical review on a topic related to Katia's doctoral research.

At first, Katia believed that composing the second essay in French would be easier than composing the other two essays in English. However, her expectation was not borne out. In fact, her third essay was the easiest to write, whereas her second essay proved as difficult if not more difficult than her first essay for three reasons. First, independent of the language in which she was composing, Katia struggled to understand her professors' expectations about the audience, purpose, scope, and organization of the comprehensive essay genre, producing no fewer than six drafts for each of the first two essays over six months. In contrast, drafting the third essay was a somewhat less painful process, as she had gained familiarity with the genre. In particular, her two former essay-writing experiences had taught her how to narrow down her topic early in the writing process rather than after several rounds of extensive revisions. By her third essay, she had also come to appreciate her professors' expectations of focusing on selected studies from a critical perspective rather than covering large bodies of literature in broad strokes.

The second challenge when writing essay two in French was that she had no language support available, because her professors could not edit her French and she had no language tutor to turn to. In contrast, she received stylistic and language feedback on her English work from her professors as well as from the language tutor (an Anglophone peer) whom she hired. Peter also commented on two rough drafts of her first essay that she was able to submit to him as part of her EAP coursework.

The third source of difficulty in composing in French stemmed from the lack of French discursive resources at her disposal. Because most of the specialized literature she had access to was in English, she found herself struggling to translate and reconceptualize knowledge claims and theoretical frameworks from English to French, a challenging task for which she was neither prepared nor rewarded. In particular, she struggled to find terminological equivalents of key English concepts such as "gender" or "households" because these concepts had no univocal equivalents in French and she was not sure which translations would be more appropriate in the context of her argument. As a result, her rough drafts were made up of French sentences peppered with English phrases waiting to be translated. These English phrases were removed from the later drafts; however, close textual analysis of Katia's writing revealed the influence of English on French phraseology, for instance with prepositions collocating with verbs as they would in English rather than in French (e.g., she would construct the French verb "*participer*" with the preposition "*dans*," a close semantic equivalent of "in," whereas concordance searches in monolingual French corpora indicate that the preposition that typically collocates with "*participer*" is "*à*," the common English equivalent of which is the preposition "to").

Some of the instructional resources and support that Katia might have found most useful when writing in French from English sources are courses and tutorials in translation, comparative English-French stylistics, and advanced French grammar. These were offered by the department of French and the faculty of continuing education. However, she could not register for these courses as part of her doctoral program because she was a full-time student of social science and they were restricted to students in other programs.

Katia's case illustrates some of the pernicious effects of disciplinary, curricular, and administrative divisions on opportunities for academic biliteracy development in English and French at an English-speaking university. The resources she would need were available on campus but not accessible to her because knowledge was compartmentalized along disciplinary and administrative lines rather than allowed to circulate across departments and disciplines.

Discussion and Implications

Hornberger's (1989, 2003) continua of biliteracy model predicts that the more the contexts of learning allow an individual to move along all the points of the continua, the greater his or her chances are for full biliteracy development. The institutional context for postsecondary education is but one context of biliteracy for the participants in this study. However it is an important one as a collective physical and discursive space that responds to other institutional and societal—governmental, legal, economic, political—influences while controlling and sometimes limiting individuals' possibilities for action and learning. A more in-depth study of the participants' experiences and contexts of learning revealed the determining influence of the institutional context over personal, interpersonal, and societal contexts on the participants' biliteracy development in English and French (Gentil, 2002, in press). For instance, regardless of their individual commitment to biliteracy and despite the vitality of French in Québec's society, the participants were able to develop academic biliteracy in both English and French at the University to the extent that their program of study provided them opportunities for using both French and English in writing and in speaking academically. These opportunities were few for Katia and virtually non-existent for Pierre, Philippe, and François because the discourse practices of their departments were monolingual English and they had no access to social and discursive academic spaces in French, such as the department of French or the French side of the LC.

According to the latest demographic data at the time of research, French-mother tongue students represented close to 21 percent of the University's student population, not counting students whose mother tongue is not French but who are fluent in French. The university president's goal was to increase this percentage to 25 percent by attracting more students from French-medium junior colleges in Québec. The University's effort to attract and keep French-speaking students was evident in the newer policies for the promotion of bilingual signage and bilingual student services on campus. Yet it is unclear how far the university was willing to go in catering for the needs of French-speaking and bilingual English-French students. Whereas bilingual communicative competencies have become a valued commodity in some Québec and Canadian workplaces (Heller, 1999), I witnessed no concerted effort on the University's part to provide students with instructional programs and resources that would help them develop the professional and academic biliteracies in English and French that they could capitalize on upon graduation. Clearly, the disciplinary and departmental divisions between FSL instruction, French literature and translation, EAP, and English L1 composition did not serve well the students like Katia, François, and Philippe who wished to extend their bilingual competencies for the workplace.

To enable bilingual students to develop academic and professional biliteracy, what appears to be needed is a cross-departmental, cross-disciplinary effort to design new structures and programs that tap into and redistribute existing resources across the curriculum. A multidisciplinary Center for Excellence in Bilingualism might be an option, but questions about its relationship with the rest of the university may be cause for debate and could lead to jurisdictional wrangling: Would the center be an autonomous unit or would it be housed within an existing faculty? If the latter, which one? And what would make a particular faculty a more suitable host? If the former, from where would it receive funding? In either case, would the center be assigned a mostly ancillary role or would it deserve a more central place among research intensive and tenure granting units? Creating new structures can cause resistance if it means taking resources away from existing units, especially when several years of cuts in government spending have caused increasing financial strictures on the University. Alternatively, and more modestly perhaps, a certificate of excellence in bilingualism offered jointly by the department of French, the LC, the WC, and the faculty of continuing education may be a more viable option. The certificate program could be designed in consultation with the corporate and governmental sectors to better ensure its marketability. It would offer instructional support for bilingual students while rewarding success by providing a plus-value on students' degrees in their disciplines. It would also ensure greater visibility and higher status for bilingual students on campus.

While some of the issues and solutions discussed in this chapter might be suitable for the particular context of this study, and for the Canadian context of postsecondary education more generally, it raises questions for other contexts as well. To be sure, the encapsulation of ESL/EAP instruction away from L1 (English) composition, English literature, and foreign language instruction, is not unique to this particular university. Despite changing demographics and numerous calls in the applied linguistics literature for overcoming the native vs. nonnative speakers' dichotomy (Harklau, Losey, & Siegal, 1999; Leung, Harris, & Rampton, 1997; Piller, 2002), it is somewhat surprising that many universities in North America continue to compartmentalize writing instruction into two separate streams for English L1 and English L2 students. If the sheer diversity of university students' language backgrounds and competencies makes it increasingly difficult to distinguish ESL from English L1 speakers, should writing research and writing instruction not adapt to this new reality? In a telling example of how history can still constrain the affordances of a mediational means long after the conditions that prevailed at the time of the development of the means have disappeared, Wertsch (1998) discusses the QWERTY keyboard. This keyboard layout was designed to slow typists down at a time when typing too fast could cause the typewriter's keys to jam. With today's electronic technology, key jamming is no longer a limiting factor, and yet the QWERTY keyboards are still being used, unnecessarily slowing typists down. New, faster designs have been conceived, but industrial pressures for standardization make it unlikely that they will replace QWERTY keyboards anytime soon. By analogy, the division of postsecondary writing instruction into L1 and L2 streams may have responded well to the students' demographics in the postwar years when ESL students were mostly international students on a visa and could easily be distinguished from English L1 domestic students. However, with the increasing numbers of immigrant and refugee ESL students and 1.5 generation students (Harklau, Losey, & Siegal, 1999), this disciplinary L1/L2 division of labor now appears to be a remnant of a past era that persists because of institutional fixtures even though it seems to be increasingly out of sync with current demographics. As such, it is a mediational structure that constrains rather than enables students' academic literacy development in English, whether English is a first or second or a first-and-a-half language for them.

New institutional structures and programs need to be designed to assist students in tapping into and expanding the literacies and language competencies they bring to the university. Despite calls in the educational literature to theorize literacy as multiple, multimodal, and multilingual and to help students negotiate the transition from the multiliteracies of the home to the multiliteracies of the workplace (e.g., Cope & Kalantzis, 2000), writing instruction in North American universities remains largely based on a monolingual, autonomous model (Street, 1984) of literacy. Diverse forms of bilingual education have been tried with various success and sometimes much controversy in primary and secondary schools (see Baker, 2001; Cummins, 2000). Particularly promising among these are Welsh programs that aim for the development of academic "transliteracy," that is, the capacity and practice of writing and talking about texts in one language from oral and written sources in another (Baker, 2003). Perhaps it is high time such bilingual education experiments were tried in postsecondary settings as well (for examples of bilingual education in postsecondary contexts, see Wesche, Morrison, Ready, & Pawley, 1990). Arguably, there is a critical mass of Spanish speakers in the U.S. to justify asking, first, whether institutional structures and instructional programs at American universities have been set up to enable bilingual Spanish-English students to develop bilingual academic and professional writing competencies in Spanish and English, and, second, how the curriculum could be redesigned to bring together foreign language instruction, first-year composition, and L2 writing instruction. To enable the biliterate development of bilingual students, redesigning the disciplinary infrastructure of L2 writing appears to be in order. Second language writing specialists have come to recognize the value of turning second language writing "into an interdisciplinary field of inquiry situated in both composition studies and second language studies simultaneously" (Matsuda, 2003, p. 25). Perhaps the interdisciplinary base of second language writing should be extended to include studies in bilingualism and bilingual education as well as in foreign language education.

NOTES

[1] To protect the confidentiality of the participants' personal information, names of people and institutional affiliations have been changed or concealed.

[2] The program of research on which this chapter is based included eight French-speaking and two Spanish-speaking apprentices and confirmed scholars in several French-speaking and English-speaking postsecondary institutions in France and Québec. For full reports, see Gentil, 1998 and 2002.

REFERENCES

Baker, C. (2001). *Foundations of bilingual education and bilingualism*. Clevedon, UK: Multilingual Matters.

Baker, C. (2003). Biliteracy and transliteracy in Wales. In N. Hornberger (Ed.) (pp. 71–90).

Bourdieu, P. (1982). *Ce que parler veut dire: L'économie des échanges linguistiques* [Language and symbolic power: The economics of linguistic exchanges]. Paris: Fayard.

Canagarajah, A. S. (2002). *Critical academic writing and multilingual students*. Ann Arbor: University of Michigan Press.

Canagarajah, A. S. (2004). *A geopolitics of academic writing*. Pittsburgh, PA: University of Pittsburgh Press.

Casanave, C. (1998). Transitions: The balancing act of bilingual academics. *Journal of Second Language Writing, 7*(2), 175–203.

Colombi, C., & Schleppegrell, M. (Eds.). (2002). *Developing advanced literacy in first and second languages*. Mahwah, NJ: Lawrence Erlbaum.

Cope, B., & Kalantzis, M. (Eds.). (2000). *Multiliteracies: Literacy learning and the design of social futures*. London: Routledge.

Cumming, A. (1994). Writing expertise and second-language proficiency. In A. Cumming (Ed.), *Bilingual Performance in reading and writing* (pp. 173–221). Philadelphia, PA: John Benjamins.

Cummins, J. (2000). *Language, power and pedagogy: Bilingual children in the crossfire*. Clevedon, UK: Multilingual Matters.

Curry, M. J., & Lillis, T. (2004). Multilingual scholars and the imperative to publish in English: Negotiating interests, demands, and rewards. *TESOL Quarterly, 38*(4), 663–688.

Gentil, G. (1998). Academic writing instruction in disciplines other than English: A sociocultural perspective. Unpublished master's thesis, McGill University, Montréal, Québec, Canada.

Gentil, G. (2002). Academic biliteracy and identity construction: Case studies of francophone science writers. Unpublished doctoral dissertation, McGill University, Montréal, Québec, Canada.

Gentil, G. (2004, May). Transnationalism and academic biliteracy: Case studies of Francophone academics in the crossfire. Paper presented at the Annual Conferences of the American Association of Applied Linguistics, Portland, OR.

Gentil, G. (2005, July). Does language of publication matter? French biologists publishing in English. Paper presented at the 14th World Congress of Applied Linguistics, Madison, WI.

Gentil, G. (2005). Commitments to academic biliteracy: Case studies of Francophone university writers. *Written Communication 22(4)*, 421-471.

Harklau, L., Losey, K. M., & Siegal, M. (Eds.). (1999). *Generation 1.5 meets college composition*. Mahwah, NJ: Lawrence Erlbaum.

Heller, M. (1999). Alternative ideologies of *la francophonie*. *Journal of Sociolinguistics, 3*(3), 336–359.

Hornberger, N. (1989). Continua of biliteracy. *Review of Educational Research, 59*(3): 271–291.

Hornberger, N. (Ed.). (2003). *Revisiting the continua of biliteracy: A framework for educational research, policy, and practice in multilingual settings*. Clevedon, UK: Multilingual Matters.

Lantolf, J. (2000). *Sociocultural theory and second language learning*. Oxford: Oxford University Press.

Lefrançois, P. (2001). *Le point sur les transferts dans l'écriture en langue seconde*. The Canadian Modern Language Review, 58(2), 223–245.

Leont'ev, A. (1981). *Problems of the development of mind*. Moscow: Progress.

Leung, C., Harris, R., & Rampton, B. (1997). The idealised native speaker, reified ethnicities, and classroom realities. *TESOL Quarterly, 31*(3), 543–560.

Maguire, M. (1994). Cultural stances informing storytelling among bilingual children in Québec. *Comparative Education Review, 38*, 115–145.

Maguire, M, & Graves, B. (2001). Speaking personality in primary school children's L2 writing. *TESOL Quarterly, 35*(4), 561–593.

Matsuda, P. K. (2003). Second language writing in the twentieth century: A situated historical perspective. In B. Kroll (Ed.), *Exploring the dynamics of second language writing* (pp. 15–34). Cambridge: Cambridge University Press.

Parks, S., & Maguire, M. (1999). Coping with on-the-job writing in ESL: A constructivist-semiotic perspective. *Language Learning, 49*, 1, 143–175.

Parks, S. (2001). Moving from school to workplace: Disciplinary innovation, border crossings, and the reshaping of a written genre. *Applied Linguistics*, *22*(4), 405–438

Piller, I. (2002). Passing for a native speaker: identity and success in second language learning. *Journal of Sociolinguistics*, 6(2), 179–206. S

Reichelt, M. (1999). Toward a more comprehensive view of L2 writing: Foreign language writing in the U.S. *Journal of Second Language Writing*, *8*(2), 181–204.

Russell, D. (1997). Rethinking genre in school and society: An activity theory analysis. *Written Communication*, *14*(4), 504–554.

Scribner, S., & Cole, M. (1981). *The psychology of literacy*. Cambridge, MA: Harvard University Press.

Silva, T. (1993). Toward an understanding of the distinct nature of L2 writing: The ESL research and its implications. *TESOL Quarterly, 27*, 657–677.

Spack, R. (1988). Initiating ESL students into the academic discourse community: How far should we go? *TESOL Quarterly, 22*(1), 29–51.

Statistics Canada. (2001). Census 2001. Retrieved November 3, 2003 from http://www.statcan.ca/english/census01

Street, B. (1984). *Literacy in theory and practice*. Cambridge: Cambridge University Press.

Swales, J., & Feak, C. (1994). *Academic writing for graduate students: A course for nonnative speakers of English*. Ann Arbor, MI: University of Michigan Press.

Troyka. L. Q., Buckley, J., & Gates, D. (1996). *Simon & Schuster handbook for writers* (1st Canadian Ed.). Scarborough, ON: Prentice Hall.

Vignola, M.-J. (1998). The first and second language writing processes of French immersion graduates. In S. Lapkin (Ed.), *French second language education in Canada* (pp. 120–143). Toronto: University of Toronto Press.

Vygotsky, L. S. (1978). *Mind in society: The development of higher psychological processes*. In M. Cole, V. John-Steiner, S. Scribner, & E. Souberman, (Eds.). Cambridge, MA: Harvard University Press.

Whalen K., & Ménard, N. (1995). L1 and L2 writers' strategic and linguistic knowledge: A model of multiple-level discourse processing. *Language Learning, 45*, 381–418.

Wertsch, J. (1991). *Voices of the mind*. Cambridge, MA: Harvard University Press.

Werstch, J. (1998). *Mind as action*. Oxford: Oxford University Press.

Wesche, M. B., Morrison, F., Ready, D., & Pawley, C. (1990). French immersion: postsecondary consequences for individuals and universities. *The Canadian Modern Language Review, 46*(3), 430–451.

Wittgenstein, L. (1953). *Philosophical investigations* (G. Anscombe, Trans.). Oxford: Basil Blackwell and Mott.

9 Different Writers, Different Writing: Preparing International Teaching Assistants for Instructional Literacy

Kevin Eric DePew

If we were to take a sample of various higher learning institutions, we would find very little consistency in the institutional bodies that facilitate (and administer) bilingual and multilingual students' use of academic English. As we know, multilingual students—depending on whether they are international students, immigrant students, or generation 1.5 students—can experience disparate language development issues. We also understand that multilingual students at the undergraduate and graduate levels have different linguistic needs, even if they share similar communicative problems. Moreover, these L2 students' academic success relies upon proficiencies in both oral and verbal modes.[1] As we can see, teaching each L2 student how to communicate effectively at English-speaking universities in the United States raises many diverse challenges.

Some universities have only equipped their ESL faculty with a single office charged with accommodating all multilingual communication issues. In spite of the diverse issues that multilingual students bring to the academy, these microinstitutions often do not have the funding or expertise to address the array of language learning issues that they face. Other universities, however, have multiple administrative bodies that address different communication issues (e.g., writing/speaking, graduate/undergraduate, student/instructor). These administrative offices often get housed across the campus and are often connected to (and funded by) a wide range of programs and departments: international student programs, English departments, education departments, communication departments, foreign language departments, intensive English programs, programs that screen and mentor international teaching assistants (ITAs), as well as others. In these cases, the disciplinary division (Matsuda, 1999) and different funding sources can impede coordination between these offices.

These are the administrative contexts that international graduate students confront as they prepare to teach in the American classroom. Because of the "problem" that these graduate students generate when they teach across the disciplines (as instructors of their own course, as teaching assistants, as recitation leaders), most campuses have established programs to screen potential ITA candidates and to provide oral English mentoring to those international graduate students who have been assessed as potentially comprehensible instructors.[2] Although these courses focus mostly on improving the graduate students' oral English, we know from our own instructional practices that writing is a significant feature of most classroom pedagogies. But where do these potential ITAs learn the instructional literacy—the reading and writing practices used to teach content material and manage the course?[3] In most ITA mentoring courses, writing is subsumed by oral communication and gets taught merely as a compensatory strategy. Furthermore, most second language writing courses are for international undergraduate students (e.g., first-year writing) and focus on the "academic literacy" of student writers. As a result, ITAs rarely get taught how to effectively use writing in the classroom because this instruction often falls between the disciplinary cracks.

In this chapter, I will illustrate that ITAs are *different writers* than the usual second language writers discussed in the literature. Likewise, I would like to see scholars and administrators across the campus, including those from second language writing programs, collaborate to address the *different writing* that these graduate students do in the classroom context. When university administrators fail to make (and support) institutional changes that develop ITAs' instructional literacy they do a disservice both to the international graduate students, who they should be professionalizing, and to the undergraduate students these ITAs teach (or may have taught).[4] To support this assertion, I will further describe the potentially contentious context that ITAs work within and academia's response to this problem. Then I will establish writing's limited presence in current ITA mentoring, in spite of its prevalence in most classroom instruction, especially with the recent ubiquity of new computer-mediated writing technologies. I will conclude with suggestions that the various stakeholders who admit and mentor ITAs may want to consider as they field student complaints and address these complaints through ITA mentoring.

"THE FOREIGN TA PROBLEM"

Bailey in her 1984 edited collection, *Foreign Teaching Assistants in U.S. Universities,* describes the complaints generated about graduate students with accented English as "the foreign TA problem." Bailey's articulation of this situation as a "problem" is double-edged. She originally positions the term in quotations, a rhetorical strategy that supports her critical inquiry of students', parents', administrators', professors', and politicians' (potentially) prejudiced perspectives of this instructional situation. Yet Bailey herself gets mired down in this culture of the "foreign TA problem" when she overly praises the American TAs that the students preferred over their ITAs. She and other researchers studying ITAs are charged with the responsibility of solving this "problem," and, consequently, this responsibility institutionally positions them to see the situation as a problem. As a result, some ITA scholarship reflects and perpetuates this culture of the "foreign TA problem."

To understand instructional literacy's importance to ITA mentoring we need to understand how these instructors' oral English gets problematized and how many stakeholders contribute to the culture of the "foreign TA problem." Concerned about the quality of education that they receive from *graduate* instructors who do not speak "standard English," students vocally question various administrators about whether the university is giving them their money's worth. To achieve recognition, students "easily tap into the philosophy that the customer is always right"; therefore, their "instructional needs must be met if their tuition and their parents' tax dollars are to be judged well spent" (Bailey, 1984, p. 4; see also Fitch & Moran, 2003). Students' parents (and sometimes other taxpayers) will air similar grievances in letters written to politicians and university administrators. Bailey reports that one parent wrote, "As an overburdened taxpayer, I know of no good reason why I should be subsidizing the education of foreign students—send them home!" Another argued, "As a tax-paying Californian, I resent supporting a policy which dilutes the teaching process by such obvious abrogation of common sense; putting square pegs in round holes was never my idea of efficiency" (cited in Bailey, 1984, pp. 5–6). As an audience sympathetic to these complaints, institutional leaders have responded to this pressure with mandates, such as the flurry of state and university regulations that established ITA screening and mentoring programs during the 1980s. Like the university administrators, faculty and administrators within the disciplines are audience to many student complaints about ITAs; they, too, would like to see the "problem" curbed. Some of the faculty in Fox and Gay's study (1994) expressed their frustration with students who quit attending class because they could not understand their ITAs; others from this study complained that they were now compelled to surveil ITAs' instruction to ensure that course policies and procedures got executed properly. Although these stakeholders point fingers at each other, ITAs ultimately get identified as the problem. But are they solely responsible for the unsatisfactory communication between themselves and their students?

Some ITAs' accented spoken English *does* make it difficult for many domestic students to understand them. However, research, including my own, suggests that the problem's lore has become more real than the articulated problem (De Pew, 2003; Rubin, 1991). How, then, do we account for this disparity? Scholars, such as Ard (1989), Kaplan (1989), and Rubin (1991), argue that the stakeholders who complain about the "problem" also contribute to it. For instance, the student audience, as communicative interlocutors, has to be held responsible for successfully receiving the message. Rubin (1991), through an empirical study, found that students are predisposed to hear an accent when they see a foreign instructor. In this study, Rubin compared the affective responses and comprehension of different groups who heard the same lectures (delivered by a woman from Ohio) while staring at different pictures of "the instructor": one saw an Asian woman and the other saw a Caucasian woman. The groups who saw the Asian instructor reported hearing an accent and scored lower on comprehending the lectures. From these results Rubin concluded, "ethnically Asian instructors who speak [Standard Academic English] apparently confront similar dysfunctional attitudes as those who speak with marked nonnative accents" (1992, p. 519). Rubin's study allows us to assume that some undergraduate students approach some ITA-led courses expecting to have difficulties.

Rubin's study also suggests that these attitudes may be endemic to academic enculturation. Responding to the "Oh-No Syndrome" that students commonly experience upon learning they will be instructed by an ITA, Fitch and Moran (2003) studied how students' narratives about ITAs shape cultural milieu. After listening to several student focus groups describe their experiences with ITAs, they learned that negative tales—that positioned students as the victims and the ITAs and the university as the antagonists—were common; therefore, a poor grade was rarely articulated as the students' responsibility. Sometimes students would characterize themselves as heroes who overcame this academic challenge or because they were not as cruel to the ITA as their peers. Fitch and Moran (2003) also emphasize that these narratives demonstrated how little the students knew about their instructors or other ITAs—both culturally and academically—including their accomplishments.

In other studies that solicited students' perceptions of their ITAs, students reported that they expected their instructor would be "disorganized or unfocused because their spoken English did not use appropriate stress, intonation, pauses, and transitions" (Twale, Shannon, & Moore, 1997, p. 62). Furthermore, students' personalities can exacerbate the problem, such as highly competitive students who see ITAs' lack of linguistic preparation as a "barrier to their [own] acquisition of vital knowledge" (Bresnahan & Kim, 1993, p. 5). Many of these students have not developed a "competence in understanding unfamiliar varieties of English which exhibit variant phonology, syntax, and intonation" and therefore cannot uphold their responsibility in the communicative collaboration between instructor and student (Bresnahan & Kim, 1993, p. 4).

Other stakeholders can also participate in improving the communicative relationship between ITAs and their students. Parents can resist fostering attitudes and values that support students' intolerance of their diverse instructors. Professors in the disciplines, the stakeholders responsible for these graduate students' professionalization, can proactively respond to students' complaints by preparing ITAs to teach within their discipline. Kaplan (1989), however, asserts that other exigencies of academic culture would not sustain this practice; faculty members probably received little pedagogical training themselves and "learned to teach by doing it, and they fail to see why [ITAs] can't do as they did" (p. 115). Furthermore, ITAs reported to Stevenson and Jenkins (1994) that they received little support from their supervisors in their disciplines. This unproductive cycle could potentially be broken by establishing mentoring for all of these future academics. In spite of the best existing efforts to prepare ITAs for the classroom, politicians and university-level administrators offer little support; they "want faculty involved in ITA instruction to provide programs that are effective, cheap, and keep complaints about teaching from reaching them" (Ard, 1989, p. 133). By withholding financial support and providing minimal moral support, these stakeholders become an obstacle for administrators and faculty who are working to resolve any problems.

I realize that my characterization of these stakeholders have been painted with broad strokes and do not represent the multitude of individuals—from students up to university-level administrators—who support the presence of ITAs because of their multiple contributions to the academy. However, the pictures that I have painted explain why ITAs—due to their "imperfect" oral English—bear the brunt of the "foreign TA problem." Moreover, I have represented some of the exigencies that make the academic culture, at many campuses, inhospitable to ITAs.

ITA Mentoring Programs and Pedagogies

In the literature about ITA mentoring curricula, writing has not been emphasized as a pedagogical practice. Since most complaints stem from ITAs' oral proficiency and most administrators and faculty of these programs tend to have master's degrees in TESL (a discipline that prioritizes oral communication), the curricula's emphasis on oral competencies seems to be a natural response.[5] While some mentoring programs may have considered expanding their curricula to include other modalities, the absence of appropriate resources for these programs has probably discouraged these programs from doing more than addressing the source of students' complaints. Because these programs need to demonstrate results in a short period of time (e.g., a year or a semester), it also makes sense for program administrators and faculty to address the "problem." As a result, writing is mostly absent from the scholarship about ITA mentoring curricula; when it is discussed, scholars present it cautiously as a compensatory strategy.

For example, Ard (1989) strongly believes that ITAs should use compensatory strategies to facilitate the communicative process. Students, he believes, will receive information present through multiple modalities, such as "body language, gestures, writing on the board, handouts, transparencies, tone of voice, volume of voice, pausing, the actual words, examples, analogies, and transition words" (p. 131). He continues, "A student does not need to understand all of these sources of information to catch the point. Perhaps one will do" (p. 131). Although Ard's list of compensatory strategies includes three examples of written communication (writing on the board, handouts, transparencies), many of these compensatory strategies relate to oral communication and dominate the scholarship about ITA mentoring curriculum. As I will later point out, the ubiquity of computer technologies on college campuses since Ard published his claims could surely add several more literacy-based strategies to this list and shift the balance of modalities that get adopted as compensating strategies.

Other scholars have researched the effects of compensatory strategies, including writing. Hoekje and Williams (1992) recommend more contextual strategies that address "effective language usage *while performing the role of TA*" (p. 247). To achieve these ends, Hoekje and Williams propose pragmatic strategies to ITAs, such as planning presentations—which requires writing—and writing frequently mispronounced words on the board. They do not, however, explain how the ITA will identify these errors, but I presume that they envision a model where ITAs receive help from their mentors. Halleck and Moder (1995), also believe that compensatory strategies, such as writing, are quite useful. However, according to their research data, these strategies are only useful to ITAs who have achieved a certain level of language proficiency. Positioning literacy in the ITA mentoring pedagogy only as a potential compensatory strategy begs the question: what role does literacy actually play within most classroom instruction?

Fitch and Moran (2003), I believe begin to address the other roles that literacy can play in the classroom. Among their recommendations for altering the campus culture (and the ITA narrative), they proposes additional instructional strategies. In particular they recommend having "ITAs provide outlines or notes to their students or to accompany their lectures with overhead slides or PowerPoint presentations. This will allow students to 'follow along' with class lectures. Moreover, such a strategy will reassure students that the ITA is indeed committed to students' learning" (p. 308). For Fitch and Moran (2003), the instructor's use of written texts to communicate does more than just hide an accent or increase students' comprehension; it helps the ITA set the tone for her classroom. With the modern classroom offering a plethora of literacy tools, ITAs have multiple opportunities to demonstrate their commitment to students' learning—if they are taught how to use these tools effectively.

Literacy's Prevalence in the Classroom

Arguing that literacy should have a place in the second language classroom, Harklau (2002) asks us to

> picture what would happen in almost any classroom where second language learning is taking place, if we suddenly took away all literacy-related materials: all texts and other books, all worksheets and handouts, all writing on the board, all overheads, all writing implements. I suspect there are few classrooms where this absence would go unremarked. (pp. 335–336)

Likewise, if the second language learner moves to the front of the classroom as an ITA, we would still see a pedagogical environment that fails to fulfill its potential; literacy practices are just deeply entrenched within the pedagogical context. In addition to the items that Harklau lists, instructors also communicate with their students by handwriting formative and summative evaluations on the work that students submit.

More recently, advances in computer technologies have given instructors new media, such as email, websites, chatrooms, PowerPoint slide shows, electronic comments in Microsoft Word, and other discipline specific software, to communicate with their students. Furthermore, those instructors who take full advantage of courseware packages, such as WebCT and Blackboard, can conduct most of their course through writing. We are seeing a pedagogical shift, for better or for worse, in which Internet writing technologies (e.g., email, websites, courseware) make the instructor as present outside of the classroom as inside the classroom. And this virtual presence is mediated through the written word. With all of these ways that writing has been normalized as a pedagogical strategy, I believe that instructional literacy needs to be emphasized in ITA mentoring courses. Otherwise, these courses are not only inadequately preparing these instructors for the classroom, but they are ignoring, as Fitch and Moran (2003) argue, significant strategies that can be used to facilitate communication and potentially alleviate tension with their student audience.

I anticipate, based upon my experience, that administrators and faculty from ITA mentoring programs would legitimately counter that they are not writing experts and that changing the focus of their pedagogy may encourage ITAs to hide behind the written word. Institutionally, most ITA mentoring programs have not been set up to support a change in the established pedagogy. As I have already explained, when students have complained about their instructors' oral English, the university responds by bringing in experts—those with degrees in TESL—who can teach oral proficiency. Likewise writing experts, especially those who study graduate level second language writers, mostly examine the pre-professional writing these students do as emerging scholars. They rarely examine the instructional literacy practices of teaching assistants which demonstrates just one more example of the disciplinary divide that Matsuda (1999) has described. Thus the institutional chasms that separate ITA mentoring and writing scholars further prevents any productive cross-disciplinary discussions.

Administrators' are also concerned that ITAs might only present themselves in writing to avoid revealing their accented English. For example, they do not want ITAs to avoid talking to their classes by relying heavily on handouts, overheads, and PowerPoint slides. While we cannot ignore that this concern also stems from the issue of disciplinary expertise, we cannot overlook that instructors' responsibilities are significantly facilitated by the spoken word. Instructors still need to explain the course material, answer students' questions, and address spontaneous concerns. Emerging instructors therefore need to learn to balance between oral and written modalities. But to strike this balance, writing needs to be more than a compensatory strategy that supports oral communication; it should be a complimentary strategy that becomes part of an instructor's multi-faceted repertoire. By delivering the content through writing and the spoken word, instructors with accented oral English increase their audience's opportunities to receive the intended message. Let me illustrate this point with an anecdote from my own research.

A Case Study

Some time ago I developed a research project to examine how ITAs used writing, especially with digital writing technologies (i.e., any digital application that allows an individual to communicate through verbal and visual modalities), to compose their instructional identities.[6] This research was conducted at a large Midwestern land-grant university that has a large international student population at both the undergraduate and graduate level. Over the course of this project, I conducted three case studies in which I examined many features of the rhetorical situation throughout the semester.[7] During the fall semester of 2001, I studied how Aiping, an Asian ITA teaching first-year composition in a networked computer classroom, composed his identity for a specific student audience.[8]

Initially most students did not respond to Aiping's accent. From the base-line questionnaire that I performed at the end of the semester's second week, I learned that most students formed their first impression of Aiping from his nationality and his personality. For example, one student found it significant that he was "being taught English by someone who has not grown up with English," but he thought it would be "good to have a new type of teacher." Similarly another student questioned "Why is this foreign guy teaching English?," but she also recognized "because he's learned English recently he has a lot of insight, and interesting comments." Like similar responders, these students acknowledge Aiping's obvious markings, but his difference seemed to inspire more curiosity than disdain. Two students, however, did comment on his linguistic proficiency. One of these students who had worked in a Chinese restaurant mentioned that he had difficulty understanding him and the other mentioned, "I found him amusing. His English is not too good; he did not know common English phrases." So only 2 of his 19 students initially found him difficult to understand. Later in the semester, many of the students' opinions unfortunately changed for the worse. By mid-semester, many students—8 of 17 respondents—identified Aiping's pedagogical weakness as his ability to speak and understand English, especially idioms. At the end of the semester, 9 of 16 students reiterated these sentiments and the student who originally found him amusing punctuates these criticisms by exclaiming, "He barely can speak modern English and English is what he is teaching."

The students' initial reaction to their international instructor counters scholars' assertions that some students automatically dismiss the TAs once they recognize them as "different." One would think that if the students could not understand the instructor's accent, this problem would have been identified by the end of the second week. The students' delayed criticisms also counter the scholars who claim that students tend to adapt to their instructor's accent after the first few weeks. Students in research studies have commonly reported that ITAs were difficult to understand at the beginning of the semester, but after a few weeks students were able to adjust by "making the appropriate phonological substitutions and even . . . [became] accustomed to systematic grammatical errors" (Williams, 1992, p. 694; see also Plakans, 1997). Time, according to, Twale, Shannon, and Moore (1997), also allows ITAs to gain situational experience that they use to improve their performance, a factor demonstrated by the higher ratings the researchers saw given to more experienced ITAs. But why did the students in Aiping's class reverse this trend from the second week to the ninth week of the semester? I speculate that several different factors—ranging from students receiving their first evaluated essay (Kaplan, 1989), to personal disagreements with the instructor, to the tragedies of September 11th—could have contributed to these changed attitudes. Likewise, I cannot discount that Aiping's accent *may have* become more pronounced over the course of the semester, especially as he began to use content related terminology that the students may have been unfamiliar with. Whether these changes reflect attitudinal or linguistic shifts, many students became quite opinionated about Aiping's oral language proficiency.

In spite of their negativity towards Aiping's accented oral English, many students who complained about his accent in the second and third questionnaires also praised Aiping's ability to communicate his instructions through writing. Throughout the semester, Aiping maintained a course website, responded to students' email inquiries, and visually supplemented his announcements and lectures with projected PowerPoint slides and Web pages. By the middle of the semester, 8 of Aiping's students explicitly described the instructions on his Web pages as "good," "clear" and "helpful." Half of these students also considered his accent to be a detriment. By the end of the semester, 9 of the 16 respondents complimented his website. The student who worked in the Chinese restaurant stated that the "instructions are clear & helpful & he puts them up on the website if you missed or cannot understand them." In reference to Aiping's feedback, the student who originally questioned the value of being taught by a "foreign guy" described Aiping as "an educated person who can speak English well via email." Both of these students echoed 5 other students who gave similar praise, but considered Aiping's oral accent to be his instructional weakness. Furthermore 8 of the 9 students who criticized his accent on the last questionnaire described how Aiping taught them new features of writing, such as writing strategies, organization, and how to write with certain technologies. One of these students explained, "I learned a lot about writing and the steps it takes to write a good paper." In spite of their criticisms, these students are learning the subject matter and Aiping's instructional writing is facilitating this process.

When I asked Aiping why he chose to teach in a computer-mediated classroom, he initially responded that he liked the technology, he wanted to teach a different type of class, and it gave him an opportunity to learn the technologies. But in later conversations when we discussed how his students' perceived him, he stated, "I admit that I do not speak like a native speaker, but I try to *compensate* by using the website. I give instructions in a clearly stated form" (emphasis added). Aiping, feeling that he has more control over his written English than his oral English, uses the technology to appear more professional. The students' responses demonstrate how this strategy does and does not succeed; although they do not see *him* as more professional, they see the written manifestations of his pedagogy as professional. Does this mean that Aiping is hiding behind his instructional writing? Aiping's delivery demonstrated otherwise. During my observations, Aiping would present his lesson orally while projecting the principles and instructions through a LCD projector. At times he would even use the cursor to highlight his talking points on the Web page or PowerPoint slides as he presented the item orally; his re-purposing of this function helped to keep the students oriented. Moreover, a lot of instruction occurred outside of the classroom walls and outside of the scheduled class time through electronic media (i.e., email, the course website) With these strategies I see Aiping's instructional writing as more than a compensation strategy; writing, as with many instructors in this new millennium, has become a primary mode of instruction.

Aiping's composition class, of course, is only one case study. And Aiping has the advantage of being a writing teacher studying the English language, as well as being mentored in a composition program that supports both instructional and the technological literacy. Few ITAs outside of English receive this type instructional or linguistic support as they professionalize in their disciplines. In spite of these advantages, this case study provides us with two lessons. First, it highlights the beneficial literacy strategies instructors already employ and that ITA mentoring programs should explore. Second, it demonstrates that various fields of writing—composition studies, second language writing, computers and writing, writing program administration, professional writing—can collaborate with ITA mentoring programs strategies to prepare ITAs for the *new* classroom.

Recommendations for ITA Mentoring

Since the establishment of the ITA mentoring course in the early 1980s, the nature of the classroom has changed. And I believe the curriculum for mentoring ITAs should reflect these changes. At this point in pedagogical history, asking whether writing should be included in the ITA mentoring curriculum is no longer a relevant question. Instead, those who mentor ITAs will want to ask what aspects of writing should they teach ITAs and how will they include this instruction into their already dense curriculum. I will provide a few recommendations that ITA mentoring programs can build upon.

First, make writing a significant component of ITA mentoring. As I have illustrated in this chapter, writing already plays a significant role in instructional literacy. But we cannot assume that the individuals we place in front of the classroom will automatically know the best ways to utilize writing strategies in the classroom. ITA mentoring programs, depending on resources, such as time and money will have to decide how to overhaul the current structure to accommodate this new instruction. Furthermore, the advent of the various digital writing technologies that I have described has made instructional literacy more complicated than just writing on the board. At some institutions, instructors can draw upon an expanded repertoire of media to communicate their lesson and manage their classes. But with these options comes the responsibility of teaching these international instructors how to use some of these applications. I anticipate that administrators and faculty of ITA mentoring programs would argue that teaching instructional technology is not their job; I would, however, respond that if ITA mentoring programs are charged with the responsibility of preparing international graduate students to effectively communicate with the English-speaking students, then they have to teach their mentees how to use the tools that they *will* use to fulfill these responsibilities. Likewise these responsibilities can be shared by creating alliances, as I describe below.

Second, ITA mentoring program will want to recognize that ITAs are professional writers. As teaching assistants, recitation leaders, and instructors of record, these instructors institutionally fulfill professional roles that require them to produce genre-driven texts. These instructors, therefore need to learn these genres, and in some cases, the various digital writing technologies that support certain genres. This point builds upon the previous point: not only do we need to teach ITAs how to use certain writing technologies, but we need to teach them how to use them effectively. As an ITA mentoring administrator once remarked, "We don't want to encourage ITAs to just silently stand in front of the classroom clicking through PowerPoint slides." ITA mentors can solve this problem by teaching these future instructors how to compose informative PowerPoint presentations, as well as how to balance oral, verbal, and visual for an effective delivery (Tardy, 2005).

Similarly, these instructors could be taught how to effectively compose readable documents. For example, Figure 1 and Figure 2 have the same content, but have been formatted differently.[9] At first glance the text in Figure 1 all seems to run together; without reading the text, the heading, "Recommendation," looks like it can be part of the previous paragraph. This slows down quick orientation and information retrieval by the audience. In contrast, the design strategies (e.g., the visual contrast, the clear hierarchies) used for Figure 2 facilitate the audiences' ability to read this document. Again knowledge of document design is not within the expected expertise for ITA mentors. Yet, these figures illustrate that knowing how to professionally present information in writing can affect the audiences' comprehension. Just like most ITAs' oral accent, a poorly designed document can be understood, but a student audience will have to work harder at making meaning. Teaching ITAs other instructionally relevant professional writing principles, such as Web authoring design and the protocols of email, may help them to exceed their student audiences' expectation and facilitate learning, as illustrated by Aiping's use of writing. These strategies can give ITAs the appearance of communicative competence that their accented oral English may not.

I want to conclude with my final recommendation: ITA mentoring programs can respond to the pressures of the twenty-first century

> **Tips for Helping International TAs
> by Kevin Eric De Pew, Old Dominion University**
>
> Purpose
>
> Most international teaching assistants (ITAs) are not taught instructional literacy in ITA mentoring courses. Writing, if it is taught, often gets taught as a compensatory strategy. Yet writing is a common pedagogical strategy. We see writing included in writing on the chalk/white board, grading assignments and tests, emails, courseware (e.g., WebCT, Blackboard). With writing being a common feature of instruction, ITA mentoring programs should develop strategies for formally teaching writing, especially discipline specific instructional literacy.
>
> Recommendations
> 1. Teach ITAs how to write and the different genres of instructional literacy.
> 2. Prepare ITAs to be professional writers by teaching them how to compose rhetorically effective texts.
> 3. Get the administrators and faculty from the ITAs' disciplines more involved in their international graduate students' professional development.

Figure 1. Minimally formatted handout

classroom by forming alliances across the university and sharing the responsibility for their ITAs' pedagogical preparation. For 20 years, stakeholders have pointed fingers at each other, but student and parent complaints still persist and the ITAs receive the brunt of fallout. In the meantime, the nature of the classroom has changed and the typical mentoring curriculum of primarily developing oral competency has become outdated. Ideally, universities will begin to provide ITA mentors the appropriate resources to programmatically reconstruct the infrastructure in ways that reflect these pedagogical changes. Unfortunately, in the current political climate this agenda would be quite unpopular.

> **Tips for Helping International TAs**
> by Kevin Eric De Pew
> Old Dominion University
>
> **Purpose**
> Most international teaching assistants (ITAs) are not taught instructional literacy in ITA mentoring courses. Writing, if it is taught, often gets taught as a compensatory strategy. Yet writing is a common pedagogical strategy. We see writing included in
>
> - writing on the chalk/white board
> - grading assignments and tests
> - emails
> - courseware (e.g., WebCT, Blackboard).
>
> With writing being a common feature of instruction, ITA mentoring programs should develop strategies for formally teaching writing.
>
> **Recommendations**
> 1. Teach ITAs how to write and the different genres of instructional literacy.
> 2. Prepare ITAs to be professional writers by teaching them how to compose rhetorically effective texts.
> 3. Get the administrators and faculty from the ITAs' disciplines more involved in their international graduate students' professional development.

Figure 2. Well formatted handout

Therefore, if ITA mentoring programs want to respond to the new classroom, they need to pull expertise from other corners of the campus. To fulfill the first two recommendations ITA mentoring programs will want to collaborate with various writing programs, including second language writing experts. Depending upon their own programs' resources, these writing experts can either instruct ITA mentors how to teach writing principles to ITAs or they can provide this instruction to ITAs themselves. Furthermore, compositionists with second language writing expertise can provide useful literacy instruction for this population of language learners. In some cases, advanced graduate students in these disciplinary emphases would relish the opportunity to work with other graduate students who are developing real-world writing strategies. Likewise allegiances can be made with computer science faculty who can teach the potential instructors how to operate the digital writing technologies commonly used in the classroom.

Most importantly, ITA mentors will want to encourage administrators and faculty in these graduate students' disciplines to actively participate in these students' professional development. Advocates of the writing within the disciplines movement argue that the ones most qualified to teach a field's discourse convention are the professionals within that disciplines; therefore, these professionals should have a stake in fostering their students' understanding of these conventions. This philosophy is equally applicable to ITAs' preparation for the English-speaking classroom. If these departments want to reap the benefits of having international diversity in their programs, they will also need to support these students. With some creative collaboration, I believe we can support these different writers and the different writing that they do.

Notes

[1] I have chosen the term "L2 students" to collectively describe all students who both read and write in a language other than their mother tongue at the American academy. While this term does not account for the multiple linguistic proficiencies that some individuals have, it does not separate speakers from writers.

[2] While some programs would use the term "training" to describe the oral and cultural instruction that international graduate students receive, I prefer "mentoring" because it avoids some of the norming metaphors implied by the former term (see Foucault, 1977). Mentoring, on the other hand, connotes that an experienced individual is imparting expertise and knowledge on a novice individual. I understand that in practice, programs have been pedagogically designed to linguistically normalize ITAs before they become instructors; however, I hope this articulation will prompt some administrators to critically consider the design of these courses.

[3] Both the terms *instructional literacy* and *pedagogical literacy* have been used in education to describe the act of teaching literacy; I am using the former term to describe the literate practices that instruction entails.

[4] Let me provide some full disclosure at this point. I have only briefly worked as an ITA mentor (i.e., eight weeks) and my primary field of study is not TESL. Thus I am not disciplinarily from the ITA mentoring context. On the other hand, I have taught and piloted various second language writing courses (i.e., developmental writing workshops, first-year writing, busi-

ness writing), and I have a background in rhetoric with research interests in second language writing. Furthermore, for an extensive research project, I reviewed the literature on ITA training, studied how three ITAs use writing in their pedagogy, and learned how these ITAs' students responded to them. One could argue that I am looking at this issue from the outside. Therefore, I hope that my audience sees my argument as an outsider's alternative perspective rather than an uninformed mandate.

[5] As a side note I want to emphasize that I respect the MA in TESL as a terminal degree and believe that it does not intellectually diminish an individuals capacity to do these jobs. I do however believe that since the degree does not put the individual in tenurable position, these administrators and instructors can be institutionally handicapped. These working conditions often foster a situation in which the individuals are not externally motivated or compensated for studying their programs. Also since many of these programs are underfunded (potentially the result of not having administrators in power who can argue for adequate resources), these individuals also have little time to do such studies. Without administrators' and faculty's contributions, we loose a valuable epistemological perspective to the greater conversation about ITA mentoring.

[6] The focus of this project was on the process strategies individuals use to compose their subjectivity using various digital writing technologies. I specifically chose ITAs as a research population because of the rhetorical situation in which they would compose this subjectivity (i.e., a milieu that articulates them as a "problem") and because I wanted to do research that could potentially benefit the representative population.

[7] I collected data with each case study by doing three interviews with the instructors about their intended strategies, conducting three questionnaires taken by the student audience, and observing class sessions every other week. The questionnaire I used entailed open-ended questions that could have been applied to any instructor of any ethnicity. Unlike many questionnaires that students have taken to evaluate their ITAs in other studies (Fox & Gay, 1994), I wanted to avoid closed-ended questions about ITAs that would prompt students to discuss the instructors' "differences." Instead I believed that the open-ended questions would allow the students to come to these discussions of "difference" on their own. This would allow me to gauge how important this issue was for these students.

[8] The participant's name is a pseudonym. I have chosen to report on what I learned from Aiping's class because of the three studies, his experience was most typical to the literature. Aiping had only been speaking English for the eight years that he had been in United States. At the time of the study he was in his third year at the university (where he had been majoring in English as a Second Language in the English Linguistics graduate program) and the third semester in the composition classroom.

[9] Figure 1 represents some of the strategies I have seen instructors, of all ranks and nationalities, use for classroom handouts and conference handouts.

References

Ard, J. (1989). Grounding an ITA curriculum: Theoretical and practical concerns. *English for Specific Purposes, 8,* 125–138.

Bailey, K. (1984a). The "foreign TA problem." In K. M. Bailey, F. Pialorsi, & J. Zukowski/Faust (Eds.), *Foreign teaching assistants in U.S. universities* (pp. 3–15). Washington, DC: National Association for Foreign Student Affairs.

Bailey, K. (1984b). A typology of teaching assistants. In K. M. Bailey, F. Pialorsi, & J. Zukowski/Faust (Eds.), *Foreign teaching assistants in U.S. universities* (pp. 110–125). Washington, DC: National Association for Foreign Student Affairs.

Bresnahan, M. I., & Kim, M. S. (1993). Predictors of receptivity and resistance toward international teaching assistants. *Journal of Asian Pacific Communication, 4,* 3–14.

DePew, K. E. (2003). *The rhetorical process of digital subjectivities: Case studies of international teaching assistants negotiating identity with digital media.* Purdue University. unpublished dissertation.

Fitch F., & Morean, S. E. (2003). "Not a lick of English": Constructing the ITA identity through student narratives. *Communication Education, 52,* 297–310.

Foucault, M. (1977). Discipline and punish: The birth of the prison (Alan Sheridan, Trans.). New York: Vintage Books.

Fox, W. S., & Gay, G. (1994). Functions and effects of international teaching assistants. *The Review of Higher Education, 18,* 1–24.

Halleck, G. B., & Moder, C. L. (1995). Testing language and teaching skills of international teaching assistants: The limits of compensatory strategies. *TESOL Quarterly, 29,* 733–758.

Harklau, L. (2002). The role of writing in classroom second language acquisition. *Journal of Second Language Writing, 11,* 329–350.

Hoekje, B., & Williams, J. (1992). Communicative competence and the dilemma of international teaching assistant education. *TESOL Quarterly, 26,* 243–269.

Kaplan. R. B. (1989). The life and times of ITA programs. *English for Specific Purposes, 8,* 109–124.

Matsuda, P. K. (1999). Composition studies and ESL writing: A disciplinary division of labor. *College Composition and Communication, 50,* 699–721.

Plakans, B. (1997). Undergraduates' experiences with and attitudes toward international teaching assistants. *TESOL Quarterly, 31,* 95–119.

Rubin, D. L. (1992). Nonlanguage factors affecting undergraduates' judgments of nonnative English-speaking teaching assistants. *Research in Higher Education, 33,* 511–531.

Stevenson, I., & Jenkins, S. (1994). Journal writing in the training of international teaching assistants. *Journal of Second Language Writing, 3,* 97–120.

Tardy, C. (2005). Expressions of disciplinarity and individuality in a multimodal genre. *Computers and Composition, 22,* 319–336.

Twale, D. J., Shannon, D. M., & Moore, M. S. (1997). NGTA and IGTA training and experience: Comparisons between self-ratings and undergraduate student evaluations. *Innovative Higher Education, 22,* 61–77.

Williams, J. (1992). Planning, discourse marking, and the comprehensibility of international teaching assistants. *TESOL Quarterly, 26,* 693–711.

Yook, E. L., & Albert, R. D. (1999). Perceptions of international teaching assistants: The interrelatedness of intercultural training, cognition, and emotion. *Communication Education, 18,* 1–17.

10 Globalization and the Politics of Teaching EFL Writing

Xiaoye You

Over the last two decades, English writing instruction in non-English dominant countries has showed great interest in adapting Anglo-American norms of writing and writing pedagogies for the local contexts.[1] This phenomenon has prompted L2 writing specialists to consider some important political issues in EFL writing. Kachru (1995) argues that the institutional varieties of English used in the Outer-Circle countries—such as India, Pakistan, and South Africa—have developed their own grammatical and textual forms to express their contexts of culture. Therefore the norms of writing grown out of Inner-Circle countries are no longer *the* standard for English writing practices in Outer-Circle contexts. In addition, Leki (2001) questions the legitimacy of the large investment required of both institutions and individuals to teach English writing in non-English-dominant contexts. She suggests the need for dialogue with EFL students about the role of writing in their lives as well as the need to make English writing enhance learner options, making it a powerful means of achieving the learners' personal goals. Studying the daily operations of an English teaching division in a Chinese university, You (2004) has observed severe tension between institutional stipulations and classroom writing instruction. Pressured by the institutional requirements for teaching English writing, the administrators, teachers, students and academic publishers maneuvered through constraining material conditions, subverting the requirements to achieve their varying interests. Issues of rhetorical standards, legitimacy of English writing instruction, and the tension between institutional requirements and grass-root level instruction constitutes the political dimension of English writing instruction in non-English-dominant countries. These discussions have enlightened us not only to the unique political nature of EFL writing but also to how EFL writing professionals respond to institutional stipulations for teaching English writing.

This chapter seeks to explore the politics of teaching English writing in non-English-dominant contexts in relation to the prevailing discourse of globalization. Globalization, whether it is the reality or simply an imagination of our world, has become a rather popular term to describe how people, images, technologies, ideologies, and capital spill over traditional political boundaries and create novel "uncertain landscapes" through their complex interaction (Appadurai, 1996, p. 43). Against these new, uncertain landscapes, many countries have heightened their requirements for English education at both secondary and tertiary levels, and invariably they connect the heightened requirements with the rhetoric of globalization (Jeong, 2004; Matsuura, Fujieda & Mahoney, 2004; Peng, Zhou, & Fu, 2002). It is crucial to examine how the rhetoric of globalization underwrites English writing instruction, including how English literacy is reconceptualized in relation to globalization, how literacy should be taught, and how it is actually taught within the limits of local material conditions.

In what follows, I will examine the teaching of English writing in China, a non-English-dominant country whose history of English writing instruction can be traced all the way back to the 1860s (You, 2005). I will scrutinize an educational decree on college English teaching published by the Chinese Ministry of Education in early 2004 and investigate its ramifications on English writing instruction in two Chinese universities. As China wholeheartedly welcomes globalization, I hope this inquiry will shed light on our understanding of how globalization has shaped, and may continue to shape, English writing instruction in non-English dominant countries in general.

REDEFINING ENGLISH LITERACY

Ever since China joined the World Trade Organization (WTO) in 2001, the influences of globalization can be strongly felt in the Chinese educational sector. English is described by the Chinese mass media as an international language for global political, economic and cultural transactions. Responding to the arising demands of globalization, the Ministry of Education issued a new educational decree, "Teaching Requirements for College English Curriculum," in January 2004. The decree lays out the goals and requirements for college English teaching, suggests major adjustments of curricular elements and teaching modes, and emphasizes well-coordinated assessment and administration.

The decree offers a good entry point for examining how English literacy is defined in the discourse of globalization. Compared with English teaching standards and syllabi published previously, "Teaching Requirements for College English Curriculum" includes not only the teaching of language knowledge and language skills, but also the teaching of language learning strategies and cross-cultural communication skills. Why are cross-cultural communication skills added in the new requirements? The answer was implied in an article published right before their release, written by Zhang Yaoxue, Chair of the Department of Chinese Higher Education. Zhang (2003) defines English as a means for international communication. He says, "The world economy is increasingly globalized; our country has joined the WTO; scientific exchanges become internationalized; international communications are getting more and more frequent; all of which has made English a daily tool just like a driver's license" (Primary Conditions Section, para. 6). The phrases, "a daily tool" and "a driver's license," have completely erased any ideological connotations of English that used to connect this language with English-dominant countries. With a driver's license, someone is entitled to operate a vehicle for traveling from one locale to another. With a good command of English, someone is capable of communicating across national boundaries. The projected image of English language as a tool for international communication thus warranted the inclusion of cross-cultural communication skills in the reconceptualization of English literacy.

English literacy is further defined in specific terms for college English teaching, with a clear emphasis on English for academic purposes (EAP). Students with different entry levels are not expected to graduate from college with the same level of language ability. Different from previous syllabi—which define listening, speaking, reading, writing and translation at two levels with quite vague terms (see College English Syllabus Revision Team, 1985, 1999)—the new requirements set three well-articulated levels, that is, the basic, relatively high, and higher levels for these language skills. More strikingly, there is significant elevation of requirements for these language skills. Besides being expected to use English for daily communication purposes, like students in English-dominant countries, students are also expected to use English for academic purposes. For example, at the relatively high level, students need to "comprehend English lectures in their disciplines given by foreign experts, grasping the central points and main ideas" (Teaching Requirements Section, para. 9) in terms of listening comprehension. Regarding reading comprehension, they should "be able to read and understand summative literature in their disciplines" (para. 11). As for writing, the students are expected to "be able to write English abstracts for their theses, and be able to, through consulting reference books, write disciplinary reports or papers with clear structure and rich content" (para. 12). Table 1 clearly shows the EAP-orientation of the writing requirements at both the relatively high and higher levels. The new demand for teaching EAP goes in unison with an ambitious bilingual education project currently underway in Chinese higher education. As part of this project, some high-ranking universities have been ordered by the Ministry of Education to increase the number of major courses taught in English (Zhang, 2003).

Table 1. Requirements for English Writing at Three Exit Levels

	Basic Level	Relatively High Level	Higher Level
Types of writing	Practical writings (such as, registration form, application form, health card, invitation, note and notice)	Practical writings, summaries, academic reports, and theses	Technical reports, and theses in one's discipline
Written competence	Be able to describe personal experiences, events, observations, and feelings.	Be able to write academic papers, reports, and theses in one's discipline.	Be able to express one's thoughts freely on general topics with clear structures, rich contents, and strong logicality.
Written competence demonstrated in assessments (within 30 minutes)	Be able to write a short passage of 120 words according to a general topic or an outline provided.	Be able to write a short passage of 160 words on a given topic.	Be able to write an expository or argumentative passage of 200 words.

(The Ministry of Education, 2004)

Implied but clear in the decree is that students are also expected to learn to use modern information technologies to assist their language learning. With reference to teaching modes, Teaching Requirements for College English Curriculum state, "The new teaching modes should rely upon modern information technologies, particularly network technology. In the new teaching mode, English teaching should encourage individualized learning, learning without being constrained by time and place, and learning on the student's own initiative" (Teaching Modes Section, para. 1). Students can choose the learning materials, and they can record and assess their progress. Studying English in an information technology-facilitated environment, on the one hand, the students will have the opportunity to develop individualized learning strategies vital to their academic success; on the other hand, more importantly, they will learn modern information technologies that will constitute their future workplace. Like cross-cultural communication skills, conceptualized in broader terms, computer/network literacy makes up part of English literacy.

The new definition of English literacy in Teaching Requirements for College English Curriculum echoes discussions of English teaching in some other countries. For example, in a report submitted to former Japanese Prime Minister Keizo Obuchi in the year 2000, the Commission on Japan's Goals in the 21st Century claimed that the possession of global literacy skills determines whether or not a citizen would expect to enjoy a better life in the 21st century. The new literacy defined by the Commission includes the mastery of modern information technologies, such as computers and the Internet, and a good working knowledge of English that helps a person with "learning about and accessing the world" (Matsuura, Fujieda, & Mahoney, 2004, p. 471). In the Chinese context, global literacy is particularized as a good command of English language skills for both academic and cross-cultural communication, as well as familiarity with modern information technologies. However, in the thrust to redefine English literacy in the discourse of globalization, the issue of which version of the world Englishes should be promoted in the local contexts continues to be ignored at the institutional level, leaving the issue to open interpretation and consequently varying practices in teaching.

Reforming Curriculum, Pedagogy and Assessment

Besides refiguring English literacy in light of globalization discourse, Teaching Requirements for College English Curriculum also strives to reform current English curricula, pedagogy and assessment, all of which are indispensable means for achieving the new literacy.

In terms of the English curriculum, two major shifts can be easily noted in Teaching Requirements for College English Curriculum. First, it is emphasized that the English curricular system should promote computer/network-based courses. They may be comprehensive English courses, courses for each language skill, culture-based courses, or ESP courses. Second, English courses are no longer conceptualized simply as offering the students basic knowledge about the language, but rather they are the media that "allow the students to learn about science and technology and Western society and culture" (Curricular Arrangements Section, para. 4). Thus the shift towards computer/network-based courses with a clear emphasis on content-rich subject matter maps out a concrete curricular infrastructure for achieving the new literacy.

When it comes to pedagogy, there is a strong emphasis on integrating information technologies into the traditional classroom. The decree encourages the development of listening- and speaking-oriented pedagogical modes based on individual computers, local area networks, or even the Internet. Further, according to the decree, the pedagogical modes should underscore student-centered teaching, encouraging individualized and autonomous learning styles in the students. Clearly the decree sees the integration of information technology into English classrooms as an excellent opportunity to alter teacher-centered instruction and to give the students more control over how they are going to learn the language. However, there are two understated, practical reasons for promoting information technologies and student-centered pedagogical modes. Zhang (2003) points out in his article that development in network technology can help to solve two current thorny problems in college English teaching. First, "as the number of college students increases, the issue of lacking enough English teachers is becoming significant . . . Right now, the proportion of English teachers to college students has reached 1:130" (Current Situation Section, para. 2). Second, quality English teachers are stretching thin because more and more college graduates are allowed to teach English in Chinese colleges. Information technologies are considered better than traditional methods in promoting the students' individualized learning and therefore have been hailed as the best solution to some major problems in college English teaching. Will the use of information technologies truly encourage more individualized learning and alleviate the shortage of quality English teachers? The institutional justification for promoting information technologies in English teaching needs to be closely examined in future research.

Working towards the new literacy, the decree articulates student-centered assessment for college English teaching for the first time. Besides the traditional summative evaluation, such as midterms and finals, the decree introduces methods for process-based, student-centered evaluation. The university can observe, evaluate, and monitor the students' progress through both in-class and extracurricular records, the students' self-learning online records, portfolios, interviews, and teacher-student conferences. For each exit level, Teaching Requirements for College English Curriculum provides benchmarks for self- and peer-evaluation of the five language skills. At the relatively high level, for example, the students can gauge their writing ability by answering "yes" or "no" to the following four statements:

- I can write a summary or an outline for a passage on a general topic, express my own opinions on a heated issue, and explain the reasons for either supporting or opposing an argument.
- I can write for daily purposes, conforming to the standard structure and expression of a particular genre.
- Based on reference materials, I can write disciplinary reports, expositions, and speech scripts with clear structure and rich content.
- Within half an hour, I can write a 160-word narrative, descriptive, expository or argumentative piece with complete content, clear structure and fluent language. (Appendix II Section, Chart II)

The introduction of process-based and student-centered evaluation has the potential to lead to student-centered teaching and learning. The process-based evaluation closely connects learning and assessment, stimulating the students throughout their entire learning process rather than having them focus on midterms and finals.

After Teaching Requirements for College English Curriculum was published, the requirements were first implemented in 180 participating universities as a year-long nationwide experiment while other universities continue to practice traditional ways of teaching English (see You, 2004 for the traditional ways to teaching English writing in Chinese universities). The Ministry of Education appropriated funding for each participating university to purchase textbooks and software programs from three Chinese publishers. At the end of this nationwide experiment, it is time to ask how the new requirements have affected college English teaching in general and writing instruction in particular in those participating universities, and what English teachers think of the new requirements. It is equally important to ask whether the new requirements have helped to solve some old issues in English writing instruction in Chinese colleges (You, 2004). Any institutional stipulation on English writing instruction has to come to terms with the local material conditions.

New Literacy in Context: A Reality Check

Data collection for the current research took place at two Chinese state universities. University A is a comprehensive university ranked by various Chinese educational agencies as one of the top 50 among over 1,000 Chinese universities and colleges. It participated in this nationwide experiment and was considered by peers as a model school in implementing the computer/network-assisted English teaching. It was visited several times by interested officials and English teachers from other schools during the year, as one of my informants reveals. University B is a regional teacher's university, which did not participate in this experiment. Investigating two universities, with one not participating in the experiment, will help us understand the complexity of some issues in English writing instruction.

Through classroom observations, interviews with six English teachers from the two universities during and after the experiment, and a review of textbooks, I have identified concrete measures taken by both university administrators and English teachers responding to the newly redefined English literacy. Both universities have built networked classrooms and their traditional classrooms have been remodeled to include a computer and an LCD projector and were considered multimedia classrooms thereafter. University A invested over 120,000 U.S. dollars to build a networked classroom with about 100 desktops for English teaching. Five teachers teach six sections in the networked classroom, with a total number of 550 first-year students participating in this year-long experiment. These students were specially placed in the experimental classes because they entered the university with higher college entrance examination scores than their peers. Selecting high English-proficiency level students for the experimental teaching needs to be taken into consideration in later discussions. In University A, audio-visual and speaking components are taught in the networked classroom for two hours every week. Reading, writing, and translation are taught in the multimedia classroom for another two hours. At the same time, students are tutored in the multimedia classroom for another two hours. University B, like many other Chinese universities, has several smaller-sized networked classrooms. However, they are not exclusively designed for English teaching and used by teachers of other subjects as well. An English teacher needs to reserve a networked classroom ahead of time. English teachers in both universities always teach in the multimedia classrooms when they do not teach in the networked classrooms.

Both universities use the same textbook, *New Horizon College English* series (Zheng, Zhou, & Tong, 2002), compiled specifically for teaching English in a networked environment. The series were published in three different media—traditional textbook, CD-ROM, and an online version (http://nhce.fjnu.edu.cn/). The three versions were designed to match three different contexts for students learning English—the multimedia classroom, the networked classroom, and the student's dorm. A test bank is integrated into the CD-ROM, so the students can evaluate their language skills at any time. There are two books for each level (four levels in total designed for four semesters): *Listening and Speaking Manual*, and *Reading and Writing Manual*. The *Reading and Writing Manual* has 10 theme-based units in which students study three passages, vocabulary, structure, writing, and translation. The readings cover topics of a truly international nature, such as cultural shock, marriage across nations, environmental protection, and studying abroad. However, they touch little upon Chinese society. The writing sections are structured in a progression—from constructing paragraphs to composing texts. The writing tasks do reflect the student's everyday life, such as "college life" and "from a hero to a nobody" (referring to some freshmen facing the transition from high school to college).

Teaching in networked classrooms, all six teachers agree that their students have effectively improved their listening and speaking ability, which was hard to achieve in traditional classrooms or multimedia classrooms. In the networked classroom, students can watch and listen to conversations and repeat after correct pronunciations as many times as they want.

As for writing, the six English teachers all emphasize English writing as an indispensable skill in its own right in worldwide business and communication instead of as a handmaid to the development of other language skills. However, compared with instruction in other language skills—such as listening, speaking, and reading—much less attention has been devoted to writing. At University A, a network-based software program was used to teach writing. The software can conduct spell check and preliminary evaluation of the student's writing. But according to Ms. Wang,[2] who teaches in the networked classroom at University A, preliminary evaluation shows rather low reliability. The students benefited the most from reading and commenting on each other's writings through online forums. After talking to the six teachers, I have identified four major obstacles to writing instruction across the two universities throughout the entire experiment period.

First, having to teach different language skills in large classes leaves little time for writing instruction. Ms Wang says, "Having to teach reading, listening, speaking, and translation all in the same class, there is simply no time to take care of writing." She assigns students four short-essay tasks in one semester. She says, "There are more than 80 students in my class, I don't have time to read so many essays." Mr. Li teaches five classes with a total of 250 students at University B. He assigns two to three writing tasks a semester. How does he deal with 500 or 750 essays a semester? He says, "I don't read those that are written in bad handwriting; I don't read those that have a disorganized structure; for the rest, I only read their topic sentences." Hoping to teach five language skills all in one class thus reduces the time devoted to teaching English writing.

Second, writing instruction continues to be confined by the rather traditional conceptualization of education in the country, that is, educational means to acquire transferable knowledge. The teacher and the students are positioned at the two ends of the knowledge pipeline; one end is the supplier and the other end the receiver. Some teachers take lecturing about the *techne* of writing as their legitimate responsibility rather than organizing systematic, procedured writing tasks for the students to practice the *techne*. Talking about tapping the potential of the traditional classroom instruction, Zhang (2003) says, "The [traditional] classroom continues to play an important role in the new teaching modes. The teacher can *lecture* on grammar, reading comprehension, writing, and translation skills, which can be conducted in a large lecture hall" (Aims and Measures Section, para. 8). To lecture on writing, both Ms. Wang and Mr. Li assign a writing task, select a few student sample papers, prepare some handouts or copy them on the blackboard, and discuss both the strengths and weaknesses of the papers in the class.

Third, Teaching Requirements for College English Curriculum encourages placing students of different entry levels in different classes and allows them to move up and down. This practice is causing detrimental effects on some students' motivation for learning English, as Ms. Zhang at University A suggests. Most college students were achievers in high school. When they are placed in English classes according to their English proficiency levels, those placed in the middle- or low-level classes feel a diminished sense of self-esteem. Studying together with other low-level students, they feel like a loser and perform poorly in process-based assessments. For example, according to Mr. Li, while 76 percent of sophomore students in his Class A passed the national College English Test, only 20 percent in his Class B and a few in Class C did so. For students who are cherished as little emperors or little empresses in their families and praised as good students in high schools, their motivation to learn is shaken loose by the placement system. However, Ms. Wang has observed a somewhat different picture among the high proficiency-level students studying in the networked classroom. Due to such extrinsic motivations as studying abroad, going to graduate schools, or seeking jobs, the students in the experimental classes are highly motivated by the opportunities offered by the networked English course. Many students showed great initiative in learning English in their spare time. Apparently the placement system works differently with high-proficiency and low proficiency students.

Fourth, the decree encourages individualized styles of learning, which poses a new challenge to some students. The Teaching Requirements for College English Curriculum advises that "in the new teaching mode, English teaching should encourage individualized learning, learning without being constrained by time and place, and learning on the student's own initiative" (Teaching Modes Section, para. 1). In reality, individualized learning style is difficult to foster in many students. They were guided closely by their teachers in high school and tended as precious pearls by their parents. Once they enter college, with little attention from the teachers and with their parents living far away, they easily get lost, disorientated in the mounting coursework and the unprecedented amount of freedom. Ms. Tang, a teacher in University A who does not teach the experimental classes, says, "With little experience of individualized learning style in high schools, the students are very unsatisfied with their English teachers, feeling they are not learning anything." However, Ms. Wang has a different observation. Thanks to the computers, the network, and the self-evaluation system, her high proficient students have showed self-discipline in their studies and developed individualized learning styles. Her observation suggests that proficiency level and educational technologies do play important roles in forging individualized styles of learning.

In terms of the teachers' attitudes towards the new requirements, there are mixed feelings. Some teachers are pleased that the networked teaching stimulates both the teacher and the students by injecting something new into the enterprise of college English teaching. Ms. Wang says, "Educational reforms like this one stimulate the teachers, enhance intercollegiate exchanges, and eventually improve the teachers' quality." Some teachers have expressed doubts or disappointments. Ms. Tang comments sharply on the reorientation of Chinese higher education. She says, "Education has become the training camp for employment; it is a product for sale. We teach simply for teaching's sake. Without much face-to-face interactions between the teacher and the students, humanized teaching is lost in the large-size classroom and networked computers." Apparently disagreements have occurred over where the educational decree is leading college English teaching.

New Literacy as an Institutional Imagination

Conceivably, there is a clear gap between institutional stipulations and actual classroom instruction. In light of the investigation at two universities, the new requirements appear to be working effectively with teaching listening and oral skills, but not with writing instruction in any substantial manner, if not making it worse by cramming many students into large lecture halls. Old issues—such as large class size, heavy teaching loads, a traditional concept of education as knowledge-cramming, and unmotivated students (see You, 2004)—continue to affect writing instruction in the new wave of college English reform. This study has clearly shown the limits of an institutional imagination consisting of both the new definition of English literacy and the suggested teaching practices.

However, more importantly, this study has revealed the power of institutional imagination. The new requirements and the nationwide experiment initiated discussions of what English literacy means and how to achieve it in a non-English-dominant country in the backdrop of globalization. The idea of English as an international language (EIL) has taken a deep root among university teachers and students. They understand the growing importance of the language, although still disagreeing on what new English literacy means exactly for average Chinese college students. The new requirements prompt them to think about the issue of new English literacy and to imagine how they should teach it. Ms. Wang says, "Although the experiment only took place in a few classes, it stimulates every teacher to consider what aspects of the experiment can be adapted into his or her own classes." The teachers' traditional view of language teaching has been apparently shaken loose by the experiment. English teaching means more than cramming knowledge about different language skills into the students. It also means skillful management of information technologies to facilitate effective learning. The new requirements and the experiment have clearly motivated serious discussion of college English teaching in China.

Finally, I want to suggest, as English becomes an international language, English writing instruction in EIL contexts is taking a historical turn. English writing skill s are considered a more and more practical tool, like a driver's license or a personal computer. What type of English writing should be taught in colleges? Why does it matter in the student's life? How can it be taught effectively so that students are able to write in English for international communication? What resources are available to both the teachers and the students? These are old questions waiting for new answers. At the same time, EIL writing is already confronted with many local issues, resulting from the conflicts caused by institutional requirements imposed from the top and classroom constraints at the grass-roots level. L2 writing specialists need to understand both the educational goals set by policy makers as well as the local constraints. They should participate in the institutional imagination by answering those seemingly old questions and working closely with local professionals to turn their imagination into reality.

Notes

[1] I would like to thank Xu Xiaoyu and Chen Ping for their help in this research. I also benefited from constructive comments from Yichun Liu, Christina Ortmeier-Hooper, and David Blakesley.

[2] The names of the English teachers used in this chapter are aliases.

References

Appadurai, A. (1996). *Modernity at large.* Minneapolis: University of Minnesota Press.

College English Syllabus Revision Team. (1985). *Daxue yingyu jiaoxue dagan (Gaodeng xuexiao ligongke benke yong)* [College English syllabus (for science and technology majors)]. Beijing: Gaodeng Jiaoyu Chubanshe [Higher Education Press].

College English Syllabus Revision Team. (1999). *Daxue yingyu jiaoxue dagan (Xiuding ben) (Gaodeng xuexiao benke yong)* [College English syllabus (Revised edition) (for four-year colleges)]. Beijing: Gaodeng Jiaoyu Chubanshe [Higher Education Press].

Jeong, Y. (2004). A chapter of English teaching in Korea. *English Today, 20,* 40–46.

Kachru, Y. (1995). Cultural meaning and rhetorical styles: Toward a framework for Contrastive Rhetoric. In G. Cook & B. Seidlhofer (Eds.), *Principles & practice in applied linguistics* (pp. 171–184). New York: Oxford University Press.

Leki, I. (2001). Materials, educational, and ideological challenges of teaching EFL writing at the turn of the century. *International Journal of English Studies, 9* (2), 197–209.

Matsuura, H., Fujieda, M., & Mahoney, S. (2004). The officialization of English and ELT in Japan: 2000. *World Englishes, 23*(3), 471–487.

Peng, J., Zhou, X. & Fu, Z. (2002). English for international trade: China enters the WTO. *World Englishes 21*(2), 201–216.

The Ministry of Education. (2004). Daxue yingyu kecheng jiaoxue yaoqiu [Teaching requirements for college English curriculum]. Retrieved June 17, 2004 from http://www.edu.cn/20040120/3097997.shtml

You, X. (2005). Writing in the "devil's" tongue: A history of English writing instruction in Chinese colleges (1862–2004). Unpublished doctoral dissertation. Purdue University.

You, X. (2004). "The choice made from no choice": English writing instruction in a Chinese university. *Journal of Second Language Writing 13*(2), 97–110.

Zhang, Y. (2003). Guanyu daxue benke gonggong yingyu jiaoxue gaige de zai shikao [Reconsidering the reform of college English teaching]. Retrieved June 17, 2004 from http://www.edu.cn/20030804/3088972.shtml

Zheng, S., Zhou, G., & Tong, J. (2002). *Xin shiye daxue yingyu* [*New horizon college English*]. Beijing: Foreign Language Teaching and Research Press.

The Politics of Second Language Writing Assessment

11 The Politics of Implementing Online Directed Self-Placement for Second Language Writers

Deborah Crusan

Within the field of writing assessment, placement of students into composition classes at the university maintains its status as one of the most ethically and politically charged areas of assessment. Placement testing at the college level has tremendous consequences for students and, because it is so charged, remains a thorn in the side of many writing program administrators (WPAs) as they struggle to keep assessment local and contextualized within their programs. WPAs often wrestle with issues relating to institutionalized definitions of "good" writing and a one-size-fits all mentality toward assessment; for example, institutions viewing writing and the writer as static might turn to evaluation that standardizes writing. Because placement testing is so consequential, it deserves our attention. Particularly, those of us who place students in writing programs and those of us who teach writing should examine and understand the political arena in which we find ourselves when we assess writing for high-stakes purposes.

I have long *recognized* that assessment is inherently political (Crusan, 2002a, 2002b, 2003). However, recently I have begun to truly know what before I had merely recognized. It seems that lately, at every turn, I recognize anew, and very personally, assessment's problems—methodological, practical, ethical, socioeconomic, political. I appreciate that evaluation is far from neutral (Hamp-Lyons, 2001, 2002; Haswell, 2004a; Huot, 2002; White, 2005), that assessment is "a form of social action" (McLeod, Horn, & Haswell, 2005, p. 556); tests are a dominant force impacting both individuals and society. Shohamy (2001) cautions us that tests are capable of defining knowledge, imposing curricula, changing behaviors, and all too often serve a gate-keeping function limiting access to those minorities and occasionally majorities considered undesirable by dominant groups. Further, I agree that all stakeholders in any assessment system might not necessarily have the same agendas (Williamson & Huot, 2000). Especially with writing placement, institutions, teachers, and students are at odds in the ways they use and need placement, and writing program administrators often find themselves somewhere in the middle trying to do the right thing (Haswell, 2004). It is on this gate-keeping function of assessment, that of placement, especially placement of second language writers, that this chapter focuses.

As an open-enrollment institution, Wright State University struggles to accurately place students coming from diverse populations (including both native and nonnative speakers of English) and a spectrum of high school English programs ranging in quality and rigor from very good to very poor. For years, the university relied upon a one-shot essay as the sole means of assessing incoming students' writing ability. We were aware of caveats associated with this form of placement—lack of predictive ability, too much emphasis on one rhetorical mode, high-stakes decisions based on a snapshot of students' writing, and lack of interrater reliability (Haswell, 2004; White, 1995), but using a single essay was considered better than the alternative—a multiple choice assessment. Or so we thought. A recent NCTE Task Force report (Ball,, Christensen, Fleischer, Haswell, Ketter, Yagelski, & Yancey, 2005) discusses concerns regarding the new SAT Writing Test (and the existing ACT essay examination). The report cites many problems with the test, most concerning L1 writers. These problems include:

- The writing required for a timed essay has little instructional validity.
- The scores on the timed essay have little predictive validity for first-year course success or for retention.

If a short, holistically scored, impromptu essay can cause concerns for L1 writers, the costs for second language writers must be even more profound. Certainly second language writers, grappling with linguistic problems, fare much worse on these kinds of tests. The Task Force questioned both the reliability and the validity of the SAT; we must question them as well when we use a single timed essay for placement of second language writers.

Unfortunately, although we are attempting to phase it out, we at Wright State continue using the one-shot essay as a placement instrument for second language writers. However, as a program administrator, I am witness to the ravages of this kind of writing placement. Even though my colleagues and I are careful to construct prompts that are neither too simple nor too complex, are easily accessible, are engaging to the writer, are free from cultural bias, are not abstract, are not trite or highly emotional (Kroll & Reid, 1994; Reid, 1993), problems continually surface. Although graduate students in my assessment class and I have developed a scoring rubric (and continue tweaking it every quarter) for our second language writing placement instrument based on the content of the courses and the kinds of writing students will do in our specific second language writing courses, I still feel a pang of self-doubt when I read and score placement essays. An uneasiness persists even though I employ multiple raters, insist on high interrater reliability, and discuss with colleagues the results of most of the placements.

Though most placements seem indisputable and incontrovertible, my qualms with the one-shot essay for second language writing placement refuse to go away, especially in light of the recent recommendations advocating the use of multiple measures when assessing writing for any purpose (Haswell, 2004a, 2004b). And when a student questions her placement, my uneasiness (read guilt) increases ten-fold.

In recent years, our university administration has begun to consider the one-shot essay method of placement too costly in terms of both time and money (at least for native speakers of English). Feeling bureaucratic pressure, the writing programs committee, after reviewing the seminal work of Royer and Giles (1998), began investigating the feasibility of directed self-placement (DSP) as an alternative to our more traditional writing placement. Royer and Giles (1998) define DSP as an alternative to traditional placement in which students choose appropriate composition courses after they are given information about all courses offered and have carefully examined their writing habits and abilities.

Royer and Giles (1998) advocate DSP for placement of first year composition students. DSP seats accountability squarely on the shoulders of those who purportedly know their writing skills better than anyone else: the writers themselves. Royer and Giles (1998) argue that "teachers are pleased when the placement responsibility lies with the students, for the relationship is thus clearer, less muddied with the interference of test scores and with predictions for success or failure from everyone except the student" (p. 67). These claims appear to hold true. Writing programs continue to adopt and adapt DSP as their means of performing the delicate university writing placement operation. Further, these institutions report evidence (cf. Blakesley, Harvey, & Reynolds, 2003; Chernekoff, 2003; Cornell & Newton, 2003; Frus, 2003; Pinter & Sims, 2003; Tompkins, 2003) that DSP, at least in their contexts, works as well or better than other means of placement tried in the past.

In the face of this evidence, the writing programs committee felt that, if implemented, DSP could serve our L1 students well and contain administrative pressure. Unfortunately, because of resistance (which I will explain later) from some in the second language writing community, second language writers were not included in DSP; rather, they were still required to write an essay. But first, let's explore Wright State's interpretation of DSP.

Directed Self-Placement at Wright State University

DSP at Wright State looks something like this. We schedule DSP writing placement sessions throughout the year. Testing services sends out DSP schedules to all newly admitted students, who select which session to attend. At the sessions, DSP counselors (all writing instructors from the English department) greet students and give an overall explanation of the session. At this point, DSP counselors ask nonnative speakers to self-identify; nonnative speakers then are required to write an essay (more on this later).

Meanwhile, native speaker students watch a PowerPoint presentation, which informs them about the composition classes we offer and what kinds of writing skills students need in order to succeed in each class. Further, the PowerPoint and DSP counselors impress upon students the importance of selecting the "right" course to match their abilities. With the guidance and input of actual instructors in the writing program, students answer questions about the kind of readers and writers they are and consider their past writing and reading experiences. Native speakers answer a Yes/No questionnaire (see Appendix A) and place themselves using the information from the PowerPoint, the answers to the questionnaire, their new knowledge of the courses, and their honest examination of their writing abilities. During the entire process, students are gently reminded to "be sure to choose the class that places you where you *need* to be rather than where you *want* to be" (Wright State University Guided Self-Placement PowerPoint, 2004, p. 5) and are coached and engaged in dialogue regarding their choices.

We believe that DSP works as well as or better than the one-shot essay used in the past. After using this placement system for several quarters, the results of an institutional study (see Table 1 and Table 2) showed that, on average, students who placed themselves in courses were apparently doing at least as well as students who had been placed using the old system of the one-shot essay.

Table 1. Students who placed into 101 either by essay test or DSP and took 101 performed almost identically over a three year period.

	1999 writing sample	2000 writing sample	2001 guided self placement
Students earning A, B, or C	85.4%	88.2%	86.7%
Students earning D, F, or W	14.6%	11.8%	13.3%
Average English GPA	2.755	2.805	2.773
TOTAL # of students	1269	1058	1055

Table 2. Students who placed into a developmental writing course (or whose answers on the DSP questionnaire suggested they should consider taking a developmental writing course) but who decided to take 101 instead. Note that, with DSP, the percentage of students who succeeded increased.

	1999 writing sample	2000 writing sample	2001 guided self-placement
Students earning A, B, or C	75.1%	79.3%	87.1%
Students earning D, F, or W	24.9%	20.7%	12.9%
Average English GPA	2.348	2.413	2.579
TOTAL # of students	339/21	445/30	278/21

We think there are many reasons for this. First, there seems to be a flaw with the *timing* of writing placement. Usually, when we ask students to take writing placement tests, they are already being cognitively overloaded from almost every corner of the university. They are under tremendous stress from other placement tests (math, foreign language). Further, they are being asked to process an astonishing amount of information regarding their majors, course selection, roommates, and meal plans, and make other crucially important decisions that will seriously impact their futures.

Students seem to be doing at least as well with DSP for another reason. During the time when we were still using the single essay as a means of placement, many students blithely ignored their placements. For example, some students who placed into developmental writing classes based on the essay they had written chose instead to enroll in English 101, the first of the two required native speaker composition courses at Wright State. Fueled by the need to show that they could succeed, many students who ignored their original suggested placement did well in the higher-level course they *self*-selected. This reinforces the importance of student agency in placement.

Most first year L1 composition teachers at Wright State find DSP a welcome change from the single essay used in the past or even worse, a multiple-choice test. However, some of the teachers have mixed feelings about DSP. A few have voiced objections based on the quality of writing they have seen in their classes. One teacher claimed that students coming from a developmental writing class (English 092) into English 101 were much better writers than those students who placed themselves directly into English 101. The students coming from the developmental writing class were found to have fewer issues concerning both development and mechanics. Further, the teacher claimed that many of her students have recognized their limitations and admitted that they might have placed themselves higher than they should have. Parental pressure is another issue at work with DSP. Parents, concerned about rising tuition costs and the time it will take their students to graduate, may push the students to choose the highest level class in the hopes of decreasing the time to graduation.

Nevertheless, it still seems that DSP is a good fit for the native speaker population. For the most part, students are faring quite well with their self-placement. However, placement has not been working out so well for our second language writers. Placement decisions for L2 writers still hinge upon that one essay upon which we base an all too important decision with too little data.

Placement and Second Language Writers

When I began my duties as Director of ESL Programs, I was determined in my quest for equity in writing placement; in other words, I viewed as discriminatory the exclusion of second language writers from any form of self-placement. As I have argued elsewhere, specialists in second language writing should examine the placement practices used by their institutions and insist that they be included in any placement decisions, all the while consistently advocating for second language writers (Crusan, 2002a).

Some of my second language writing colleagues have been less than supportive about employing DSP for L2 writers. They base their argument on their past experience in contending with the difficulties, emotions, and consequences associated with second language writing placement. They argue that college ESL students might make poor decisions about their language proficiency for vastly logical reasons. An education in the U.S. is quite expensive for international students. Very often, much of the financial burden for their educations fall mainly on their families still in foreign countries. This fact might certainly cloud an ESL student's judgment. Since they want to save time and money on their educations, they make unrealistic appraisals of their proficiency and what they can accomplish.

My colleagues further argue that the training in writing some second language writers receive might be quite limited and different from the training native English speakers receive; teachers expect L2 writers to produce text in perhaps very different ways from the texts they produced in their L1; that is, the creation of meaning in English might look different from the creation of meaning in students' first languages. Opponents to self-placement for second language writers believe that students who bypass courses that can prepare them for the expectations of the university might be setting themselves up for failure.

Some of my second language writing colleagues remind me that self-placement is culturally insensitive, arguing that we cannot force some students to make decisions about their placement as notions such as face-saving and humility come into play. Others reason that students would not voluntarily place themselves in ESL classes because of the additional time and money. ESL students traditionally pay very high out-of-state tuition. Many of them feel that they need to take courses that both bear credit and count toward graduation. Second language writers often argue that not having to enroll in ESL writing courses, especially those that do not count toward graduation, will save time and money and allow them to take other, more important (in their eyes) courses. Therefore, the argument goes that students will place themselves either too high or too low, and the result will be chaotic at best.

My L1 colleagues had been somewhat more supportive of the inclusion of second language writers in DSP than many of my L2 colleagues. Possibly, this hinges on their self-professed lack of knowledge of the needs or abilities of second language writers and their deference to me as the 'expert' in matters pertaining to second language writers. It might be, too, that my colleagues are expressing the fear that many L1 composition specialists exhibit when asked to deal with second language writing issues. They seem happy to have someone upon whose shoulders these perceived problems might rest a little lighter than on their own.

However, my agitation at the exclusion of nonnative speakers from self-placement continues. I understand the hesitation of some of my colleagues when they list reasons DSP would be a serious misstep for second language writers. A portion of their reticence may be based on their less than satisfactory experiences with poorly designed or inappropriate self-assessment tools. However, self-assessment instruments, if carefully developed and used appropriately, may indeed be useful for second language writers (Strong-Krause, 2000). In her eyes, self-assessment has several advantages over traditional placement:

- Less time and considerably less money involved than with traditional assessment;
- Test security issues eliminated;
- Student involvement in decision making increases responsibility for learning;
- Students certainly know their combined language abilities better than any test might show. (Strong-Krause, 2000)

Further, student attitude plays an enormous part in student success, another reason that second language writers should be allowed to self-place. In a study of university placement, Crusan (1999) asked second language writers to answer a writing attitude survey regarding their placement. The placement measure was a 50 item multiple-choice instrument. Twenty-nine students (23 percent) believed that their placement was incorrect, that it was too low. Interestingly, students in the study did not complain about their placement, possibly thinking that it was not appropriate to complain. Generally speaking, ESL university students, unlike their native English speaking counterparts, have a higher regard for authority, a deeper respect for teachers, and rarely question decisions (Zamel, 1995). Additionally, students are often unaware of course content and are not willing to risk their academic careers without more specific information. For these students to disagree with their placement might be seen as an insult to their teacher and a threat to their chances of obtaining a college education using a language not their own, a task already fraught with difficulty. It is easy to see how students felt a lack of agency in this example.

Frankly though, I can understand the reticence of my second language writing colleagues (and other second language colleagues who are not involved deeply in writing research but who still have many questions) regarding the use of DSP for nonnative speakers of English.

Another Mandate Changes the Face of Placement

Nothing, however, is certain except change. Almost as soon as the writing programs committee implemented DSP, the administration again began applying pressure, this time insisting that we put writing placement online. That, coupled with the exclusion of L2 students from the DSP process, resulted in rethinking the entire DSP process. The writing programs committee felt forced to search for alternative solutions and began the painfully slow process of creating and implementing (for both L1 and L2 writers) an innovative system we currently call Online Directed Self-Placement (ODSP).

In the past few months, we have been developing ODSP with the help of grant money and the subsequent hiring of computer programmers. ODSP is a multi-dimensional, uniquely weighted online directed self-placement instrument, which weighs indicators and variables germane to the university student population; that is, it applies multiple measures (Haswell, 2004a). We define online directed self-placement as an *online* process in which students provide basic demographic information and respond to a questionnaire. L1 and L2 students have separate questionnaires addressing issues most important to each population. The nonnative speaker questionnaire (see Appendix A), comprised of 15 questions, queries students on issues both cognitive and affective. Students must chose to answer *Strongly Agree, Agree, Disagree,* or *Strongly Disagree* to questionnaire items. We weighted the questionnaire in two ways; the first weight places an importance from 1 (lowest)—4 (highest) on the *question*. The second weight places a ranking on each *answer* to each question. For example, one of the questions on the non-native speaker questionnaire declares, "I regularly translate from my native language when writing in English." We determined that this statement was very important, so the question is worth four points (the higher the final combined score, the higher the placement). Further, for this statement, Strongly Agree would be worth one point; Agree, two points; Disagree, three points; Strongly Disagree, four points. The ODSP program calculates a score for each item and then for the questionnaire as a whole. The program then pulls available data from the university mainframe: test scores (e.g. SAT—including the new essay score, ACT—including essay score if available, TOEFL—including the separate writing score of 0–30), high school GPA, and high school class rank. The online program uses an algorithm to calculate a placement (not seen by the student) by combining the weighted questionnaire score with a weighted data score (combination of test scores, GPA, and class rank). The program then instructs students to contact their advisor to discuss placement results. While ODSP is not entirely self-placement, it does afford students some agency and "includes the students' own self as an essential component in the placement decision" (Royer & Giles, 2003, p. 56).

In many ways, ODSP answers critics who argued that DSP did not serve the second language writer. ODSP has a number of inherent advantages over the DSP process. For instance, ODSP is less dependent upon academic staff time and resources; prospective students can go online anytime before registration without having to go to a counselor-fronted placement session. This allows students to answer the questionnaire at their own pace (with the answers to frequently asked questions concerning each of the ODSP questions available simply by placing the cursor over the question). Because of the many variables it considers, ODSP seems a valid and reliable means of placement, especially for the second language writer. I believe wholeheartedly that ODSP will be successful, and I look excitedly to this uncharted future. We will discover the viability of ODSP when we pilot the process in early 2006.

However, at present, many issues remain unresolved, among them time, funding, and issues of territory and access. Further, we are ever mindful of lurking dangers—the possibility of lack of reflection on the parts of the students and the wholesale adoption of self-assessment without careful study of the consequences (Schendel & O'Neill, 2000). In my eyes, however, the promise of inclusion of second language writers in ODSP, affording them agency and a sense of belonging, is emotionally exciting, intellectually stimulating, and highly relevant to the field of second language writing assessment. If ODSP for second language writers is half as successful as I expect it to be, it heralds a breakthrough in the field of second language writing assessment.

Of course, many questions remain unanswered, and until we are able to perform validity studies, some of which we have begun, we cannot say with absolute certainty that this method of placement is either completely safe or accurate. However, we have labored to make ODSP serve the student; we have carefully considered "how to shape the message the placement system sends to students" (Harrington, 2005, p. 26). We have also fought to keep writing assessment in the hands of writing teachers, heeding White's (1996) warnings to involve ourselves (the writing teachers and program administrators) in the construction, supervision, and appraisal of writing tests.

REFERENCES

Ball, A., Christensen, L., Fleischer, C., Haswell, R., Ketter, J., Yagelski, R., & Yancey, K. (2005). *The impact of the SAT and ACT timed writing tests* [Electronic version]. Retrieved May 30, 2005 from http://www.ncte.org/about/gov/cgrams/insight/120774.htm

Blakesley, D., Harvey E. J., & Reynolds, E. J. (2003). Southern Illinois University Carbondale as an institutional model: The English 100/101 stretch and directed self-placement program. In D. J. Royer & R. Gilles (Eds.), *Directed self-placement: Principles and practices* (pp. 207–242). Cresskill, NJ: Hampton Press.

Chernekoff, J. (2003). Introducing directed self-placement to Kutztown University. In D. J. Royer & R. Gilles (Eds.), *Directed self-placement: Principles and practices* (pp. 127–148). Cresskill, NJ: Hampton Press.

Cornell, C. E. & Newton, R. D. (2003). The case of a small liberal arts university: Directed self-placement at DePauw. In D. J. Royer & R. Gilles (Eds.), *Directed self-placement: Principles and practices* (pp. 149–178). Cresskill, NJ: Hampton Press.

Crusan, D. (1999). *Effective assessment for placement of English as a second language writers into composition courses at the university level.* Unpublished doctoral dissertation. University Park, PA: The Pennsylvania State University.

Crusan, D. (2002a). An assessment of ESL writing placement assessment. *Assessing Writing: An International Journal, 8,* 17–30.

Crusan, D, (2002b). The quagmire of assessment for placement: Talking out of both sides of our mouths. *TESL Reporter, 35*(2), 37–48.

Crusan, D. (2003). The persistence of indirect assessment for placement and its effects on ESL writers. *TESOL in Action, 17,* 13–15.

Frus. P. (2003). Directed self-placement at a large research university: A writing center perspective. In D. J. Royer & R. Gilles (Eds.), *Directed self-placement: Principles and practices* (pp. 179–191). Cresskill, NJ: Hampton Press.

Hamp-Lyons, L. (2001). Fourth generation writing assessment. In T. Silva, & P. K. Matsuda (Eds.), *On second language writing* (pp. 117–127). Mahwah, NJ: Lawrence Erlbaum Associates.

Hamp-Lyons, L. (2002). The scope of writing assessment. *Assessing Writing: An International Journal, 8,* 5–16.

Hamp-Lyons, L. (2003). Writing teachers as assessors of writing. In B. Kroll (Ed.), *Exploring the dynamics of second language writing* (pp. 162–189). Cambridge: Cambridge University Press.

Harrington, S. (2005). Learning to ride the waves: Making decisions about placement testing. *WPA: Writing Program Administration, 28*(3), 9–29.

Haswell, R. (2004a). *Post-secondary entry writing placement: A brief synopsis of research* [Electronic version]. Retrieved March 3, 2005 from http://comppile.tamucc.edu/writingplacementresearch.htm

Haswell, R. (2004b). *Post-secondary entrance writing placement* [Electronic version]. Retrieved June 21, 2005 from http://comppile.tamucc.edu/placement.doc

Huot, B. (2002). *(Re)Articulating writing assessment for teaching and learning.* Logan, UT: Utah State University Press.

Kroll, B., & Reid, J. (1994). Guidelines for designing writing prompts: Clarifications, caveats, and cautions. *Journal of Second Language Writing, 3*(3), 231–255.

McLeod, S., Horn, H., & Haswell, R. (2005). Accelerated classes and the writers at the bottom: A local assessment story. *College Composition and Communication, 56*(4), 556–580.

Pinter, R., & Sims, E. (2003). Directed self-placement at Belmont University: Sharing power, forming relationships, fostering reflection. In D. J. Royer & R. Gilles (Eds.), *Directed self-placement: Principles and practices* (pp. 107–125). Cresskill, NJ: Hampton Press.

Reid, J. M. (1993). *Teaching ESL writing.* Englewood Cliffs, NJ: Prentice Hall Regents.

Royer, D. J., & Gilles, R. (1998). Directed self-placement: An attitude of orientation. *College Composition and Communication, 50*(1), 54–70.

Royer, D. J., & Gilles, R. (Eds.). (2003). *Directed self-placement: Principles and practices.* Cresskill, NJ: Hampton Press.

Schendel, E., & O'Neill, P. (1999). Exploring the theories and consequences of self-assessment through ethical inquiry. *Assessing Writing, 6*(2), 199–227.

Shohamy, E. (2001). *The power of tests: A critical perspective on the uses of language tests.* Harlow, England: Pearson Education Limited.

Strong-Krause, D. (2000). Exploring the effectiveness of self-assessment strategies in ESL placement. In G. Ekbatani & H. Pierson (Eds.), *Learner-directed assessment in ESL* (pp. 49–74). Mahwah, NJ: Lawrence Erlbaum Associates.

Tompkins, P. (2003). Directed self-placement in a community college context. In D. J. Royer & R. Gilles (Eds.), *Directed self-placement: Principles and practices* (pp. 193–206). Cresskill, NJ: Hampton Press.

White, E. M. (1996). Power and agenda setting in writing assessment. In E. M. White, W. D. Lutz, & S. Kamusikiri (Eds.), *Assessment of writing: Politics, policies, practices* (pp. 9–24). New York: The Modern Language Association of America.

White, E. M. (2005). The scoring of writing portfolios: Phase 2. *College Composition and Communication, 56*(4), 581–600.

Williamson, M. M., & Huot, B. (2000). Literacy, equality, and competence: Ethics in writing assessment. In M. A. Pemberton (Ed.), *The ethics of writing instruction: Issues in theory and practice* (pp. 191–209). Stamford, CT: Ablex.

Wright State University. (2005). *Institutional assessment: Entering student questionnaire.* Retrieved February 12, 2005 from http://goto.wright.edu/assessment/bpra/institutional/esq.html

Zamel, V. (1995). Strangers in academia: The experiences of faculty and ESL students across the curriculum. *College Composition and Communication, 46*(4), 506–521.

Appendix A

English Self-Placement Questionnaire
WRIGHT STATE UNIVERSITY

MARKING INSTRUCTIONS
- Use a No. 2 pencil or Blue or Black Ink Pen.
- Do not use pens that SOAK through the paper.
- Fill the response completely.
- Erase cleanly any marks you wish to change.
CORRECT: ● INCORRECT: ⊘ ⊠ ◐ ◑

Last Name: *
First Name:

* Please bubble in the first 3 digits of your LAST NAME.

The statements in this questionnaire are designed to help you decide which writing course is right for you. Please answer honestly so that you can make the best decision for your needs.

1 = Yes / Agree   2 = No / Disagree

TODAY'S DATE
MONTH | DAY | YEAR
Jan, Feb, Mar, Apr, May, June, July, Aug, Sept, Oct, Nov, Dec

Please respond to ALL items.
1. I enjoy reading newspapers, magazines and books regularly.....
2. In high school, I wrote several essays per year..........................
3. My final high-school GPA was 2.9 or above................................
4. I have used computers for drafting and revising essays..............
5. My ACT-English score was 20 or above....................................
6. I consider myself a good reader and writer................................
7. Generally, I don't read when I don't have to...............................
8. I did not do much writing in high school.....................................
9. My final high-school GPA was 2.7 or below................................
10. I'm unsure about the rules of writing..
11. My high-school rank was not in the top half of my class............
12. My ACT-English score was below 20.......................................
13. I don't think of myself as a strong writer..................................
14. In my high-school classes, I wrote mostly letters and memos....

SOCIAL SECURITY NO.

If you answered YES to **most** of the statements 1 through 6, please bubble in ENGLISH 101   ⇨   ENG 101

If you answered YES to **one or more** of the statements 7 through 14, you should consider a development writing course.   ⇨   TURN THE PAGE AND COMPLETE THE BACK SIDE

If you answered YES to **more than two** of statements 7 through 14, it's best to enroll in a developmental course.   ⇨   TURN THE PAGE AND COMPLETE THE BACK SIDE

Writing Advisor Approval: _____ Date: _____

OVER ⇨

Figure 1.

Choosing a Developmental Writing Course

The statements in this questionnaire are designed to help you decide which writing course is right for you. Please answer honestly so that you can make the best decision for your needs.

1 = Yes / Agree   2 = No / Disagree

1. I have a history of problems with reading and/or writing...........
2. I often need help finding ideas to write about.........................
3. I find it very hard to write more than a page or two when telling a story or developing and idea..
4. Often, I don't finish the reading that I am asked to do in school..
5. I don't like to read out loud because I can't read smoothly..........
6. I often have trouble understanding books written for my grade level...
7. I am sometimes told that I write too much like I speak................
8. I don't notice problems with my writing (missing words, wrong words, incomplete sentences, incorrect sentences) even when I have time to work on and revise my writing..............................
9. I'm not sure where to end and start sentences............................
10. I tend to let someone else do most or all of the writing in a group project..
11. Computer spell-check programs don't help me; they can't tell what words I mean, or they suggest words that don't say what I mean...
12. I have an identified learning disability that affects my reading and writing...

If you responded YES to **1 or 2 statements** - consider taking <u>DEV 092</u>. ⇨ DEV 092

If you responded YES to **3 or 4 statements** - you should probably take <u>DEV 082</u>. ⇨ DEV 082

If you responded YES to **5 or more statements** - you should probably take <u>DEV 072</u>. ⇨ DEV 072

Please return all the materials to the writing advisor. Thank you.

Figure 2.

Appendix B

Online Directed Self-Placement

ESL Questions

1. I am nervous about writing in English.

    Strongly Agree   Agree   Disagree   Strongly Disagree

2. I like using computers to draft and revise writing.

    Strongly Agree   Agree   Disagree   Strongly Disagree

3. I wrote two or more essays/papers in English in the last year.

    Strongly Agree   Agree   Disagree   Strongly Disagree

4. I regularly read newspapers, magazines, or books in English.

    Strongly Agree   Agree   Disagree   Strongly Disagree

5. I can revise my papers written in English without the help of a native speaker of English.

    Strongly Agree   Agree   Disagree   Strongly Disagree

6. I have written an essay/paper/book review/memo in English in response to something I have read.

    Strongly Agree   Agree   Disagree   Strongly Disagree

7. I'm eager to share my papers with classmates and get their feedback to help me revise.

    Strongly Agree   Agree   Disagree   Strongly Disagree

8. I am unsure of the rules of writing in English, and I struggle with grammar and punctuation.

    Strongly Agree   Agree   Disagree   Strongly Disagree

9. I find it very hard to write more than a page or two when telling a story or developing an idea.

    Strongly Agree   Agree   Disagree   Strongly Disagree

10. I feel confident of speaking in English in front of native speakers.

    Strongly Agree   Agree   Disagree   Strongly Disagree

11. I worry about sharing my writing with native speakers of English.

    Strongly Agree   Agree   Disagree   Strongly Disagree

12. I have difficulty organizing my ideas in English.

    Strongly Agree   Agree   Disagree   Strongly Disagree

13. I am successful at using a variety of sentence structures in English.

     Strongly Agree   Agree   Disagree   Strongly Disagree
14. I regularly translate from my native language when writing in English.
     Strongly Agree   Agree   Disagree   Strongly Disagree
15. I feel confident about my vocabulary in English.
     Strongly Agree   Agree   Disagree   Strongly Disagree

12 Investing in Assessment: Designing Tests to Promote Positive Washback

Sara Cushing Weigle

The thought of tests makes many writing teachers uneasy, and for good reason. From their own experience both as teachers and as students themselves, teachers know that tests can make students anxious and do not always allow students to demonstrate their best writing. A typical timed impromptu writing test, in which students are asked to write on a previously unseen topic within a fairly short time frame, is often seen as unfair as it is unrepresentative of many of the skills that teachers try to foster in their students. Furthermore, teachers often feel more comfortable in the role of nurturing and supporting their students in their growing writing competence than evaluating and assigning a grade or number to their students' work.

When tests of writing ability are mandated from an authority beyond the classroom, as is the case at many postsecondary institutions, anxiety is often increased for both teachers and students. Teachers often feel pressured to spend time on test preparation rather than teaching writing skills they believe are more important because they do not want their students to perform poorly on the test. Teachers may also feel professionally undermined for at least two reasons. First, an externally mandated assessment makes a strong statement about what type of writing is valued, and this may not be—indeed, often is not—the type of writing that teachers want to focus on in class: writing as a process of discovering meaning, writing from sources, or writing as revision.

The effects of externally mandated tests on instruction have been recognized for a long time, but they have only recently become an object of research. In the field of language testing, the influence of tests on teaching and learning is known as washback (Wall, 1996; Cheng, Watanabe, & Curtis, 2004). Washback is a complex phenomenon and can be regarded as positive or negative, depending on whether the implementation of a new test leads to improvements in instructional practices or detracts from them. An example of positive washback in writing assessment was the introduction of the Test of Written English (TWE) to the TOEFL examination; before the TWE was required at many institutions, students often came to the U.S. with the ability to perform very well on discrete-point tests of grammar and usage but with very little experience with writing in English. Once colleges and universities began to require a writing sample for admission, however, test preparation courses needed to change in order to prepare students for the writing test, and students wanting to take the TOEFL needed to practice actual composition, not simply answering multiple choice questions.

On the other hand, negative washback occurs in situations where the type of writing that is valued by teachers (and presumably by students as well) is not what gets tested. An example is the practice of requiring a timed impromptu essay at the end of a composition course that focuses primarily on the writing process. In this case the assessment method does not match the teaching focus, and teachers will feel pressure to "teach to the test" despite their belief that this sort of writing is not as useful for students.

Speaking specifically of language testing, Messick (1996) states that "for optimal positive washback there should be little, if any, difference between activities in learning the language and activities involved in preparing for the test" (pp. 241–242). This is a sentiment that most writing teachers would agree with in terms of writing assessment, whether they are teaching English language learners or native speakers: Students learn to write by writing and should be assessed in terms of what they have written throughout the course, not asked to perform some other writing task under what are often stressful and inauthentic conditions.

Nevertheless, testing is a fact of life for students and teachers. If testing is necessary, then, is it possible to design tests that promote positive washback? In this chapter, I will discuss briefly the history of mandatory writing assessment at the postsecondary level, give some critiques of the timed impromptu essay test as a means for ensuring that college graduates have met minimum writing standards, and describe an alternative to the timed impromptu essay that is being used successfully at one institution. In the conclusion, I argue that teachers need to be critical consumers of mandated assessments and provide some suggestions for how teachers and administrators can improve testing at their institutions.

Mandatory Writing Assessment

White (1994) traces the trend in mandatory writing assessment at the postsecondary level to two main factors: the expansion of postsecondary education to traditionally underrepresented segments of the population, often through open enrollment, and complaints by employers that college graduates lacked the writing skills they needed to perform well on their jobs. As a result of these factors, many colleges and universities felt pressure to ensure that, regardless of the skills they had when entering the institution, students were well equipped with writing skills when they left.

Institutions across the U.S. have met this challenge in a variety of ways. Some institutions require students to submit portfolios of their written work, while others require students to take a certain number of writing-intensive courses. Still others, including the university system of Georgia, require all students to take a standardized essay examination during their first or second year of studies. However, as White (1984) and others have argued, this solution is one of the least satisfactory, for several reasons. A proficiency test required at mid-degree, as opposed to an entry-level placement test, requires consensus on what constitutes "good writing" across a range of campuses and degree programs, and such a consensus is difficult if not impossible to come by. Furthermore, standards on such a test are inevitably fairly low, as the test is a barrier to graduation for some students and, as White notes, it is politically difficult to fail a large number of students. These factors make a standardized proficiency examination problematic as a way of ensuring that students are acquiring sufficient writing skills at the college level and beyond.

In addition to these concerns about writing proficiency examinations in particular, critiques of timed impromptu essay tests in general have often been raised by scholars in writing assessment. These critiques generally center around issues of reliability, validity, and authenticity. In terms of reliability, a single-prompt writing test is, essentially, a one-item test (Hamp-Lyons, 1991), and thus cannot meet the standards for reliability that are found in discrete-point multiple choice tests or other selected response test types. An important component of reliability for writing tests is inter-rater reliability, which can be increased through the use of multiple raters, extensive training, and clearly articulated scoring guides with model responses at each scoring level (see Weigle, 2002).

A more serious problem with writing tests is the difficulty of ensuring that different prompts are of equal difficulty, and thus that students scores are not affected by factors related to differences in prompts. Writing prompts or tasks vary on a number of dimensions, such as subject matter, genre, rhetorical task, and cognitive demands that may affect scores on writing tests in complex and unpredictable ways (Henning, 1991; White, 1994; Weigle, 2002). Because of this complexity, it is difficult to isolate specific factors that affect scores in a consistent ways, although research suggests that "rhetorical task" in particular may be one of these factors: differences between narrative tasks and argumentative tasks have been found both in the scores awarded and in the language used to accomplish these task types (Crowhurst, 1980; Quellmalz, Capell, & Chou, 1982; Hake, 1986).

As for authenticity, research on writing in undergraduate courses (e.g., (Carson, Chase, & Gibson, 1992; Leki & Carson, 1997) suggests that graded writing is virtually always done in response to other texts that have been read and/or discussed orally. Thus the task of writing an essay on a previously unseen topic, with little or no opportunity to explore the topic through interaction with other texts on the topic, is a highly inauthentic task as it does not represent the contextual factors of authentic academic writing.

Finally, the validity of the "snapshot" approach to writing (Hamp-Lyons & Kroll, 1996) is limited, as a single essay does not allow the assessment of the total range of a writer's ability because it does not provide opportunities for students to express themselves in more than a single genre for a single purpose. An additional validity concern about essay examinations has to do with the reductive nature of holistic scoring because giving a single score to an essay reduces the complex multifaceted nature of reading to a single number (Charney, 1984; Huot, 1988; Hamp-Lyons, 1991).

Much of the research on timed impromptu essays has been conducted with native speakers. For NNS, timed impromptu essays may be even more problematic, particularly when their essays are scored along with NS essays. Several studies have documented difficulties that NNS have had on mandated writing proficiency examinations compared with their NS peers (Ruetten, 1994; Johns, 1991; Byrd & Nelson, 1995). Research suggests that raters who lack training or experience with ESL writing may give undue attention to sentence-level errors (Sweedler-Brown, 1993) and that faculty from different disciplines may use different criteria for judging NNS writing (Mendelsohn & Cumming, 1987; Santos, 1988; Brown, 1991). Furthermore, using a single scale to grade essays is particularly problematic for NNS, who may develop different aspects of writing skill at different rates (Hamp-Lyons, 1991).

As noted above, the critique of timed impromptu essays that is perhaps of most concern to writing teachers is the separation of assessment from instruction. If teachers believe that good writing is rewriting and want to foster the process of writing and revision among their students, they feel undermined when an externally mandated timed impromptu essay examination gives a different message: Good writing is a good first draft. An even more insidious message, perhaps, of the timed impromptu essay is that it is permissible, and even encouraged, to express a strong opinion on a topic that one has not read or thought much about and for which one has no ready access to data that will support one's point of view. This message can easily undermine a teacher's insistence on critical reading and the use of appropriate sources as essential components of academic writing skills.

The stated mandate of external writing assessments is frequently quite limited compared to the writing skills that composition teachers feel are essential for university students. For example, the published goal of the Regents test in the university system of Georgia is to ensure that students meet "certain minimum skills in writing" (http://www2.gsu.edu/~wwwrtp/overview.htm). It is interesting to note that these skills are not explicitly identified; the directions to students simply state: "[t]he purpose of the Essay Test is to find out how well you can write an essay" (http://www2.gsu.edu/~wwwrtp/essainst.htm).

In contrast, a sample syllabus from first year composition at Georgia Southern University (GSU) (http://www2.gsu.edu/~wwwgea/Teaching_Resources/1101_a.html) includes the following list of learning outcomes:

- engage in writing as a process, including various invention heuristics (brainstorming, for example), gathering evidence, considering audience, drafting, revising, editing, and proofreading
- engage in the collaborative, social aspects of writing, and use writing as a tool for learning
- use language to explore and analyze contemporary multicultural, global, and international questions
- demonstrate how to use writing aids, such as handbooks, dictionaries, online aids, and tutors
- gather, summarize, synthesize, and explain information from various sources
- use grammatical, stylistic, and mechanical formats and conventions appropriate for a variety of audiences
- critique their own and others' work in written and oral formats
- produce coherent, organized, readable prose for a variety of rhetorical situations
- reflect on what contributed to their writing process and evaluate their own work

Clearly, this list of objectives is much more comprehensive than anything that can be tested within 60 to 90 minutes, and there is a discontinuity between the skills that composition teachers feel are important (to say nothing of faculty from other disciplines) and the skills required to write a short impromptu essay. Given this discontinuity, along with the political reality of externally mandated assessment, a worthwhile goal is to create an assessment that goes beyond the limited definition of writing in this mandate so that teachers can feel good about devoting class time to test preparation, since the test is more fully aligned with the curriculum. In the next part of the chapter I will describe one attempt at designing a test with a view towards achieving this goal.

Description of Regents Test and Alternate Regents Test

The Regents testing requirement in the university system of Georgia has been legislatively mandated since 1972. Students must take the Regents Reading and Writing Tests as soon as they have completed 30 semester hours of coursework; if they have not passed both parts of the test by the time they have completed 45 hours they must enroll in an appropriate remedial course every semester until they have passed both the reading and the writing tests (http://www.gsu.edu/~wwwrtp/semester.htm).

The writing test consists of a 60-minute timed impromptu essay on the student's choice of four short prompts selected from a large bank of approved prompts, which are available on-line (http://www.gsu.edu/~wwwrtp/topics.htm). In principle, each form of the test should contain at least one prompt that requires general knowledge of current issues (e.g., Should convicted lawbreakers be required to serve their full sentences without parole?) and one that can be answered on the basis of personal experience (e.g., Is there any job that you would absolutely refuse to take? Explain.) (http://www.gsu.edu/~wwwrtp/essadev.htm, retrieved 10/15/03).

The test is scored using a four-point holistic scale, with scores of 2 or higher being passing marks. The writing tests from all campuses are scored together by trained raters, thus reducing the risk of different standards being used on different campuses. Each essay is rated by three raters; an essay passes if two of the three raters give it a passing score.

The consequences of failure on the Regents test can be quite serious. Students must take a test preparation course each semester that they do not pass. Until recently, this course was not covered by financial aid, so students had to pay for the course out of their own pockets. Even more seriously, students cannot graduate without passing the test, even if they have completed all other graduation requirements.

Washback

Washback from the Regents test can be seen in the syllabi for both the Regents test preparation course and the regular first-year composition course. Because test preparation courses are strictly focused on helping students pass the test, the course syllabus typically concentrates on simulating examinations and choosing topics. Another issue regarding test preparation courses is that they are often taught by the least experienced teaching assistants, who may have had little or no training in writing instruction.

In addition, since students are encouraged to take the Regents test after completing their first-year composition requirement, these first year courses typically include a week preparing students for timed writing examinations, even if they do no other timed writing in the course.

Testing for Nonnative Speakers

While the same statewide test is required for native speakers throughout the university system, procedures for testing NNS vary from campus to campus. Until recently, the alternative test for NNS at GSU was a variation of the regular Regents test with some modifications, including longer testing time, local scoring by trained ESL raters, and a smaller set of approved prompts to reduce the possibility of cultural bias. However, faculty members from the Applied Linguistics/ESL department who taught the Regents test preparation course and rated the exam felt strongly that the test was an inappropriate measure of writing ability for these students. For one reason, raters noted that many of the approved prompts elicited problematic essays that may not have represented students' abilities accurately (see discussion below). Another problem with the testing procedures in place was the fact that the test was scored on the same holistic scale as the regular Regents test, and failing scores were not useful for diagnostic purposes, as students and their teachers would have no way of knowing whether their failure in the test was due to linguistic or rhetorical problems.

Problems with Prompts

The prompts used for the Regents writing are solicited by a statewide Testing Subcommittee and reviewed to meet specific criteria. For instance, prompts should not contain difficult vocabulary, require specialized knowledge, involve highly controversial or emotional subjects, or encourage students to identify their institutions in their essays. Prompts are also chosen with a view towards providing students a variety of topics to choose from.

However, the prompts are not pilot tested before being used operationally, nor does the Regents testing program publish data on which prompts are chosen most frequently or how students perform on individual prompts. While the implied presumption is that test prompts are equivalent in difficulty, they represent a number of different discourse modes, including argumentation, exposition, and narration. One study (Weigle, 2004) suggests that, at least for nonnative speakers of English, there is a relationship between the prompt one chooses and the probability of passing the test; that is, students are more likely to get passing scores on some prompts than on others.

As an illustration of some of the difficulties with the approved prompts, the following are example "current issues" prompts:
- Should Georgia's sales tax be removed from groceries and other necessities? Discuss.
- Attack or defend the practice of advertising by doctors and lawyers.
- Should convicted lawbreakers be required to serve their full sentences without parole? Discuss.

One obvious problem with these prompts is that many 19 to 20 year old students do not have the background knowledge to discuss them cogently, as they concern complex social issues that students of this age group may never have thought about in depth, much less had to write about in 60 minutes. Since students do not have access to empirical data during the test that could be used to support one point of view or the other, they are forced to rely on their own experience or what they have heard from others as support for their thesis in prompts of this nature. While raters may be willing to accept anecdotal evidence as support in a timed essay, the danger exists that students may come to believe that anecdotal evidence is sufficient for persuasive writing in other situations.

Many of the more personal prompts are problematic as well, but for somewhat different reasons. Consider the following two prompts:
- Do you enjoy shopping? Why or why not?
- If you could have a household robot, for what jobs would you want it programmed? Discuss.

In the 1999–2000 school year, these two prompts appeared on the Regents test for nonnative speakers. Among the 18 prompts that were chosen by at least 10 students, the average pass rate was 75 percent. For the "shopping" prompt, however, the pass rate was only 42 percent (5/12)—the lowest of any prompt—while for the "robot" prompt the pass rate was 90 percent (10/11). These numbers are small but suggestive of differences due to the nature of the prompts themselves. While there may be several reasons for the difference in pass rates, raters who scored the essays that year commented that most students attempt to write a traditional five-paragraph essay for both of these prompts. It is fairly easy to come up with three distinct household jobs for which one might program a robot and to write a few sentences about each job; it turns out to be somewhat more difficult to come up with three distinct reasons for why one likes to shop. Furthermore, students who chose the shopping topic may have unwittingly given raters the impression that they were not serious students, simply by virtue of having chosen this very non-academic topic, and this impression may have affected some raters' scores, though of course this is only speculation.

Description of GSTEP Regents

Starting in 2001, a new test has been used at GSU both for placing matriculated students into ESL courses, where appropriate, and as an approved alternative to the Regents test for nonnative speakers. The test was designed with the potential for positive washback in mind, and I will describe it here.

Test Format

The Georgia State Test of English Proficiency (GSTEP) was developed in the early 1980s as a traditional discrete-point four skills language test. It was revised in 1999–2000 by a committee headed by an assessment specialist in consultation with ESL teachers, applied linguistics faculty, and a working group of faculty members from disciplines across the university. The committee's mandate was to revise the test to fit within the constraints of current assessment practices: It was to be paper and pencil based, administered at a single sitting to a large group of students and scored within a few days. At the same time, however, the test developers wanted the test to reflect more closely the reading and writing skills needed by university students: in particular, analyzing an author's perspective in reading, synthesizing information from different input sources, and using source texts to support an argument. One important reason for assessing these skills was so that these skills, would be taught in the test preparation courses and, more importantly, that students who had to take the test preparation course would learn not just the narrow skills needed to pass the regular Regents test but skills that would serve them well in other academic courses.

The revised GSTEP has three main sections: a listening section, a multiple-choice reading section, and an integrated reading/writing section, which is the section of the test that is used to fulfill the Regents writing requirement and thus the only section of the test described in detail in this chapter. When this section of the test is used for placement purposes, it is scored for both reading and writing (see

Weigle, 2004 for details), but for Regents writing purposes, it is only scored for writing.

The format of the integrated reading/writing test is as follows. First, examinees are presented with two 300- to 350-word passages presenting different viewpoints on a particular topic (e.g., computers in education, genetic engineering). Examinees read the passages and answer eight open-ended questions about the passages: six dealing with the individual passages and two requiring test takers to compare or contrast the ideas in the two passages. Afterwards, they are asked to write an essay in which they take a stand on the issue raised in the readings, using information from at least one of the two passages to support their position. Appendix A contains a sample test form; note that for reasons of test security this is a practice form rather than an operational form.

This test differs from the traditional timed impromptu essay test in a number of ways. First, as a source-based writing test, it is more representative of academic writing than an impromptu test is, since reading and writing are so highly inter-related in academic writing. Providing sources also provides common background information for test takers, potentially reducing the possibility of content bias. Having a source text also serves to activate writers' schemata. The test uses multiple sources so that students have the opportunity to synthesize information from different sources, an important academic task. Furthermore, some research suggests that providing more than one reading passage as input for writing results in higher quality essays than using a single text (Feak & Dobson, 1996).

Another distinctive feature of the test is the practice of using short answer rather than multiple-choice questions to assess comprehension of the reading passages. This was done for three main reasons. First, short answer questions are an authentic genre of writing for many undergraduate students in their content courses (Carson, Chase, & Gibson, 1992; Leki & Carson, 1997). Second, questions have been raised about the validity of multiple-choice as a format for testing reading, particularly for nonnative speakers of English (Bernhardt, 1991). Third, the short-answer questions were designed to help prepare test takers for the essay portion of the test, by having them express the main points of the passages in their own words and explicitly compare the two arguments.

Test takers are given two scores for their responses to the short-answer questions based on two holistic scales: one for content and the other for language (see Tables 1 and 2). A distinctive feature of these scales is that they relate to the short-answer items as a whole rather than as individual items; that is, raters are asked to evaluate whether a student's responses overall indicate various degrees of reading comprehension (in the case of content) or language proficiency/writing ability (in the case of language).

Table 1. GSTEP Short answer scoring rubric: Content

5	Responses demonstrate full and sophisticated understanding of both texts. All items addressed completely and accurately.
4	Responses demonstrate good understanding of both texts. Most items addressed completely and accurately, though some responses may be undeveloped.
3	Responses demonstrate minimally adequate understanding of both texts. Some responses may be brief or off-target; at most one or two items are not attempted.
2	Responses demonstrate partial misunderstanding of at least one text. Several answers may be brief and/or off-target but some responses are accurate.
1	Responses demonstrate inadequate understanding of both texts. Several items not answered or responses are off-target.

Table 2. GSTEP Short answer scoring rubric: Language

5	Responses demonstrate excellent command of English. Few errors in grammar or vocabulary; responses consist primarily of student's own words.
4	Responses demonstrate good command of English. Some errors present that do not interfere with comprehension; there may be some reliance on source text language.
3	Responses suggest minimally adequate command of English. There may be several distracting errors but responses are generally comprehensible; there may be heavy reliance on source text language.
2	Responses suggest lack of command of English. Many errors, some of which interfere with comprehension; extensive copying from source texts.
1	Responses demonstrate lack of command of English. Responses that are present are mostly incomprehensible or are copied from source texts.

The essays are graded on an analytic scale comprising four aspects of writing, each with 10 points: content, organization, language range and complexity, and language accuracy (see Appendix B). The content and organization scores are added together to make a single "rhetoric" score (maximum points equals 20), and the accuracy and range/complexity scores are combined to make a single "language" score (maximum points equals 20).

Essays are read by two raters, with a third rater adjudicating if the scores on Rhetoric or Language differ by more than three points (when the essays are graded for placement purposes) or when the two ratings fall on either side of the decision point (when the test is used for Regents testing purposes).

For both the short answers and the essays, the raters' scores are averaged, and the average score is converted into a band score from 1 (lowest) to 7 (highest). Students receive an overall band score for rhetoric (based on the essay) and one for language (based on the average of the essay and the short answer scores). The passing scores for Regents testing were arrived at by a committee of experienced Regents raters from both the applied linguistics program and the English department at GSU; the consensus of the committee was that the standards for rhetoric should be higher than those for language in recognition of the fact that many nonnative speakers of English can learn to organize an essay and develop their ideas satisfactorily even if they have not yet acquired native-like control over some of the more problematic aspects of sentence-level grammar.

The GSTEP has now been used for Regents testing purposes for several years; in the next section of the chapter I will report briefly on the performance of the test based on data collected over the first three years of the test's use.

Reliability and Pass Rates

As reported in Weigle (2004), the pass rate for the new test is about 90 percent, compared with 75 percent for the older test, and there appears to be very little difference across test forms in this rate. In contrast, on the older version of the test, pass rates across different forms of the test (each with four different prompts) ranged from 65 percent to 95 percent. Furthermore, the test has proven to be quite reliable, with a third reader needed to adjudicate differences in scoring only 2 percent of the time.

Students who fail the test tend to do so on the basis of rhetoric rather than language. As noted above, the standards for rhetoric are higher than for language, which probably accounts for this result. However, students who fail on the basis of language almost always also fail on rhetoric as well; at the level of proficiency at which students are likely to fail on the basis of language there are often many sentence-level errors that interfere with comprehension, making it difficult for raters to discern the main ideas or overall organizational structure of the essay.

A few students have failed the test more than three times. A close look at their records reveals that these students tend to have low scores on the language scale, indicating low language proficiency overall; they tend to avoid writing-intensive courses and to have frequent withdrawals from courses. Students who fit this profile may benefit from language-intensive courses to improve their overall language proficiency: The other alternative is to tighten admission standards so that such students are not admitted to the university in the first place. The risk of that strategy, of course, is in denying admission to other students who manage to succeed despite lower language proficiency. In any case, the test seems to be correctly identifying students at overall risk in their academic careers and does not seem to be functioning as an unreasonable stumbling block to graduation.

Washback

As Wall (2000) notes, "It should not be assumed that a 'good' test will automatically produce good effects in the classroom, or that a 'bad' test will necessarily produce negative ones" (pp. 505–506). The introduction of a new test by itself will not guarantee that classroom instruction will change (for better or worse); other important factors include teacher experience and training, resources and classroom conditions, and management practices of the school (see Alderson & Wall, 1993; Wall, 2000). A full-scale study of washback of the new GSTEP has not yet been undertaken; however, an inspection of the syllabus for the GSTEP Regents writing test preparation course reveals that more time is devoted to critical reading, using sources in writing, and paraphrasing and less time to the traditional five-paragraph essay format and strategies for prompt selection as compared with earlier iterations of the course. It would, of course, be valuable to investigate not only whether the test preparation course has changed, but whether students who take the course that prepares them for the GSTEP Regents are able to transfer the skills learned in this course to their other academic work more than the skills taught in the traditional test preparation course, which focuses primarily on passing the regular impromptu essay examination.

Dilemmas

In the four years since we have introduced the Regents GSTEP writing test, we have had a positive response to the test from teachers, raters, and students. The pass rate on the test is higher than on the old version, and more importantly, the test appears to be more reliable in terms of differences across prompts. However, there are still a number of dilemmas in continuing to use the new test on an ongoing basis.

The first of these dilemmas has to do with identifying students who are candidates for the Regents GSTEP and encouraging them to enroll in the appropriate test preparation course. As is the case at many institutions, students self-select into either regular or ESL sections of the test preparation courses and do so for myriad reasons. A limited number of ESL sections are offered each semester, so some students may prefer an ESL section but are not able to enroll in one because of their schedule. Other students may not want to identify as ESL students and so they choose to enroll in the regular Regents course instead. One problem that arises as a result is that students may be in a course that is primarily preparing them for a test that they will not ultimately take, as the regular Regents courses focus only minimally on the GSTEP, and vice versa.

Another dilemma with the new format for the test is that, when asked, students generally prefer a choice of topic rather than being required to write on a single topic (Polio & Glew, 1996; Jennings, Fox, Graves, & Shohamy, 1999). Furthermore, the equivalence between forms is difficult to judge; while the scores given across different forms appear to be equivalent, determining whether reading passages are equally difficult is a complex proposition.

An equally serious problem is the very real issue of practicality. Test development and administration are expensive and time-consuming, and the budget for testing is limited. The university provides funding for test administration, but additional forms of the test need to be developed every two or three years, and this is not an inexpensive proposition. To accomplish this task a number of steps must be taken. First, appropriate reading passages that meet the specifications of length, difficulty, topic, and genre must be found and edited as necessary. Then short answer and essay questions must be drafted. Potential new forms must be pretested with students who are comparable to the test population but not actually students who will eventually have to take the Regents test. In the past we have made arrangements with colleagues at other institutions to pretest new forms with their students, but this is not always logistically feasible. Even when suitable students are found for pretesting, they may need motivation to take the test. We have arranged for students at other institutions to administer a potential new form of our test as part of a diagnostic procedure at the beginning of a semester, an arrangement that can be of benefit to both institutions. Where this is not possible, an appropriate incentive must be found, such as a cash payment or extra credit for a course assignment.

Once a potential new form of the test has been pretested, raters must be found to rate the pretests. The rating process is important at this stage so that raters can identify questions that are ambiguous, elicit responses that are difficult to score, or are otherwise problematic. Finally, statistical expertise is needed to determine whether scores on newly developed forms are equivalent to scores on existing forms. All of these steps require resources that may not be easily available, yet they are essential for any on-going testing program to maintain test security and to replace outdated or overused forms.

Conclusion

If writing assessments are mandatory and involve high stakes for students, it is imperative that they be valid and fair. In this regard, the test described in this chapter can be seen as an advance over the regular Regents test for NNS. In particular, the prompts are carefully developed and pretested to ensure equivalence across forms—something that is not done for the statewide Regents test—and the test was designed to assess the kind of writing that is more valuable in other types of academic writing. In this way the test allows for positive washback: The skills required for the test reflect more accurately those that are valued in the classroom, and, for those students who are required to take a test preparation class, the course offers them more of an opportunity to learn skills that they can apply to academic writing across the curriculum.

What Can Teachers Do?

Many classroom teachers feel that externally mandated assessments are beyond their control and that they are helpless to effect changes. However, there are several actions that classroom teachers can take to mitigate the negative effects of standardized writing tests. Initially, it is important for teachers to become informed about the testing policies at their own institutions. It is easy to assume that by virtue of being standardized, tests are automatically valid and reliable. As I have discussed in this chapter, however, valid questions can and should be raised about how tasks are set, how reliable the procedures for administering and scoring the tests are, and whether the test has been validated for the purpose for which it is being used. Teachers should be aware of what administrative bodies are responsible for developing and administering tests and what avenues exist for challenging the status quo where relevant.

It is also important to recognize that high quality tests are not inexpensive to produce. Teachers should not be expected to develop valid and reliable assessments that have serious consequences for students in their spare time. If asked to participate in test development projects, teachers should insist on seeing a realistic budget (including course release, when possible) and a feasible timeline.

There is also plenty of scope for collaboration among different institutes in terms of identifying appropriate reading passages and developing prompts for writing assessment. I have already spoken of the possibility of pretesting forms of the test at other institutions; if this were done on a larger scale across several campuses the possibilities for creating high quality assessments would be greatly enhanced. Even if the format for testing differs at different institutions, it would be a wonderful thing to have a password-protected bank of reading passages on a variety of topics that could be used in different places, and if agreements for pretesting could be made among programs in different states or areas of the country.

Tests that promote positive washback, in that they promote the teaching and learning of useful academic writing skills, are feasible, but not inexpensive. A source-based writing test is more costly to develop, administer, and score than a traditional timed impromptu essay, but I would argue that investing in such a test brings benefits that outweigh the costs. Students and teachers both benefit when the gap between instruction and assessment is as small as possible.

References

Anderson, J.-C. & Wall, D. (1993). Does Washback exist? *Applied Linguistics, 14*(2), 115-129.

Bernhardt, E. (1991). *Reading development in a second language: Theoretical, empirical, and classroom perspectives.* Norwood, NJ, Ablex.

Brown, J. D. (1991). Do English and ESL faculties rate writing samples differently? *TESOL Quarterly 25*, 587–603.

Carson, J. G., Chase, N. D., & Gibson, S. U. (1992). Literacy demands of the undergraduate curriculum. *Reading Research and Instruction, 31*(4): 25–50.

Charney, D. (1984). The validity of using holistic scoring to evaluating writing: A critical overview. *Research in the Teaching of English, 18*, 65–81.

Cheng, L., Watanabe, Y., & Curtis, A. (Eds.) (2004). Washback in language testing: Research contexts and methods. Mahwah, NJ: Laurence Erlbaum & Associates.

Crowhurst, M. (1980). Syntactic complexity and teacher's ratings of narrations and arguments. *Research in the Teaching of English, 13*, 223–31.

Hake, R. (1986). How do we judge what they write? In K. L. Greenburg, H. S. Weiner, & R. A. Donovan (Eds.), *Writing assessment: Issues and strategies* (pp. 153-167). New York: Longman.

Hamp-Lyons, L. (1991). Scoring procedures for ESL contexts. In L. Hamp-Lyons (Ed.), *Assessing second language writing in academic contexts* (pp. 241-276). Norwood, NJ, Ablex.

Hamp-Lyons, L., & Kroll, B. (1996). Issues in ESL writing assessment: An overview. *College ESL, 6*(1), 52–72.

Henning, G. (1991). Issues in evaluating and maintaining an ESL writing assessment program. In L. Hamp-Lyons (Ed.), *Assessing writing in second language contexts* (pp. 279–291). Norwood, NJ, Ablex Publishing Corp.

Huot, B. (1988). The validity of holistic scoring: A comparison of talk-aloud protocols of expert and novice holistic raters. Unpublished doctoral dissertation. Indiana University of Pennsylvania.

Jennings, M., Fox, J., Graves, B., & Shohamy, E. (1999). The test-takers' choice: An investigation of the effect of topic on language-test performance. *Language Testing, 16*(4), 426–456.

Leki, I., & Carson, J. (1997). Completely different worlds: EAP and the writing experiences of ESL students in university courses. *TESOL Quarterly, 31*(1), 39–70.

Mendelsohn, D., & Cumming, A. (1987). Professors' ratings of language use and rhetorical organizations in ESL compositions. *TESL Canada Journal, 5*(1), 9–26.

Polio, C., & Glew, M. (1996). ESL writing assessment prompts: How students choose. *Journal of Second Language Writing, 5*(1), 35–49.

Quellmalz, E. S., Capell, F. J., & Chou, C. P. (1982). "Effects of discourse and response mode on the measurement of writing competence." *Journal of Educational Measurement, 19*, 241–258.

Santos, T. (1988). Professors' reactions to the academic writing of nonnative speaking students. *TESOL Quarterly, 22*(1), 69–90.

Sweedler-Brown, C. O. (1993). ESL essay evaluation: The influence of sentence-level and rhetorical features. *Journal of Second Language Writing, 2*(1), 3–17.

Wall, D. (1996). Introducing news tests into traditional systems: Insights from general education and from innovation theory. *Language Testing, 13*(3), 334–354.

Weigle, S. C. (2002). *Assessing writing*. Cambridge. UK: Cambridge University Press.

White, E. (1994). *Teaching and assessing writing: Recent advances in understanding, evaluating and improving student performance* (2nd ed.). San Francisco: Jossey-Bass.

Appendix A: Sample GSTEP form

Directions: Read the following two passages that are arguing for two different sides of the same issue. After you finish reading, you will write the answers to 8 questions based on the reading passages. In this section you will be graded on content and language: what you say and how you say it. You will have 45 minutes.

A. Excerpt from an essay published by the BioDemocracy and Organic Consumers Association

B. Excerpt of an essay entitled "Kill the Frankenstein Myth" by Robert W. Tracinski, a senior writer for the Ayn Rand Institute in Marina del Rey, California.

Directions: Answer the following questions based on the readings. There are several possible ways to answer each question. You should use your own words as much as possible; you will not find the answers written word for word in the readings. Your answers will be graded on content and accurate use of English. Be sure to write complete sentences. NOTE: Your answer will be marked down if it contains fewer than 10 words or if your answer consists mainly of words taken directly from the readings.

NOTE: On the actual test there is more room to write responses!

1. What is the main argument in passage A?

2. What are some of the most important effects of genetic engineering, according to passage A?

3. According to Passage A, how do biological pollutants differ from chemical pollutants?

4. What is the main argument in passage B?

5. What are some of the most important effects of genetic engineering, according to passage B?

6. Why are genetically modified foods sometimes called "Frankenfoods," according to Passage B?

7. How do the opinions of the two authors compare with regard to the use of genetic engineering to make plants resistant to viruses or bacteria?

8. How might the author of Passage B respond to Passage A's prediction that "never again will people know the joy of eating naturally produced, fresh foods"?

Part 2: Writing an Argumentative Essay

Directions: Write a well-organized academic essay on the topic below. Your essay will be graded on content, organization, and appropriate use of English. You may refer to the reading passages while you are writing. You may use this space for notes. Write your essay on the lined paper. You will have 45 minutes to write your essay.

Essay Topic

Some people believe that genetically modified plants are dangerous to our health and to the environment. Others believe that genetic engineering is an important tool in feeding the world's population. Which position do you support? Use specific information from *at least one* of the two articles to support your ideas.

Appendix B: GSTEP Essay Scoring Rubric

RHETORIC		LANGUAGE	
Content	Organization	Language: Accuracy	Language: Range and Complexity
9–10 The treatment of the assignment completely fulfills the task expectations and the topic is addressed thoroughly. Fully developed evidence for generalizations and supporting ideas/arguments is provided in a relevant and credible way. Uses ideas from source text well to support thesis.	9–10 Clear and appropriate organizational plan. Effective introduction and conclusion. Connections between and within paragraphs are made through effective and varied use of transitions and other cohesive devices.	9–10 The essay is clearly written with few errors; errors do not interfere with comprehension. Includes consistently accurate word forms and verb tenses. Word choices are accurate and appropriate.	9–10 Uses a variety of sentence types accurately. Uses a wide range of academic vocabulary. Source text language is used sparingly and accurately incorporated into writer's own words.
7–8 The treatment of the assignment fulfills the task expectations competently and the topic is addressed clearly. Evidence for generalizations and supporting ideas/arguments is provided in a relevant and credible way. Ideas from source text used to support thesis.	7–8 Clear organizational plan Satisfactory introduction and conclusion. Satisfactory connections between and within paragraphs using transitions and other cohesive devices.	7–8 The essay is clearly written but contains some errors that do not interfere with comprehension. The essay may contain some errors in word choice, word form, verb tenses, and complementation.	7–8 The essay uses a variety of sentence types. Good range of vocabulary used with at most a few lapses in register. Some language from the source text may be present but is generally well incorporated into writer's own words.

RHETORIC		LANGUAGE		
Content	Organization	Language: Accuracy	Language: Range and Complexity
5–6 The treatment of the assignment minimally fulfills the task expectations; some aspects of the task may be slighted. Some relevant and credible evidence for generalizations and supporting ideas/arguments is provided. Ideas from source texts are included but may not be explicitly acknowledged as such.	5–6 Adequate but simplistic organizational plan. Introduction and conclusion present but may be brief. Connections between and within paragraphs occasionally missing.	5–6 Is generally comprehensible but contains some errors that distract the reader; at most a few errors interfere with comprehension. The essay may contain several errors in word choice, word form, verb tenses, and complementation.	5–6 Somewhat limited range of sentence types; may avoid complex structures. Somewhat limited range of vocabulary. May include extensive language from source text(s) with an attempt to incorporate text language with own language.
3–4 The treatment of the assignment only partially fulfills the task expectations and the topic is not always addressed clearly. Evidence for generalizations and supporting ideas/arguments is insufficient and/or irrelevant. May not include ideas from source text, or may consist primarily of ideas from source text without integration with writer's ideas.	3–4 Organizational plan hard to follow. Introduction and conclusion may be missing or inadequate. Connections between and within paragraphs frequently missing.	3–4 Contains many errors; some errors may interfere with comprehension. Includes many errors in word choices, forms, word forms, verb tenses and complementation.	3–4 Uses a limited number of sentence types. Vocabulary limited. Extensive use of source text language with little integration with writer's words.

RHETORIC		LANGUAGE	
Content	Organization	Language: Accuracy	Language: Range and Complexity
1–2 The treatment of the assignment fails to fulfill the task expectations and the paper lacks focus and development. Evidence for generalizations and supporting ideas/arguments is insufficient and/or irrelevant.	1–2 No apparent organizational plan. Introduction and conclusion missing or clearly inappropriate. Few connections made between and within paragraphs.	1–2 Contains numerous errors that interfere with comprehension. Includes many errors in word choices, forms, word forms, verb tenses and complementation.	1–2 Uses simple and repetitive vocabulary that may not be appropriate for academic writing. Does not vary sentence types sufficiently. May rely almost exclusively on source text language.

The Politics of the Profession

13 Mapping Postsecondary Classifications and Second Language Writing Research in the United States

Jessie Moore Kapper

Contemporary second language writing scholarship theoretically responds to and reflects different contexts in which second language writing occurs, including different geographic locations and educational settings. A close examination of the field's scholarship, though, suggests that many of these contexts are underrepresented in publications focused on second language writers who are working and studying in the United States. As a result, second language writing scholars likely have neither a comprehensive knowledge of the varied geographical and educational settings in which second language writing occurs, nor a representational understanding of second language writers.

In what follows, I present mappings related to the geographical and educational contexts of second language writing scholarship in the United States—focusing on correlations between institutions' Carnegie classifications and the amount of second language writing scholarship the institutions produced in the 1990s and the early 2000s. These mappings demonstrate how institutional priorities affect the scope of contemporary second language writing research and the field's collective understanding of the writers with whom we work.

Analysis of the Fields' Professional Literature

As part of a larger study, I recently analyzed publications related to second language writing and mapped these publications against variables such as time, research methods, research foci, and cited fields.

My selection of professional literature to analyze is not intended to be exhaustive. Rather, I attempted to assess a sampling of published scholarship representative of the work in second language writing over the past seven decades. To that end, I began my analysis with scholarship that I encountered in my coursework and research projects during my graduate studies. I then added texts from edited collections, composition studies journals, second language studies journals, and the *Journal of Second Language Writing* in an effort to fill noticeable gaps related to topical areas or time periods. Although the larger project looks at second language writing scholarship on an international scale, this particular piece of the project is decidedly focused on the United States.

As a way to analyze the scope and coverage of this professional literature, I charted the geographical locations of the authors and compared the geographical density of the second language writing scholarship to the population densities and geographical distributions of international students in institutions of higher education and of U.S. Census Bureau respondents who speak a language other than English at home or who have limited English proficiency. By visually mapping these comparisons, I was able to identify gaps in the professional literature's representations of second language writers in specific geographical locations where these writers often live, work, and study, which in turn, led me to examine potential gaps in representations of second language writing that occurs in specific educational contexts (K-12, Associate's, and Master's institutions). This type of spatial analysis allows second language writing scholars to better understand the shifting settings for the field's work and to reimagine representations of the field and its boundaries. (For another example of the use of mapping in second language writing scholarship, see Matsuda, 1998.)

Geographical Distributions of Second Language Writing Scholarshipand Second Language Writers

The professional literature that I examined from the 1990s and 2000s was created by scholars working in 33 states, 22 countries and provinces, and Puerto Rico. Figure 1 illustrates the relative frequency of second language writing scholarship in each of the 50 United States, based on the authors' locations. As the figure highlights, the examined publications did not include scholarship from the states of Arkansas, Delaware, Idaho, Kentucky, Maine, Maryland, Mississippi, New

Jersey, North Dakota, Rhode Island, South Carolina, South Dakota, Utah, Vermont, Virginia, West Virginia, or Wisconsin.

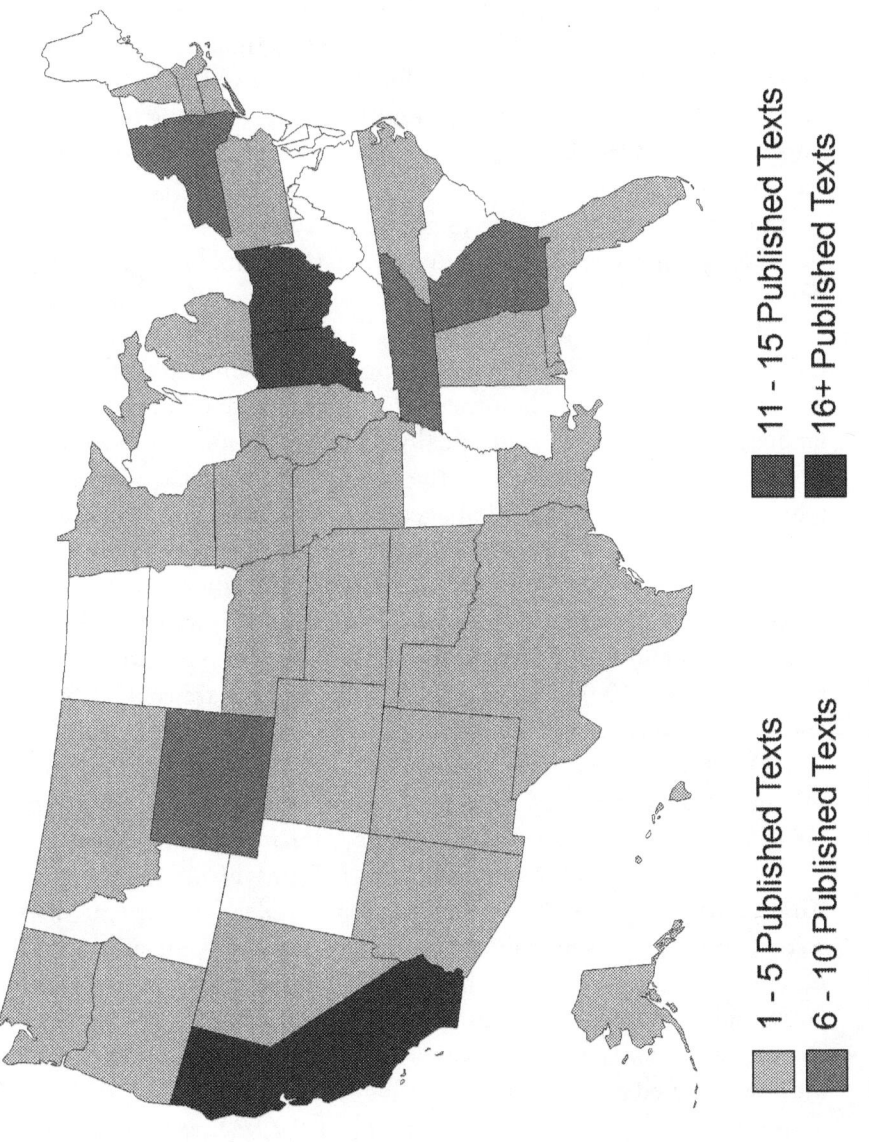

Figure 1. Frequency of publications by state.

Although California's second language writing scholars were represented 25 times in the examined professional literature, 26 states were represented by only one to five professional texts. Ten of these states (Alaska, Connecticut, Kansas, Missouri, Montana, Nevada, New

Mexico, North Carolina, Oregon, and Texas) are represented only once, and seven (Alabama, Arizona, Hawaii, Massachusetts, Michigan, New Hampshire, and Oklahoma) are represented only twice. Of the six states with six to 15 professional texts, Indiana was the site of second language writing scholarship 15 times and Ohio, 13 times. Georgia had eight examples of second language writing scholarship, New York and Wyoming had seven examples each, and Tennessee had six examples.

In part, this representation might be anticipated based on international student populations, bilingual populations, and Carnegie Foundation classifications. If a state has several institutions of higher education that attract international students, that state might be the site of more extensive second language writing research. Similarly, if a state has large bilingual populations, it also might produce more second language writing scholarship. Finally, if an institution is a Doctoral/Research University, scholars at the institution might have more intensive research and publication agendas. As the following discussion reveals, though, these assumptions hold true only part of the time.

Figure 2 shows the number of international students in higher education by state, based on data from the Institute of International Education's (2003b) Open Doors project. As might be expected, several states with over 10,000 international students also are sites of high levels of second language writing scholarship (i.e., California, Indiana, and Ohio). Similarly, New York and Georgia each has over 10,000 international students and moderate levels of second language writing publications. What is surprising, though, is that Arizona, Delaware, Florida, Illinois, Massachusetts, Missouri, Pennsylvania, Texas, and Virginia have high numbers of international students but few, if any, second language writing publications in the examined publication set. Equally surprising, Wyoming had only 491 international students in 2003, but accounted for seven of the 1990s-2000s second language writing professional texts, making it tied with New York as the fifth most represented state.

Similar discrepancies are apparent when the frequency of second language writing publications is compared to the English proficiency of the resident population. Figure 3 shows the percentage of persons five years and over who speak a language other than English at home, according to the U.S. Census Bureau's 2000 census. This data does not include international students studying at U.S. institutions of

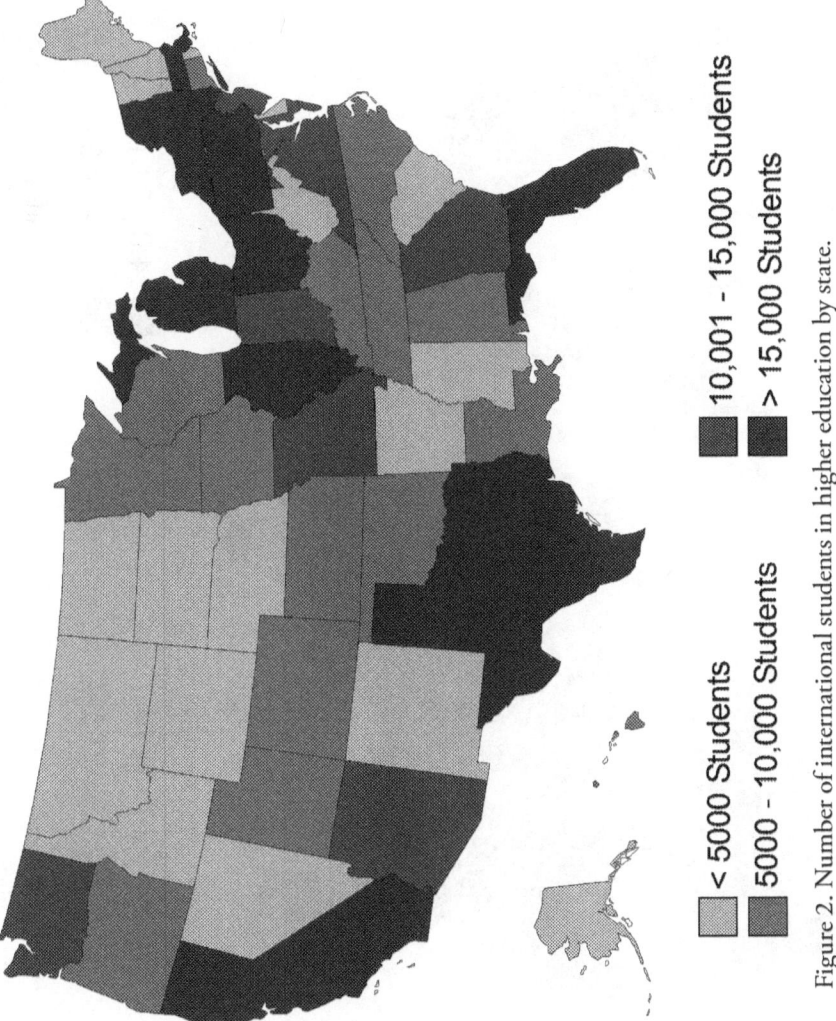

Figure 2. Number of international students in higher education by state. (Data for figure: Institute of International Education, 2003b)

higher education. Although there is a moderate to high percentage of second language speakers in Alaska, Arizona, Colorado, Connecticut, Florida, Hawaii, Illinois, Massachusetts, Nevada, New Jersey, New Mexico, Rhode Island, Texas, and Washington, these states are the sites of limited second language writing scholarship. In contrast, Georgia, Indiana, Ohio, Tennessee, and Wyoming, have very few second language speakers but generated moderate to high levels of the field's scholarship.

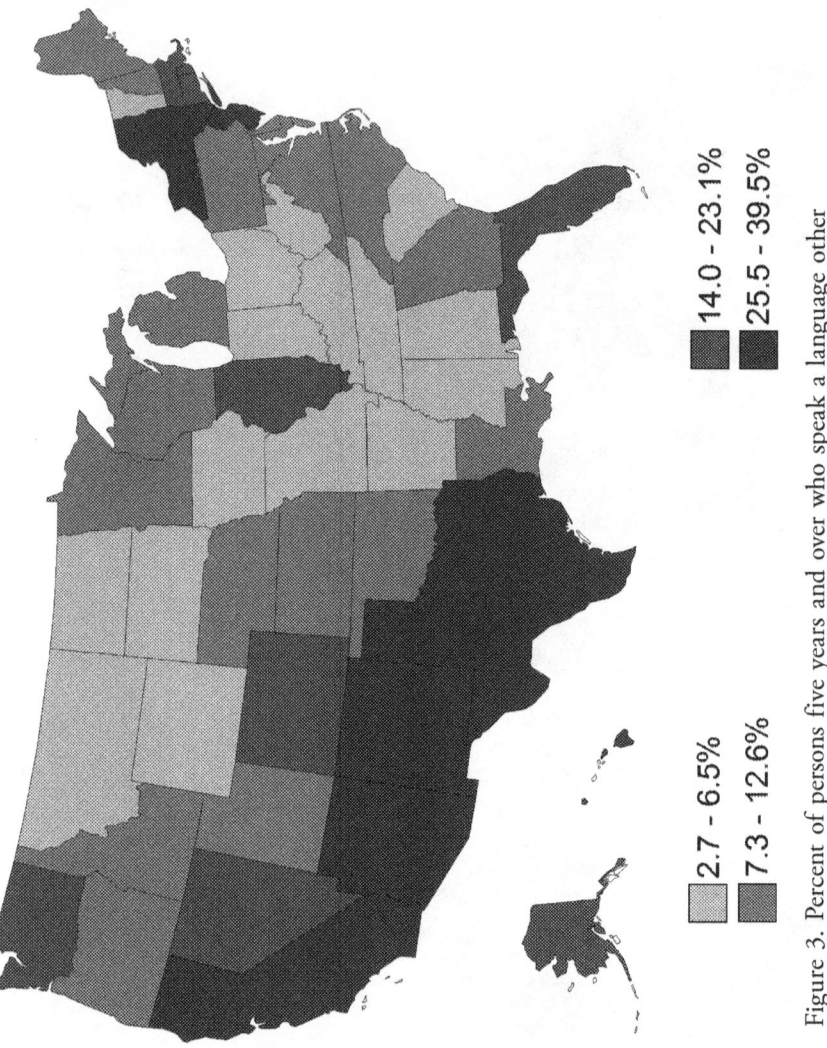

Figure 3. Percent of persons five years and over who speak a language other than English at home. (Data for figure: U.S. Census Bureau)

Figure 4 shows the percentage of limited English proficiency speakers in 2000, according to the U.S. Census Bureau. Once again, several states with larger populations of limited English proficiency speakers reflect a void in second language writing scholarship. Although 14.0—39.5 percent of the total populations in Arizona, Colorado, Connecticut, Florida, Hawaii, Illinois, Massachusetts, Nevada, New Mexico, Oregon, Rhode Island, Texas, and Washington are limited English proficiency speakers, scholars in each of these states produced only one to five of the 1990s and 2000s professional literature publications that

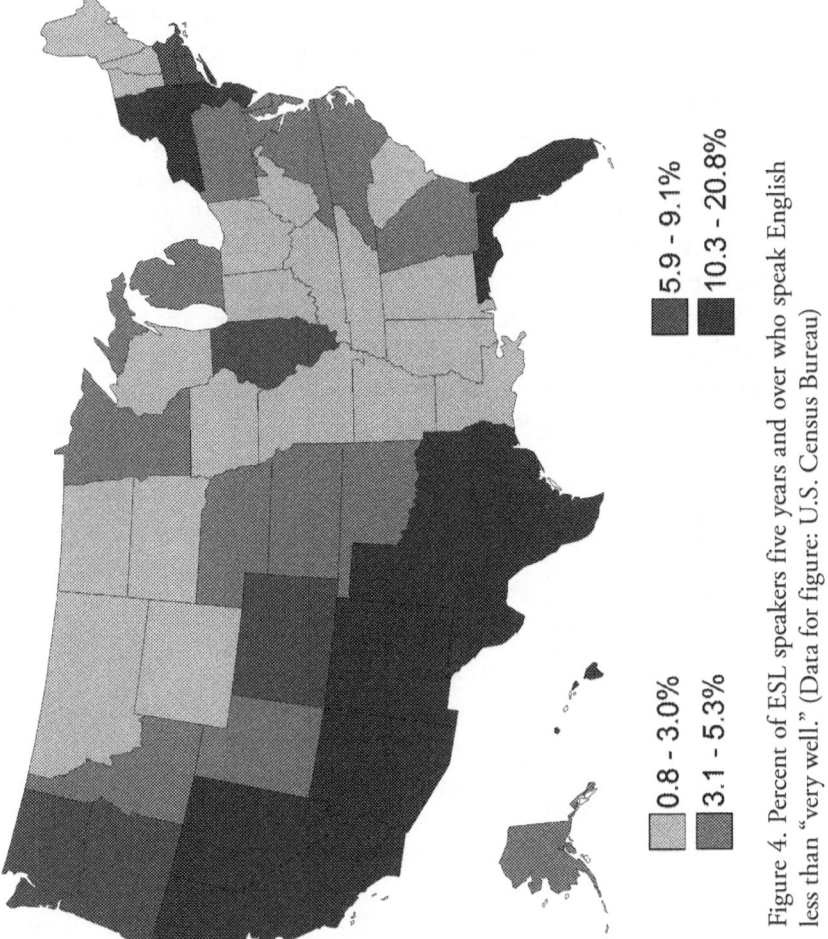

Figure 4. Percent of ESL speakers five years and over who speak English less than "very well." (Data for figure: U.S. Census Bureau)

I examined. Furthermore, despite New Jersey's high percentage of limited English proficiency speakers, no second language writing scholarship from New Jersey scholars was identified in the text collection. As Harklau, Siegal, and Losey (1999) note, California, Florida, Illinois, New Jersey, New York and Texas have large numbers of generation 1.5 students, so it is particularly surprising that Florida, Illinois, New Jersey, and Texas are not better represented in the professional literature, as shown in Figure 1.

IMPACT OF PROMINENT FIELD SCHOLARS AND THEIR INSTITUTIONS' EXPECTATIONS

Some of these discrepancies between a state's population and the amount of second language writing scholarship in the state can be accounted for by considering where prominent second language writing scholars are located. For instance, Wyoming has low populations of second language speakers and international students, but the state is the source of a moderate amount of second language writing scholarship. Since Joy Reid worked at the University of Wyoming, a Doctoral/Research University–Extensive institution, for several decades, it's not surprising that the state is well represented in the publication sample from the last two decades.

Similarly, Robert B. Kaplan, Dana Ferris, and Terry Santos contribute to the publications from California, Tony Silva and Ulla Connor add to the professional literature from Indiana, Ilona Leki publishes extensively from Tennessee, and Joan Carson contributes from Georgia. Other scholars have contributed to the publications from several states as they have moved from institution to institution and developed their careers. For instance, Paul Kei Matsuda has published articles while in Indiana, Ohio, and New Hampshire, and he likely will create a peak in publications in New Hampshire—despite comparatively low international and ESL populations—if he remains in the state.

Overall, then, these mappings suggest that the number of publications in a given state are more dependent on the scholars in the state—and their institutions—than on the state's population of language learners. Out of 140 U.S. contributions to the text sampling, 80 stem from institutions classified as Doctoral/Research University–Extensive in the Carnegie Classifications. An additional 23 contributions come from Doctoral/Research University–Intensive institutions. Doctoral institutions therefore account for the production of nearly 75 percent of published second language writing scholarship. Twenty-five of the remaining contributions (or approximately 18 percent) come from Master's College and Universities I, two come from Associate's Colleges, one originates at an Other Specialized Institution, and two come from K–12 institutions. One contribution stems from a publishing company, and the remaining contributions are not affiliated with an institution. This distribution suggests that most second language writing work occurs in Doctoral/Research Universities, where research is highly valued, even if those schools do not have large populations of second language learners. Although K–12 teachers likely are interacting with second language writers on a daily basis, their daily experiences are not broadly reflected in the fields' professional literature.

Admittedly, local and regional publications might have better representation of scholarship occurring at Master's, Associate's, and K–12 institutions than the distribution suggested by my professional literature selection. I did not include these publications in my sample, though, because I wanted to limit my sampling to second language writing scholarship more easily accessible internationally and nationally to second language writing scholars. While some readers might consider this sampling a limitation of the study, local and regional research likely is represented in internationally and nationally available scholarship that has been informed and influenced by local and regional publications and presentations. Figure 5 reflects this potential trickle-up effect. However, professional literature that is available only locally or regionally will not help the field's scholars around the nation and the globe understand the second language writing that occurs in these local contexts; without access to this locally or regionally distributed scholarship, scholars only gain insight to its claims if they are

Figure 5. Trickle-up effect of second language writing scholarship

referenced in more internationally available publications. Therefore, while the mappings developed from this professional literature sampling might not represent local discourse, they do intimate the geographical distribution of second language writing scholarship available to the field as a whole.

As Table 1 suggests, the distribution of second language writing scholarship locations does not parallel the distribution of international student enrollment by Carnegie classifications. Other than under-representing second language writing at Associate's institutions, the comparisons in this table might not seem alarming, until we remember that these numbers reflect only international student enrollment and do not include the many English language learners, such as the limited English proficiency population identified by the census, who are not identified as international students. This missed population likely studies at underrepresented Associate's institutions (in ESL programs, continuing education programs, community literacy programs, etc), as well as in K-12 schools and other community literacy settings—all underrepresented sites of second language writing.

Table 1. Carnegie classifications and second language writing: Representation in text sampling versus enrollment (Enrollment information: Institute for International Education, 2003a)

	Institutional Affiliations of Authors in Sampling of Second Language Writing Published Texts	Carnegie Classifications of the 50 Institutions with the Highest International Student Enrollment
Doctoral	75%	90%
Master's	18%	3%
Baccalaureate	0%	0%
Associate's	1%	7%

The Role of Carnegie Classifications in the Production of Professional Literature

So why do the Carnegie classifications have such an impact on our field's research? Looking at the missions, goals, and "about our school" statements that schools include on their websites reinforces the distinctions between the Carnegie classifications. Doctoral institutions repeatedly refer to their research and research facilities. The University of Wyoming, where Joy Reid worked while publishing extensively, describes itself as a "Provider of . . . education, research, and outreach services. . . . An outstanding faculty, world-class research facilities" (University of Wyoming, 2004). While research is listed after education, the same statement highlights research facilities—not education facilities. Purdue University, where both Tony Silva and Paul Matsuda have worked, identifies itself as "a public, doctoral-granting research university, and Indiana's land-, sea-, and space-grant university" (Purdue University, 2004). In this statement, research supersedes any reference to education, other than connotations carried by the word "university." Similarly, Ilona Leki's home institution—the University of Tennessee—proclaims that it "offers the highest quality instruction, research, and outreach programs throughout the state of Tennessee. Undergraduate, graduate, and professional education merge seamlessly with the exploration of new knowledge and dissemination of practical information and technology to the state and its citizens" (The University of Tennessee, 2004). Research intertwines "seamlessly" with education, but it clearly has a prominent place in the institutional identity. In all these examples, although education usually is referenced before research, these institutions clearly value—and expect—the research and scholarship reflected in my text sampling.

Master's institutions, on the other hand, emphasize educational goals and opportunities. California State University, Northridge—home of Barbara Kroll—boasts that its website provides "ample evidence of Cal State Northridge's commitment to the educational and professional goals of students, and its extensive service to the community" (California State University, Northridge, 2004). Research isn't even mentioned in this claim, which emphasizes education and service. Similarly, CUNY Baruch notes that "Baruch College traces its roots to 1847, when the Free Academy, the first institution of free public higher education in the country, was founded in New York City to provide educational opportunity and superior academic programs" (Baruch College, 2003). Again, the institution emphasizes a commitment to education and academics and makes no reference to research. California State University, Sacramento, home of Dana Ferris, claims, "We are committed to providing an excellent education to all eligible applicants who aspire to expand their knowledge and prepare themselves for meaningful lives, careers, and service to their community" (California State University, Sacramento, 2004). Once more, the institutional priorities focus on education and service—not on research. Although research likely does occur at these institutions, education and teaching are most esteemed. Consistent with this observation, the texts in my study that were produced at Master's institutions focus more often on describing practice than on presenting research.

Associate's institutions, in turn, highlight addressing learner's needs and facilitating lifelong learning. Houston Community College and Northern Virginia Community College are the two associate's institutions with the highest enrollment by international students, although neither school was represented in my professional literature sampling. Houston Community College enrolled 3,507 international students in 2003, making it the school with the nineteenth highest enrollment of international students among United States institutions (Institute for International Education, 2003a). Houston Community College emphasizes

> Student Success: Opening Doors—Closing Gaps . . . The Houston Community College System is an open-admission, public institution of higher education offering opportunities for academic advancement, workforce training, career development, and lifelong learning that prepare individuals in our diverse communities for life and work in a global and technological society. (Houston Community College System, 2004)

Northern Virginia Community College enrolled 2,865 international students in 2003 and ranked 35th overall (Institute for International Education, 2003a). The school states that its mission "is to respond to the educational needs of its dynamic and diverse constituencies through an array of comprehensive programs and services that facilitate learning and workforce development in an environment of open access and through lifelong educational opportunities" (Northern Virginia Community College, 2002). Although these goals are facilitated by disciplinary research, they do not elicit research by faculty at the institution. Furthermore, the emphasis on teaching and service to the community often limits time and resources available for pursuing research.

Yet Associate's institutions, along with K-12 settings, present some of the largest gaps in our disciplinary knowledge. Therefore, if these institutions do not promote and facilitate research, it falls to disciplinary members in more research intensive settings to collaborate with teachers in underrepresented areas in an effort to fill these disciplinary gaps. And while others previously have initiated the challenge, let me reiterate their call: If we have the means (time, funding, or perhaps most significantly, an institutional value of research) to study underrepresented contexts for second language writing, it is our responsibility to solicit and support collaborations with scholars—experts—in these settings.

For the record, of the 70 presentations (and 81 presenters) listed on the website for the 4th Symposium on Second Language Writing, nine participants represent master's, associate's, or K-12 institutions (Symposium on Second Language Writing, 2004). That's a reasonable starting point.

Carnegie classifications seem to be one of the strongest influences on second language writing scholarship. Scholars working at Doctoral/Research Universities are expected to conduct research and their efforts usually are rewarded with tenure and promotion, so they have a strong incentive to contribute publications to the field's professional literature. Although the distribution of international student populations also has some impact on the amount of published second language writing scholarship from a state, state populations are a secondary influence to institutional classification. After all, even if scholars encounter large populations of second language writers, if their institutions do not value work committed to learning and writing about these populations, scholars may not be able to identify time or funding to support their research. This discrepancy is most notable in examples of the countertrend, such as the high number of second language writing publications in Wyoming, despite the low number of international students and second language speakers. Since the University of Wyoming values research, Joy Reid published extensively while employed by the institution, despite small populations of second language writers. Thus, the institutional classification seems to take precedence over the size of the second language speaking population.

A Renewed Call

Given this trend, it's time to get creative—to find ways to learn about these underrepresented populations of second language writers so that the practices of the devoted scholars working in these settings and their knowledge of their students can better inform our field's other disciplinary work. Second language writing scholars can and should:

- Collaborate with teacher researchers in underrepresented settings, such as K-12, Associate's, and Master's institutions, as well as community programs. Ask teachers in these settings about their classroom observations and practices; work together to publish reports of research, theories, or pedagogies.
- Solicit contributions from scholars working in underrepresented contexts. The ESL CoLearn partnership between the National Council of Teachers of English and Teachers of English to Speakers of Other Languages (TESOL), as well as the development of the Second Language Writing Interest Section at TESOL, provide opportunities for journal and collection editors to invite scholars working in varied geographical and institutional contexts to contribute to the field's growing body of professional literature.
- Participate in local and regional conferences. Encourage presenters to contribute to more widely disseminated second language writing scholarship.
- Work with teacher educators to establish scholastic partnerships with future K-12 teachers who likely will teach second language writers. Help new teachers establish reflective practices and acquire strategies for publishing what they learn in their classrooms.

Taking these and similar steps to fill the gaps in the field's professional literature will help scholars acquire a greater knowledge of and appreciation for the varied contexts in which second language writing occurs, strengthening our field's future research, theories, and pedagogies.

REFERENCES

Baruch College, The City University of New York. (2003). *At a glance.* Retrieved September 29, 2004, from http://www.baruch.cuny.edu/about/glance.html

California State University, Northridge. (2004). *About CSUN.* Retrieved September 29, 2004, from http://www.csun.edu/aboutCSUN/index.html

California State University, Sacramento. (2004). *Mission statement.* Retrieved September 29, 2004, from http://www.csus.edu/webpages/mission.htm

Harklau, L., Siegal, M., & Losey, K. M. (1999). Linguistically diverse students and college writing: What is equitable and appropriate? In L.

Harklau, K. M. Losey, & M. Siegal (Eds.), *Generation 1.5 meets college composition: Issues in the teaching of writing to U.S.–educated learners of ESL* (pp. 1–14). Mahwah, New Jersey: Lawrence Erlbaum Associates.

Houston Community College System. (2004). *Mission & strategic plan: 2003—2006.* Retrieved September 29, 2004, from http://www.hccs.edu/system/admin/mission0306.html

Institute of International Education. (2003a). *Open Doors 2003: Institutions with 1000 or more international students.* Retrieved September 29, 2003, from http://opendoors.iienetwork.org/?p=35937

Institute of International Education. (2003b). *Open Doors 2003: U.S. state fact sheets.* Retrieved June 23, 2004, from http://opendoors.iienetwork.org/?p=36562

Matsuda, P. K. (1998). Situating ESL writing in a cross-disciplinary context. *Written Communication, 15*(1), 99–121.

Northern Virginia Community College. (2002). *NVCC mission.* Retrieved September 29, 2004, from http://www.nvcc.edu/president/mission.htm

Purdue University. (2004). *About Purdue University.* Retrieved September 29, 2004, from http://www.purdue.edu/Purdue/about/index.html

Symposium on Second Language Writing. (2004). *Presenters.* Retrieved September 29, 2004, from http://sslw.jslw.org/2004/presenters.html

The University of Tennessee. (2004). *About the university.* Retrieved September 29, 2004, from http://www.utk.edu/aboutut/

University of Wyoming. (2004). *About UW.* Retrieved September 29, 2004, from http://uwadmnweb.uwyo.edu/UW/aboutuw/

U.S. Census Bureau. (n.d.). Percent of persons 5 years and over who speak a language other than English at home: 2000. Retrieved June 23, 2004, from http://factfinder.census.gov/servlet/ThematicMapFramesetServlet

U.S. Census Bureau. (n.d.). Percent of persons 5 years and over who speak a language other than English at home and speak English less than "very well": 2000. Retrieved June 23, 2004, from http://factfinder.census.gov/servlet/ThematicMapFramesetServlet

14 Institutional Politics in the Teaching of Advanced Academic Writing: A Teacher-Researcher Dialogue

Christine Norris and Christine Tardy

In this chapter, we take the view that both teaching and researching are infused with politics. We use the term *politics* here in a very broad sense, referring to the "relations of power in everything we do and say" (Pennycook, 2001, p. 116), including classroom and research settings. Our chapter explores how politics influence one very local second language writing context: that of one classroom with 10 students, an instructor, and a researcher. More specifically, we focus on the institutional politics of this setting at various levels, including the constraints that academic institutions exert upon course design and delivery; the ways in which the teacher's and students' identities and roles within larger institutions come to bear on classroom relationships and expectations; and the impact that disciplinary institutions and their (real and perceived) borders can have on teachers. We discuss these issues from the vantage points of both the teacher and the researcher, comparing our perspectives and interpretations in order to reach a better understanding of the complexities of the classroom. We hope that the insights gained through this dialogue will be of use to those involved in advanced academic writing courses—both rhetoric and composition specialists and applied linguists—as they consider the dynamics of institutional politics within their own contexts.

The context that we will describe is that of a graduate-level English for Academic Purposes (EAP) writing class offered at Purdue University, a North American research university with a large international student population. The majority of these students at the graduate level were educated in Outer or Expanding Circle countries (Kachru, 1985) prior to their study at Purdue; in most cases, they arrive with limited experience writing in English. In an effort to support these students and their writing development, the English department offers a no-credit, pass-fail writing course that is open to international students across the university. The course, English 002: Written Communication for ESL Graduate Students, is taught by the director of ESL writing (a tenured faculty member) and by graduate teaching assistants with interests and experience in teaching L2 writing. With the exception of an in-house writing class in the department of electrical and computer engineering, English 002 is the only ESL writing course available to graduate students. Multiple sections are offered each semester, and they are generally filled to capacity (10 students per section) with a long waiting list.

The "typical" English 002 student is a male from East Asia, studying in one of the sub-disciplines of engineering. Nevertheless, because of its status as the only writing course for most graduate students, classes may include students from fields as diverse as foreign languages and literature, biology, and civil engineering; these students may be first-semester master's students or dissertation-writing doctoral students. In many cases, students are required by their department or advisor to take the course, but a sizable number of students also enroll voluntarily with the aim of improving their writing.[1] Describing a very similar course, Frodesen (1995) points out the considerable challenges that face course instructors:

> The syllabus for a required course must not only address writing needs across disciplines; it must also adapt to students' various stages of involvement in the larger academic community and in their specific disciplines; it must address varying student motivation and expectations; it may also have to meet specific English or ESL departmental requirements for composition credit. (p. 333)

In the case of the course section we will describe, the instructor (and students) had to negotiate the additional anxiety of being under the gaze of a researcher's eye.

In the remainder of this chapter, we will explore the ways in which various political dimensions impacted the English 002 class taught by one of the authors (Christine Norris, whom we'll refer to here as "Christine"). This class was observed by the second author (Christine Tardy, whom we'll refer to as "Chris") as the first stage of a longitudinal study of the disciplinary writing development of four multilingual graduate students (see Table 1).

Table 1. Details of Participants' Educational and Linguistic Backgrounds

Participant	First language(s)	Field of Study	Degree	Year in program during English 002
John	English; Korean	electrical engineering	M.S.	2nd year
Paul	Chinese	computer sciences	M.S.	2nd year
Yoshi	Japanese	electrical engineering	M.S.	1st year
Chatri	Thai	electrical engineering	Ph.D.	2nd year

As we reflected on the project, we found ourselves struggling with the interpretation of specific classroom behavior—both Christine's and her students—and with the implications of that behavior for teaching advanced EAP. This struggle, of course, is one with which classroom-based researchers will be quite familiar. In our case, we felt that it was important not to let the researcher's voice dominate in interpreting what was occurring during the study. Following the guidelines suggested by feminist researchers such as Lather (1991), we wanted our work to validate both the researcher's and researched's understanding of the study. In what follows, therefore, we revisit the data in a collaborative effort to understand better how the perspectives of student, teacher, and researcher fit together. Through the unconventional form of a dialogue between the researcher (Chris) and the teacher (Christine), we hope to foreground the multiple perspectives involved in any writing classroom and research study, specifically considering how the impact of institutional politics is felt by various "players" in the writing classroom.

BACKGROUND TO THE RESEARCH AND COURSE SETTING

Chris: In the summer of 2002, I began preparing for my study of the development of disciplinary writing skills in a second language. I knew that I wanted to work with a small group of English 002 students and then follow their progress after the course had completed; I also knew that I did not want to research my own students, but that it may be difficult to find another teacher who would open up his or her classroom to my study. I approached Christine (whom I already knew well) to ask if she would be willing to participate in the project. I explained that her participation would involve allowing me to sit in the back of her classroom every day, to audio-record each class session (including individual student conferences with several of the students), to regularly interview four of her students about their writing experiences in her class and others, to collect the writing of those students, and to interview Christine at various points during the term. To my relief and surprise, she quickly and enthusiastically agreed.

Christine: For me, the decision to participate in Chris's research project was an easy one for several reasons. First, I do classroom-specific field work myself, and I'm a firm believer in the importance of researchers experiencing what it is like to be the subject of study. In other words, I don't think that researchers should ask their participants to do something they are not willing to do themselves. Second, in my own work I am interested in examining how the logistics of specific classes (who teaches them, when and where they teach them, and to whom) influence what kinds of writing can be taught. Finally, Chris and I share a common interest in discourse analysis, particularly as it applies to academic writing, so Chris's research overlaps with a lot of my own concerns.

Chris: Christine's semester-long course met for three 50-minute sessions per week. Like other instructors of the course, Christine taught five relatively short assignments; in the class I observed, these assignments included a writer's autobiography, a résumé and cover letter, a conference proposal, a conference poster, and a final genre of each student's choice. Also like other instructors,

Christine placed an emphasis on revision, holding one or two individual conferences with each student before a final draft of each paper was handed in.

Influences of Institutional Politics

Placement and Course Design

> Christine: English 002 is a somewhat unusual class. Since it is the only graduate ESL course available at the university, it draws students from a wide variety of disciplines. Though most of the students are from the sciences and engineering, their sub-specialties are so different that they have little to no shared disciplinary knowledge. The pass/fail grading of the course, coupled with the fact that students receive no university credit and take the course on top of a full graduate course load, means that it is difficult to justify assigning a great amount of outside work. My assignments, then, like those of most of my fellow teachers, emphasized brief yet standard academic genres that could be read and understood by people with different disciplinary backgrounds.
>
> An additional issue I had to consider in my course planning was how best to structure class meetings. My goals were to design a course that would be useful to students at different levels of graduate work and in different fields, would not take up so much time as to interfere with their work in their home departments, and would help them increase both skill and confidence in their writing. Given these goals and the unique needs of each of my students, I didn't think that designing a course that fit the more traditional full-class discussion model would be the best option. In consultation with the director of the program and my fellow teachers, I created a course that alternated between whole-class meetings and individual tutorials. Students were free to substitute assignments with other writing that they felt was more relevant to their work, and I encouraged them to bring in "real world" assignments from their home departments. My hope was that they would be able to immediately apply class work to outside projects.

Chris: When my research first began, I had guessed that issues of placement would play an important role in the writers' experiences in and attitudes about the course. Because they were all required to enroll in English 002, I suspected that the students would have some resentment about the requirement—a demand not made on their domestic peers. In fact, only one student ("John") expressed any such concern; as a Korean national who was educated in the U.S. through elementary school, John considered himself to be a native speaker of English and felt that the course was probably more helpful to those with less proficient English skills.

A second issue that I assumed might arise was related to the multidisciplinary mix of students in the class; specifically, I wondered if students would feel that a disciplinary-specific course might better address their needs. Instead, all four of the students that I worked with saw the multi-disciplinarity of English 002 as an advantage. Paul, for example, enjoyed the opportunity to collaborate with students in other fields:

> I think if all the people are from my department it would be more difficult to prepare the [presentation] slides [for one assignment] because I would think more about the technical content. *And I think diversity is very important to exchange ideas.* Because this class should be focused on the language, not the technical things, and I think by doing the pair work or collaboration, *I can learn something from others because they have some thoughts that I have not, and they will help me to broad my thoughts.* (Paul, 12/12/02, emphasis added)

Similarly, Yoshi noted that "it is interesting to speak [with] another person who has completely different background" (Yoshi, 12/04/02). Their comments illustrate the writers' general agreement that because the course was an *English* course, it need not be discipline-specific. Furthermore, the classroom diversity allowed students to become experts at times, as they shared their fields' practices and conventions and contrasted these with other students' and Christine's. In this way, the institutional influences on course design seemed to work to the students' advantage—at least in their eyes.

In response to the diversity of disciplinary backgrounds and educational level, Christine individualized the class in the ways that she's already described. Students found this individualization to be a real strength; they appreciated the feedback in conferences, and they liked having the opportunity to fulfill the assignments with writing tasks that they needed to do anyway. As a graduate student who had no way to change the constraints imposed on the course, Christine instead adopted productive methods to work within it.

Credit and Grading

> Christine: One of the major factors in the design of the course was that it was pass-fail with no credit. On the one hand, students did not have the pressure of grading and the class could be a more informal workshop setting. On the other hand, I often felt that some students did not push themselves as much as they would in a graded course. Because it was low-stakes, English 002 was clearly the last priority for many of my students, and I can't blame them for putting it last. My students had enormous amounts of high-stakes work to do, both in the courses they took and in their research labs. I felt torn between wanting the class to be more of a central part of my students' academic lives and realizing, given the high-demands of their own fields, that it was difficult for them to give the class more of their time than they were already.

> Chris: The issue of course credit came up at the start of my first interview with Christine when I asked her to describe the course as she would to another teacher. Her first response was that "[English] 002 is a no credit, pass-fail course for graduate students" (08/28/02). In the first few days of the term, she described the course to students as "a low pressure class," telling them "You have to work hard not to get credit" and "If you do the work, you'll pass." It seemed to me that Christine stressed this point to set a more comfortable and relaxing tone for the course, one that would allow students to take risks in their writing, perhaps try out new things, ask questions, and make the course meet their individual needs rather than trying to fit their needs into a more rigid format.

The students did take a relaxed approach to the course, but as a researcher, I wondered if it was at times too relaxed. At the end of the course, I asked each of the students to describe English 002 to me as they might to a peer who was considering taking it; their responses reflect an emphasis on credit and grading. Each of the writers began by describing the course as easy, saying, it is "not difficult," "not so demanding," "the workload is not high," or "you don't have to do much to pass the course." Reflecting on the course eight months after having completed it, Paul admitted that he put in less effort because of the informal nature of the course. He said to me, "Maybe we should suggest to give more pressure in that English class . . . But if they increase pressure in that class, maybe people won't take it" (08/04/03). It is also important to note that both Paul and Yoshi felt that the most important thing they had gained from the course was an increased confidence in their writing—one of Christine's goals for the course.

But the challenge for teachers becomes judging how much pressure is too much. Perhaps there is an optimal level of pressure that can allow students to increase their confidence but also encourage greater student investment. Chatri, for example, explained to me that lower expectations from the course led him to lower his expectations of his own writing. He drew a clear distinction between his writing for English 002 (and his engineering courses) and his research writing, saying:

> . . . in 002, I don't think that the instructor expect too much, so when I'm writing, I still didn't expect too much also. Right? But, when you write *this* [a conference paper], you write for *our research*, we expect very much [laughs], and we know that the reader expect very much too. (01/23/04)

Christine: For me, Chatri's quote encapsulates the difficulties of this course. On the one hand, the course can not be too demanding of the students' time and must be general enough to meet the needs of different students. On the other, if the students do not feel pressured to work, they may not put in as much effort into the class as they would otherwise.

Broader Social Spaces

> Chris: One of the most important benefits of Christine's interviews for me was that they forced me to recognize that the classroom is not a vacuum in which the teacher (and students) can filter out the other messy elements of their lives. While the students and teacher in this English writing course were not living within a larger social context as difficult or dangerous as that of Canagarajah's (1993) English class in Sri Lanka, the decisions that they made in the classroom were nevertheless linked to their lives outside of the classroom walls. Christine's interpretations of her teaching that term, for example, were heavily influenced by the pressures of her daily life at that time. She spent much of the time in our interviews berating herself for everything with which she felt dissatisfied, particularly at the end of the semester. Even a year after the course had finished, when I asked her to expand on some of her earlier comments, she again went back to the ways in which the realities of her student life had impacted her teaching at the time.

> Christine: During the time Chris was observing my class, I was completing my dissertation and looking for my first tenure-track job. Consequently, I was under a great deal of stress, and this stress manifested itself in my hyper-critical evaluation of my own teaching performance. In addition, the irony was not lost on me that I was teaching a class centered on helping students write job documents, professional presentations, and dissertations, while I myself was in the midst of composing these documents and unsure of my own ability to succeed at writing them.

> Chris: While Christine's time was stretched between job applications and dissertation writing, the students in her classroom similarly struggled with their own personal concerns. During this semester, Yoshi was acclimating to a new country while living halfway around the world from his wife and new baby whom he had not even met yet. John was consumed with researching doctoral programs at schools in other states and navigating the sociocultural conventions for asking for letters of recommendation or contacting professors with whom he hoped to work. Paul was struggling with the decision of whether to continue

on for a doctoral degree or to graduate with an M.S. and search for a job, either in the U.S. or back home in China. And Chatri was preparing for a second attempt to pass his qualifying exams so that he could move on to the next stage of his very difficult doctoral program. Certainly, they faced additional challenges and issues that I was unaware of, but the point that should be stressed is that the classroom is a complex space for each individual. Like Christine, each of these writers had their own set of circumstances that seeped into the classroom walls, influencing their classroom interactions and performance in various ways. Their outside lives influenced their choices in which genres they chose to write in, how much time they invested in various assignments, and their individual goals and expectations for the course as a whole.

Institutional Roles and Identities

> Christine: Much has been written about the power dynamic between teachers and students (see, for example, Elbow, 1998), and many teachers acknowledge the ways in which status, power, and authority influence what can be said in the classroom. However, as Susan Jarratt (1991) has noted, classroom politics are not as simple as a powerful teacher dominating a powerless student; we bring the outside world into our teaching and research, and identity issues of status, gender, ethnicity, language, and academic roles and hierarchies can create a continuing fluctuation in the politics of the classroom. Perhaps ironically, one of the most difficult parts of teaching 002 for me was my uncertainty about my own qualifications for teaching the course. First, as a doctoral student in an English department, I was teaching a course to my fellow graduate students in other university departments. Second, I was a student in the humanities teaching students who were, for the most part, from the sciences and working on projects that were completely foreign to me. Therefore, I felt it was inappropriate to teach the course as an "expert" given that I had little knowledge of their fields and was at the same level of study as my students. I did know, however, about academic writing in English, and about strategies for composing, so I focused the class on those areas, and I

adjusted my teaching persona to fit the class and my perception of my role in it.

Chris: When Christine discussed her approach to this course in our first interview, she described herself as a "peer" and "a native speaker friend who happens to have rhetorical training" (08/28/02). The students did see (and refer to) her as a *writing teacher*, but they were also relatively informal with her and often perked up in class when she shared her own experiences of writing as a graduate student. In other words, it seemed to me that she used her graduate student ethos to her advantage, foregrounding it rather than attempting to hide it.

At the end of English 002, I asked each of the students whether the instructor's lack of content knowledge in their fields influenced the course in any way. Rather than viewing this lack of knowledge as a weakness, they focused on the importance of having an instructor who is knowledgeable of how writing works and how to teach it:

> I think it's very advantageous [to have a non-engineering instructor], because, you know, *they concentrate on the English, I mean, on the wording and everything*. I mean, the content itself- if you have trouble with the content, I mean, you really shouldn't be writing it. So, usually what's wrong is the wording or some other, like, small mistake that you probably just overlooked. I mean, if you're a pretty competent writer, I guess, I think it's a really big plus. And, um, people in the same field, if they look at it, they might miss the same mistake as you do, they're used to some conventions and stuff—which may be wrong. (John, 12/10/02, emphasis added)

> . . . *I think the instructor from the English department maybe get some more writing skill to teach.* What do you call? For example, you. You are specializing in writing. You can teach, okay, how to teach the student to write a good paper. You have more skill to teach than the EE [Electrical Engineering] professor. I don't know. (Chatri, 12/02/02, emphasis added)

As a researcher, I found it even more interesting that three of the four writers claimed to modify their classroom writing for the non-specialist audience of the instructor. Paul, for example, said that he wrote for the class "in a very simple way, simple to understand" (12/12/02). Yoshi described writing "in a more general way" for Christine, trying "not to use difficult words." Furthermore, he noted that when writing for someone with shared content knowledge, he "might concentrate more to the precision of technical contents" (12/04/02). Because disciplinary writing involves knowing how to communicate within a community of experts, what are the implications of altering one's work for non-experts in a classroom setting? Is it possible for students to really practice discipline-specific writing in an English course, or instead, is the usefulness of a writing classroom that it allows writers to temporarily filter out the other "noise" of content and audience, focusing instead on form? This, to me, seemed to be the students' expectation.

Christine: In addition to the unease I felt about my (non-science) disciplinary background, I also felt some concern about how I was adjusting to the theoretical frame of the course itself. English 002, as described in the various instructional documents I received and through examining other instructors' materials, was designed with a strong theoretical base in applied linguistics. Since I am a rhetoric and composition specialist and have studied field-specific writing, there was some overlap between my background and the theory from which the course emerged. However, I still felt as if I didn't understand enough of the applied linguistics theory behind the course to make decisions about what to teach and when to teach it. Therefore, I often thought that my own decisions about what to teach seemed quite arbitrary, especially when I was helping students with micro-level concerns, as I'll explain below. I continually doubted my own ability to create a class that was going to be useful to my students.

Disciplinarity

Chris: I find Christine's struggle with disciplinary lines intriguing because it says much about the assumptions made of writing courses for second language writers. While theoretical discussions of advanced L2 writing can be found in interdisciplinary forums like *Journal of Second Language Writing* and *Written Communication,* pedagogical discussions of courses like English 002 are generally published in "applied linguistics" journals like *Journal of English for Academic Purposes* or *English for Specific Purposes.* This pedagogical literature tends to draw more heavily on scholars such as John Swales rather than, for example, Charles Bazerman. As a researcher, I've tried to ignore such disciplinary boundaries, but Christine's struggle has made me wonder whether these distinctions may be more profound for *teachers.* The most common resources for advanced L2 writing courses, for instance, are the Swales and Feak (1994, 2000) textbooks, which draw rather heavily on applied linguistics research in text analysis and corpus linguistics but say much less about, for example, forum analysis, rhetorical appeals, or *kairos*—all very important elements of advanced academic writing and much more familiar tools to rhetoric and composition scholars. In other words, pedagogical resources for graduate-level L2 writing courses seem to still follow the disciplinary division of labor model that Matsuda (1998, 1999) described in the late 1990s.

Christine: I tried to select writing tasks that I thought would be typical for graduate students across the disciplines—CVs, abstracts, conference posters. In class I asked students to examine examples of these genres from different fields and from a variety of writers and to look for patterns. What similarities and differences, for example, did they see in the ways CVs were written by electrical engineers looking for corporate jobs and art history majors looking for assistant professorships? I also asked students to think about the ways in which who they were, their relationship with their readers, and their level of disciplinary expertise, influenced their writing. For example, we spent some time discussing the pros and cons of giving oneself an English name for professional correspondence. If a student is looking for a job in the U.S., what is given up and what is gained if he anglicizes his name?

These activities are similar to ones that I had taught in my rhetoric and composition classes, and I felt relatively comfortable teaching them. Where I had difficulty was in my ability to help students adopt the word choice, stylistic features, and language of their field. I knew that there were several tools from linguistics that would be helpful to me in assisting students in their word choice, such as a number of online language corpora, but I didn't feel I understood how to use these well enough myself to spend much time in class teaching others about them. When working with students on language-level concerns, therefore, I often ended up falling back on helping students with general grammar points or referring them to their instructors or peers in their field to check on whether the way they were writing was common practice.

Chris: This question of how much to focus on language and how much to focus on more global issues is one all L2 writing teachers deal with and their practice generally depends on their comfort level in different areas and on their students' needs. Among Christine's students, I saw a range of expectations and needs. While John was purely interested in the more rhetorical elements of writing, Chatri was interested only in what he called "general writing skills"—structuring sentences, paragraphs, and sections of documents. Christine's approach to the course allowed her to address these issues to different extents with different writers. Her expertise in rhetoric and composition provided her with an interesting lens on issues like *ethos* and audience and a very dynamic understanding of text, but it did not equip her with the tools necessary for giving the kind of grammatical feedback that she (and many of the students) felt they also needed.

QUESTIONS FOR FURTHER EXPLORATION

As we have reflected on Christine's English 002 class, we've found our conversations circling around a number of core questions about the institutional politics surrounding graduate-level ESL writing courses. These questions, we feel, serve as some of the central variables influencing the class dynamics and the kinds of work accomplished in the course.

Is there an optimal level of pressure necessary for real learning? If so, how do teachers find and maintain a good balance given their institutional constraints? Teachers tend to think of course evaluations as the institutional constraint that most often discourages them from putting pressure on students. Conventional wisdom, put forth in such places as *The Chronicle of Higher Education,* argues that if course evaluations went away, teachers would feel free to put more pressure on students and that this pressure would result in a higher quality of student work.[2] Our study questions both of these truisms. Christine's reluctance to push her students had little-to-nothing to do with evaluations, and seemed to have more to do with the format of the course, who was enrolled, and under what circumstances. We wonder if more attention should be paid to how the ways in which courses are structured on an administrative level influence the kinds of work that are done in them.

How do the constraints of the classroom support and/or discourage the skills necessary for writing to and in a disciplinary community? The students in this study seemed to feel primarily that the writing classroom was intended to improve their general writing skills of grammar and organization; they believed that they would learn discipline-specific skills through disciplinary practice. In fact, research—including the longitudinal results of the present study—does suggest that disciplinary practice plays a pivotal role in disciplinary writing development and rhetorical knowledge (e.g., Haas, 1994; Prior, 1998). At the same time, many students in courses like English 002 are not actively involved in writing in their disciplines. Master's degree students like Yoshi and John often do not work on independent research projects, do not write a thesis, and (therefore) do not have a faculty mentor. In the absence of these support features, the writing classroom offers an important space for practicing writing—both general and disciplinary. Yet when students must modify their writing in order to make it understandable to the (English) teacher, they miss out on practicing one of the most fundamental elements of advanced academic writing: persuading a knowledgeable reader of the value of the content. In her case study of a graduate student enrolled in a similar course, Hansen (2000) found that the issue of audience was crucial for "Mei-Huei," who was unable to resolve the conflicts of audience, purpose, and content knowledge that she experienced when asked to write for her ESL instructor as though she were writing for a specialist. As teachers of such courses know, however, the picture is not always grim; many students express gratitude for having the opportunity to practice writing and to receive feedback from someone with writing expertise. The challenge for course instructors is to find ways to address the inherent conflicts of audience and content within the constraints of the classroom.

How can further exploration of the politics of identity and institutional roles provide insights into the learning process? In reflecting on many of Christine's self-doubts about the classroom, we were both struck with the very powerful importance of the institutional roles that she played (or, more aptly, juggled) while teaching the course. These roles as peer, teacher, native-speaker informant, rhetoric and composition specialist, job-seeking and dissertation-writing graduate student all influenced what she taught and how she taught it. At the same time, the students juggled their own roles which influenced their approaches to various tasks and assignments. The somewhat chaotic politics of identity and institutional roles are clearly significant in understanding the successes and failures of any given class; in graduate-level writing classes, the institutional roles of teacher and student may be even more ambiguous or complex than in a traditional undergraduate class. The balances of power do not flow in the typical directions, as students may hold more academic, symbolic, or even economic capital than their teachers; factors like age, ethnicity, race, gender, and linguistic background add additional layers of complexity. Our conversations with other teachers of English 002—who include native and nonnative speakers of English, graduate students and tenured faculty, rhetoric and composition, professional writing, and applied linguistics specialists—lead us to see identity as having a profound effect on the shape of the classroom and the learning processes. We believe that a careful examination of these roles—and perhaps an open classroom discussion of these roles—can benefit teachers and students, and we would like to see future studies of advanced academic writing explore this issue in more depth.

How does scholarship on disciplinary writing for advanced L2 writers favor an applied-linguistics orientation over a rhetoric-and-composition orientation? Despite our belief that ESL writing is—and must be—an interdisciplinary field of study that draws on both applied linguistics and rhetoric and composition, the disciplinary division of labor model still seems largely in place in advanced academic L2 writing instruction. Unlike first-year composition, graduate-level writing classrooms rarely include both native- and nonnative English writers; in fact, the teaching of advanced academic writing is almost exclusively an ESL (or, more aptly, multilingual) writing endeavor.[3] As a result, the bulk of literature on the subject is written within applied linguistics-oriented forums, while the subject of graduate student writing in general has not been an active area of research with composition studies (cf. Prior,

1998). We believe that a truly multidisciplinary model for advanced academic ESL writing instruction is still absent.

In what ways might collaborative research paradigms provide new insights in classroom research? Because our focus in this chapter has been on gaining new insights into the writing classroom through collaborative teacher-research dialogue, we have backgrounded the politics of our research itself. We are certainly aware that the constant presence of a researcher is not unnoticed and that it adds to the "relations of power" to which we referred at the start of this chapter. Our primary goal here, however, has been to use our different vantage points, roles, and disciplinary backgrounds to probe the institutional politics at play in Christine's classroom. Our collaborative dialogue has allowed each of us to see the same events from a new perspective, uncovering at least some of the invisible forces that might help us make better sense of the learning environment. The experience has been rewarding for us, and we hope that other researcher-teacher collaborators might adopt similar approaches in interpreting their own classroom contexts.

Notes

[1] Silva, Reichelt, and Lax-Farr (1994) describe the course as bringing together EAP, process writing, and student-centered approaches; see their article for a more detailed description of the course.

[2] See, for example, recent articles by Kamber and Biggs (2002), and Smallwood (2004).

[3] We are aware of a small number of dissertation writing and grant writing courses offered to native-English graduate students at research universities, but these courses seem to be relatively rare.

References

Canagarajah, A. S. (1993). Critical ethnography of a Sri Lankan classroom: Ambiguities in student opposition to reproduction through ESOL. *TESOL Quarterly, 27,* 601–626.

Elbow, P. (1998). *Writing without teachers.* New York: Oxford University Press.

Frodesen, J. (1995). Negotiating the syllabus: A learning-centered, interactive approach to ESL graduate writing course design. In D. Belcher & G. Braine (Eds.), *Academic writing in a second language: Essays on research and pedagogy* (pp. 331–350). Norwood, NJ: Ablex.

Haas, C. (1994). Learning to read biology: One student's rhetorical development in college. *Written Communication, 11,* 43–84.

Hansen, J. (2000). Interactional conflicts among audience, purpose, and content knowledge in the acquisition of academic literacy in an EAP course. *Written Communication, 17,* 27–52.

Jarratt, S. (1991). Feminism and composition: The case for conflict. In P. Harkin & J. Schlib (Eds.), *Contending with words: Composition and rhetoric in a postmodern age* (pp. 105–123). New York: Modern Language Association.

Kachru, B. B. (1985). Standards, codification and sociolinguistic realism: The English language in the outer circle. In R. Quirk & H. G. Widdowson (Eds.), *English in the world: Teaching and learning the language and literatures* (pp. 11–30). Cambridge: Cambridge University Press.

Kamber, R., & Biggs, M. (2002, April 12). Grade conflation: a question of credibility. *The Chronicle of Higher Education.* Retrieved December 5, 2004, from http://www.chronicle.com

Lather, P. (1991). *Getting smart: Feminist research and pedagogy with/in the postmodern.* New York: Routledge, Chapman, and Hall, Inc.

Matsuda, P. K. (1998). Situating ESL writing in a cross-disciplinary context. *Written Communication, 15,* 99–121.

Matsuda, P. K. (1999). Composition studies and ESL writing: A disciplinary division of labor. *College Composition and Communication, 50,* 699–721.

Pennycook, A. (2001). *Critical applied linguistics: A critical introduction.* Mahwah, NJ: Lawrence Erlbaum Associates.

Prior, P. A. (1998). *Writing/Disciplinarity: A sociohistoric account of literate activity in the academy.* Mahwah, NJ: Lawrence Erlbaum Associates.

Smallwood. S. (2004, January 30). Professors lose money for awarding too many A's. *The Chronicle of Higher Education.* Retrieved December 5, 2004, from http://www.chronicle.com

Silva, T., Reichelt, M., & Lax-Farr, J. (1994). Writing instruction for ESL graduate students: Examining issues and raising questions. *ELT Journal, 48,* 197–204.

Swales, J. M., & Feak, C. B. (1994). *Academic writing for graduate students.* Ann Arbor: University of Michigan Press.

Swales, J. M., & Feak, C. B. (2000). *English in today's research world.* Ann Arbor: University of Michigan Press.

15 Shifting Sites, Shifting Identities: A Thirty-Year Perspective

Stephanie Vandrick

As the theme of this volume is a focus on the politics of the institutions where second language writing programs are housed, I feel compelled to tell the story of my institution, the University of San Francisco (USF), where I have been a faculty member for the 30-plus years that the ESL program has existed there. Here I describe the many changes the program has undergone, and the contexts, causes and consequences of those changes. In those thirty-plus years, the ESL writing program, along with the rest of the ESL program, has had five different names and structures, including several changes in affiliation and reporting line: It has been an independent program, an academic department, and a part of a larger academic department; it has ranged from being entirely disconnected from the L1 writing program to being part of the same department. These changes have taken place within, and been greatly affected by, the context of larger changes within the university, including curricular changes, faculty unionization, major shifts in university administration, dramatic ebbs and flows in the number and types of international students enrolled, and emphatic changes in the mission and goals of the university. Further, the changes have taken place in the context of larger changes in the TESOL profession.

I would like to note here that although this is an essay about the shifting sites and identities of ESL within the larger institution, my own professional history is so intertwined with the story of the program that I cannot clearly separate one story from the other; thus my chapter is at least partially a narrative, with elements of a personal narrative. (For a more personal version of this story, please see Vandrick, 2003.) Note that—as part of a move against limiting the definition of research to quantitative, experimental research paradigms—personal narrative (including teacher narratives) has become an increasingly common and accepted mode of inquiry in academe, and in particular in composition studies (Fontaine & Hunter, 1993; Hindman, 2003; Roen, Brown, & Enos, 1989; Trimmer, 1997). Narratives provide some of the same kinds of data that ethnographic research, case studies, interviews, and diary studies provide. (For further discussion of the place of personal narrative in scholarly writing, please see Casanave & Schecter, 1997; Casanave & Vandrick, 2003; Connelly & Clandinin, 1999; Haroian-Guerin, 1999; Ritchie & Wilson, 2000). Here it is my intention, however, to contextualize the story in a larger framework, and I hope that this essay thereby sheds light on connections between individual stories and institutional stories, and on the implications of these stories for the future of ESL, and ESL writing, at our institutions.

The History

I will begin with a brief history of ESL and ESL writing at USF, then will list relevant factors influencing that history, and will go on to outline some of the implications of the various stages and sites the program has gone through.

The ESL program was initially established at the University of San Francisco in 1974, and was essentially an Intensive English Program that enrolled both matriculated and nonmatriculated students. It was called the "English Language Center," and was set up as an independent program that was led by an administrative director who reported to the vice president for academic affairs. The program had little connection to the rest of the university.

In the second year of the program, the full-time faculty were moved from term appointments to tenure-track appointments, an important improvement in the status of the faculty and the program, and one that was to make a critical difference.

Although the enrollment was large and the program was academically and financially successful, there was much political turmoil that led to a change in directors and to the renaming of the program, in 1976, as the "World English Center." In 1979, the center was rehoused in the college of arts and sciences and the administration-appointed director reported to the dean of that college.

A few difficult years of further turmoil later, the university decided to limit international student enrollment, and serve only matriculated students. At that point when the program was, for the first time, *not* an intensive program, the university in 1985 renamed it once again, as the "Intensive English Program."

During this time period, there were many difficulties and skirmishes between the administration and the faculty, especially about workload. Although the ESL faculty was technically declared equal to other faculty at the university, the administration both at the program level and at the university-wide level resisted according ESL faculty the same status and working conditions as "real" faculty. For one example, the ESL faculty were required to teach many more hours than other faculty did; one dean at the time justified this decision by stating that ESL faculty did not have to do any preparation, but merely walked into class, opened a grammar book, and taught. Worse, several faculty members were fired. Others who stayed were repeatedly denied tenure and then promotion. It was only with the support of the new faculty association—a union (more about this later)—that any of the faculty (in some cases only after extended appeal and arbitration processes) kept or were reinstated to their positions and were, eventually, tenured and promoted. However, many more were never reinstated, and to this day there are far fewer full-time faculty members than there were during the first years.

A few long years later, in 1992, with more changes in administration, and in particular with the understanding of a supportive new dean of arts and sciences, the program became the "ESL Department." This change was a real turning point, and was enormous in its implications. It recognized that the ESL program and faculty were equal and equivalent to other disciplines and faculty on campus, and should therefore have the same department status as, for example, history, biology, or sociology. This new status allowed the faculty to elect a chairperson and control the curriculum, policies, and budget of the department, rather than being directed by administrators.

The fourth and last (to date) change—to the fifth name, site and status—occurred in 1999, when the dean asked the ESL faculty to consider the possibility of becoming part of a newly forming department, "Communication Studies." This department would combine the communication major, the ESL program, and the L1 writing program (that up to this point had been called the Expository Writing

Program, but soon became the Rhetoric and Composition program). Although there were some political and personnel-related reasons for this proposed change, the primary reason was that such a department structure would facilitate much closer coordination and articulation among the three related programs, and would allow for curricular connections and innovations. The three programs would continue to have much autonomy, but would also work together as a department.

After much discussion, all three units agreed to this new departmental structure. (Note that the fact that the faculty was consulted at all was a huge improvement from the first 16 years of the ESL program's existence.) The ESL faculty reasoned that although in joining the larger department we would lose some of the independence we had enjoyed as a separate department, we would gain in strength, clout, and status. And although there have been some rough spots in establishing the new department, overall it has in fact turned out to be a successful and productive situation, and we look forward to even more collaboration and mutually beneficial curricular and other projects.

As a sign of the ESL program's equal role in the new department, let me note that in 2002 the coordinator of the ESL division was elected by the communication studies department faculty as its new chair, and in 2005, she was elected to another three-year term. She, a senior member of the campus faculty, whose having served as chair of the arts council and in other positions of leadership within the college and university has enhanced her credibility and visibility within the university, is recognized by all in the department to be doing an outstanding job as chair, one who has been actively instrumental in promoting and facilitating cooperation among the three units.

OTHER RELEVANT FACTORS IN THIS STORY

There are several relevant factors that were involved in the program faculty's ability to make these last two positive changes in our position, status, and effectiveness at the university: the first change being becoming a department, and the second change being becoming stronger through joining a larger department. The most important of these change-promoting factors are as follows.

1. Unionization

First and probably foremost in importance is the fact that the faculty at the university became unionized in 1975. This was a long, hard fight, with many difficult consequences, but it was necessary and beneficial for faculty, and therefore for the atmosphere and quality of the university. The unionization came at a very good time for the ESL program and faculty: Although it also intensified the already-existing acrimony between faculty and administration, and led to many terribly difficult years, the union with its processes and protections was able to preserve the full-time tenure track positions in ESL, and helped to make—eventually—the ESL faculty's working conditions approach equality with other faculty's. I would also like to point out that much later the university's part-time faculty—including the ESL part-time instructors—also unionized, and were able to earn many protections, including a sort of modified tenure called the "preferred hiring pool," along with much-improved pay and some medical and other benefits.

I know that some academics do not approve of unions for faculty, but I believe that when working under difficult and unfair administrations, unions provide the only way to balance, at least somewhat, the power equation. In our case, the status of our program and its faculty would be far lower if it were not for the union.

2. Changes in Administration

The second most important factor in the ESL program's progress was changes in the university administration, most notably the appointment of a new dean of the college of arts and sciences who came from the faculty and had been active in the faculty association (the union). He had initially been appointed by the university administration as acting dean. Before a search for a more permanent dean was launched, a compelling majority of the college faculty—including the ESL faculty—signed a petition and wrote letters strongly requesting that he be retained as dean. The administration, clearly somewhat surprised by this display of near-unanimity, acquiesced. This event was a strong indication both of the power of the faculty under the union, and of the administration's graceful realization that it was more productive to work with the faculty rather than maintain an adversarial relationship.

This new dean was the first senior administrator at USF who treated the ESL program and faculty as equal to other programs and faculties. He was the one who facilitated our becoming an academic department, with a faculty chair. He also reduced our teaching load to match other faculty's, procured us private offices (finally!), and encouraged and supported our research and other academic and professional activities.

Please take a moment to imagine the difference it makes to have a senior administrator who supports your work and takes it as a given that you should be treated like any other program and faculty. And as trivial as it sounds to those who have fortunately been able to take these things for granted, imagine how it feels to finally—after many years—have access to travel and research funds, and to have a decent private office, with one's own computer, telephone, windows, and lock on the door!

3. University's Shifting Stance on Internationalism and Multiculturalism

Another important change was the university's widely shifting stance on internationalism and multiculturalism. In the mid-1970s, the university had one of the largest proportions of international students of any university; in addition, because of its location in the multicultural San Francisco Bay Area, there were many students from a multiplicity of ethnic backgrounds, particularly Asian. Some of the university's traditional constituencies (especially among the alumni and the board of trustees) were concerned that the university was becoming *too* diverse; the university administration apparently agreed, and drastically cut the number of international students it enrolled. In other words, the university at that time did not really see international and immigrant students—at least as such a large proportion of the enrolled students—as an asset. However, in the past 10 to 15 years, the university has—to its credit—evidenced a huge turnaround in its attitude, now seeing and strongly emphasizing the benefits of a diverse student population. One of the official strategic initiatives, according to the university catalog, is to "Enroll, support and graduate a diverse student body . . ." (USF Catalog, 2005–2007, p. 5). And in 2004 and 2005 the university president announced with pride that USF was listed in the *Princeton Review* as one of the most diverse universities in the country. This change in the university's stance was partly a response to the changing times, partly a function of USF's location in the liberal San Francisco Bay Area, partly a sign of the Jesuit Society's increasing commitment to social activism, and partly a natural consequence of the college's recent hiring of several cohorts of progressive young faculty members. Thus the ESL program and the way it has been regarded within the university has fallen and risen with the changing goals and focuses of the university.

I believe this is an important point to look at when examining the shifting locuses and statuses of ESL and L2 writing programs, and I believe that my institution—like other institutions—has historically devalued international and minority students; clearly one of the reasons that ESL is marginalized is this very devaluation of "Others." This kind of ethnocentrism is harmful not only to the students who are Othered, and to the programs that serve them, but to the larger institution as well (Benesch, 2001; Canagarajah, 2002; Morgan, 1998). It is fortunate that the situation has much improved, at my institution and at others, but TESOL professionals must be vigilant, especially in these post-September 11th days of increased U.S. government suspicion of people from outside the United States, and of people from nonwestern cultures and non-Christian religions.

4. University's Increasing Focus on Social Justice

Closely related to the university's commitment to diversity is its increasing, especially during the past 10 to 15 years, emphasis and focus on a commitment to social justice. When the university's Mission and Goals were revised a few years ago, the new statement included the following: "The University will distinguish itself as a diverse, socially responsible learning community . . ." (USF catalog, 2005–2007, p. 4) and one of the goals listed was "social responsibility in fulfilling the University's mission . . ." (p. 5); the new tagline on all the university's publicity is "Educating minds and hearts to change the world." This emphasis on social responsibility and social justice has also reinforced the ESL program's place in the university, especially as the program has enrolled students from struggling countries or backgrounds. For example, when the Dalai Lama recently came to be honored by, and speak to, the USF community, one of our Tibetan students was prominently involved in the ceremonies and publicity surrounding the event.

5. Changing Enrollment Profile

Also evolving has been the enrollment profile of the ESL Program. In the early years of the program, by far the majority of ESL students were Intensive English Program (IEP) students who had come specifically to study English. With time, a much larger proportion of the students consisted of matriculated students, and now matriculated students form the majority. Because matriculated students are much more connected to the mainstream of the university, taking classes in various departments, interacting with American students, and of course staying much longer, this trend has also promoted the visibility and status of the ESL program on the campus.

6. Credit for ESL Classes

A related development is that after many years of ESL faculty and students' fighting for students' receiving academic credit for ESL classes, a few years ago this credit was approved by the university. Up to eight credits of students' ESL classes (most commonly, ESL writing classes) count toward degree credit, and all grades in ESL classes, even beyond the eight credits, are averaged into students' grade point averages. This development makes everyone—students, faculty, and administration—take the ESL classes more seriously.

7. Flexibility Offered by a Smaller University

Another development that has helped the program is that, because the university is not large (about 4,800 undergraduates and 3,200 graduate students), there is a flexibility that allows and even promotes interdisciplinary research, teaching, and service. This atmosphere has allowed ESL faculty to be closely involved in the committee work and other administrative structures of the university; to teach non-ESL classes in other departments and even colleges as appropriate; and to work on research and otherwise engage intellectually and academically with other faculty and other disciplinary units on campus. This, again, promotes visibility and status of the ESL faculty and thus of the program.

When the ESL faculty joined the communication studies department, this moving beyond disciplinary borders was accelerated. ESL faculty—both full- and part-time—have frequently taught in both the communication and rhetoric/composition divisions, and often consult on curriculum and policies. In particular, the ESL and rhetoric/composition divisions have been able to work closely together on improving the teaching of writing at the university. They have also been able to work together on improving the status of the faculty and of the programs. For example, faculty from one unit frequently serve on another unit's faculty search committees.

8. Individual Faculty Members' Efforts

An eighth and final factor involved in the ESL—and ESL writing—program's ability to move forward has been the efforts of individual faculty members. When given the opportunity and encouragement by the new, supportive dean, faculty members welcomed the opportunity to prove the ESL faculty and programs deserving of the equality finally being granted to them. They—we—saw that we could one by one, by hard work, convince our fellow faculty, administrators, and others that the TESOL discipline was in fact a legitimate one, and that its faculty were as capable as any faculty of producing high quality research and publications, and of doing their share of the service work of the university. Every time our new publications were listed in the university newsletter; every time one of us chaired a committee or council; every time one of us got a campus award, we felt we were doing so not only for ourselves as individuals, but for the program, the discipline, and the profession.

Our fellow faculty throughout the college and university have responded very positively to us, inviting us to join them in various ways. I, for example, teach classes in women's studies and women's literature (invited by the English department), and at one point directed USF's women's studies program. At another point I directed USF's combined undergraduate/graduate teacher preparation/credentialing program. A colleague has taught linguistics classes in the communication division, as well as teacher education classes in the school of education, and has been a member of the president's budget committee and other high-level university-wide committees. For another example of cross-disciplinary connections, I belong to a reading/writing group of women faculty—from fields such as history, sociology, media studies, and French—who read and discuss feminist and other theory, and who discuss our research and writing projects with each other.

Implications for Identity Construction of Program, Faculty, and Students

Now I would like to examine more closely ways in which the changes in names, sites and structures have affected the ways that the program, faculty, and students construct their identities and perceive their roles and statuses within the university, and how they are perceived by others at the institution.

Identity Construction of the ESL/L2 Writing Discipline

As readers know, ESL, and ESL writing, have often been, like L1 writing programs, considered by many to be less rigorous, less prestigious, less "real" academic disciplines than long-established areas such as English literature, economics, and political science. (See Rose, 1985, for one of many discussions of L1 composition's marginalization, and of writing instruction being characterized as "remediation.") This is partly because these are relatively new disciplines, and partly because they are considered "service" areas rather than "content" areas.

As Linda Lonon Blanton (2002) has so vividly put it regarding ESL writing, and as I think applies to ESL as a whole as well, "In truth, ESL composition, like a foster child, has been hard to 'place' . . . college program administrators have created jerry-rigged curricular constructs that perch second language students precariously between institutional units, both in and out of the academic mainstream . . ." (p. 152). In fact, ESL writing has been further marginalized not only within institutions, but when included as part of L1 composition programs, has often been marginalized there as well. So too have the L2 students themselves, who are generally taught by part-time and often inexperienced (in ESL) faculty, as Jessica Williams (1995) and others have noted. Williams and others further note that ESL writing classes are considered "remedial," a label that has long ensured the separation and marginalization of ESL classes and students.

I don't pretend to say that this perception has changed completely at my university or in general, but I do think that much progress has been made. Some progress has been made at specific institutions such as mine; some has been made at the level of the profession and its professional organizations and publications. For examples of the latter: Tony Silva, Ilona Leki and Paul Kei Matsuda and others—many of whose work is represented in this book—have worked hard to establish second language writing as a respected area of study, a field of its own, through the Symposium on Second Language Writing held every other year at Purdue University, through the *Journal of Second Language Writing,* and through other publications and forums. They have also reached out to the L1 composition profession and community through joining committees, organizing panels, and giving papers, with such organizations as the Conference on College Composition and Communication (CCCC). Other scholars—again, including those who have written chapters for this volume—have contributed to ESL/TESOL/L2 writing scholarship, and thus to the status of the profession and the field.

Identity Construction of ESL Faculty

Relatedly, the promotion of the status of the discipline and that of the faculty reinforce each other. As Elsa Auerbach so strongly put it, "A fact of life for ESL educators is that we are marginalized . . ." (1991, p. 1). At my institution, there was initial strong resistance (from the administration and even from other faculty on campus) to granting equitable working conditions, tenure, and promotions to ESL faculty; it was only with the gradual improvement of the status of the program, the support of certain administrators who believed in equity and believed in the ESL faculty, and some hard work, that the faculty reached the position of being judged by their peers and by the administration to be deserving of tenure and promotion and other signs of academic acceptance and equity.

Identity Construction of ESL Students

Also closely related are the ways in which our ESL students' sites and identities are regarded and constructed within the institution. According to Blanton (2002), "ESL students—whether international or resident—don't understand how the system works or how and why they end up placed where they do. No wonder" (p. 152). Certainly the widely varying sites and organizational structures, and the sometimes-unclear relationships among them, have often been confusing, alienating, and even sometimes humiliating for students.

Fortunately—but only after a painfully long period of time—at my institution, the status of international students, and in particular students in ESL and ESL writing classes, has risen throughout the years as the status of the program has risen. In the early years, the program, like many ESL programs, was considered to be separate from the mainstream of the university, a program that was housed there but was not very connected to the rest of the university. Students themselves felt this separation. As the program gained legitimacy and status, and as the university's attitude toward the value of international and multicultural students and diversity became more positive, the position of ESL students rose as well.

In addition, students have benefited pedagogically, and can now see, much more than in the past, that the L1 and L2 writing programs are integrated, that the faculty of each talk to and consult with each other and back each other up on decisions about, for example, placement.

Focus on L1/L2 Parallels

I would like to focus briefly on the parallels between the evolving of the status of the L1 and L2 writing programs at USF (and at many other institutions). Both have been regarded by many as "service units" and as less than completely legitimate disciplines. Both have—in the past—been more closely controlled by administration and had less faculty control over their work than have other disciplines. Both have endured criticism from other university faculty for not preparing students adequately for the writing tasks they face during their university studies (see Janopoulus, 1992; and Zamel, 1995, 1996, among others, on this latter point). In both cases, the situation has improved at USF, because of the factors I listed above, and because the two disciplines/programs have recently worked more closely together in the new shared department structure; the two programs/disciplines have been able to lend each other strength, support, and legitimacy. As Paul Kei Matsuda (1998, 1999, 2003) and others have pointed out, the two disciplines have historically diverged in most institutions, and as disciplines, but certainly should be working more closely together both at the institutional level and across the professions.

Conclusion

Although each program's situation is different, I believe that there are some common threads in my story that may resonate for others at other institutions, and I hope that some of those threads have been evident in this chapter. I hope that I don't convey, in this essay, an overly optimistic and perhaps naïve attitude about the situation of ESL and ESL writing in academe. I cannot and will not ever forget the obstacles and problems that we dealt with in our institution, and that so many ESL and ESL writing programs have dealt with and are still dealing with in their academic homes. But I do believe that with time and effort, our still young field is establishing itself, and can and will continue to establish itself, as a legitimate, essential discipline that will continue to grow in status and influence in the future. I believe that those of us who believe in and care passionately about our profession and our students can and will make it happen.

References

Auerbach, E. R. (1991). Politics, pedagogy, and professionalism: Challenging marginalization in ESL. *College ESL, 1*(1), 1–9.

Benesch, S. (2001). *Critical English for academic purposes.* Mahwah, NJ: Lawrence Erlbaum Associates.

Blanton, L. L. (2002). As I was saying to Leonard Bloomfield: A personalized history of ESL/writing. In L. L. Blanton & B. Kroll (Eds.), *ESL composition tales: Reflections on teaching* (pp.135-162). Ann Arbor: University of Michigan Press.

Canagarajah, A. S. (2002). *Critical academic writing and multilingual students.* Ann Arbor: University of Michigan Press.

Casanave, C. P., & Schecter, S. R. (Eds.). (1997). *On becoming a language educator: Personal essays on professional development.* Mahwah, NJ: Lawrence Erlbaum Associates.

Casanave, C. P., & Vandrick, S. (Eds.). (2003). *Writing for scholarly publication: Behind the scenes in language education.* Mahwah, NJ: Lawrence Erlbaum Associates.

Connelly, F. M., & Clandinin, J. (Eds.). (1999). *Shaping a professional identity: Stories of educational practice.* New York: Teachers College Press.

Fontaine, S. I., & Hunter, S. (Eds.). (1993). *Writing ourselves into the story: Unheard voices from composition studies.* Carbondale, IL: Southern Illinois University Press.

Haroian-Guerin, G. (Ed.). (1999). *The personal narrative: Writing ourselves as teachers and scholars.* Portland, ME: Calendar Islands.

Hindman, J. E. (Ed.). (2003). The personal in academic writing [Special issue]. *College English, 66.*

Janopoulos, M. (1992). University faculty tolerance of NS and NNS writing errors: A comparison. *Journal of Second Language Writing, 1,* 109–121.

Matsuda, P. K. (1998). Situating ESL writing in a cross-disciplinary context. *Written Communication, 15* (1), 99–121.

Matsuda, P. K. (1999). Composition studies and ESL writing: A disciplinary division of labor. *College Composition and Communication, 50* (4), 699–721.

Matsuda, P. K. (2003). Second language writing in the twentieth century: A situated historical perspective. In Kroll, B. (Ed.), *Exploring the dynamics of second language writing* (pp. 15-34). Cambridge: Cambridge University Press.

Morgan, B. (1998). *The ESL classroom: Teaching, critical practice, and community development.* Toronto: University of Toronto Press.

Ritchie, J. S., & Wilson, D. E. (2000). *Teacher narrative as critical inquiry: Rewriting the script.* New York: Teachers College Press.

Roen, D. H., Brown, S. C., & Enos, T. (Eds.). (1999). *Living rhetoric and composition: Stories of the discipline.* Mahwah, NJ: Lawrence Erlbaum Associates.

Rose, M. (1985). The language of exclusion: Writing instruction at the university. *College English, 47,* 341–359.

Trimmer, J. (Ed.). (1997). *Narration and knowledge: Tales of the teaching life.* Portsmouth, NH: Boynton/Cook.

University of San Francisco General Catalog 2005–2007.

Vandrick, S. (2003). On Beginning to write at 40. In C. P. Casanave & S. Vandrick (Eds.), *Writing for scholarly publication: Behind the scenes in language education* (pp. 53-60). Mahwah, NJ: Lawrence Erlbaum Associates.

Williams, J. (1995). ESL program administration in the United States. *Journal of Second Language Writing, 4,* 157–179.

Zamel, V. (1995). Strangers in academia: The experiences of faculty and ESL students across the curriculum. *College Composition and Communication, 46,* 506–521.

Zamel, V. (1996). Transcending boundaries: Complicating the scene of teaching language. *College ESL, 6*(2), 1–11.

Coda

16 Toward a Promised Land of Writing: At the Intersection of Hope and Reality

Barbara Kroll

A central tenet of the Old Testament, a sacred text in the Judeo-Christian tradition, is the covenant that God makes with Abraham (considered the founding patriarch of the Jewish religion), in which the land of Canaan is promised to Abraham and his descendants in perpetuity. Various verses in the Biblical book of Genesis account for the term "Promised Land" in this context.* Additional Old Testament sections detail the difficulty of reaching the promised land, including the need to overcome unimaginable obstacles to reach it (one of which being a period of 40 years of wandering in the desert), and much concern about what will be found once it is (hopefully) arrived at. I reference this ancient history without any intention of trying to determine how the borders of ancient Canaan do or do not overlap with actual real estate in and around modern day Israel (where I sit as I write these words). Rather I would simply like to lift the term "promised land," which is, at its very heart, a metaphor more than a place. If we explore this metaphor, we will see its remarkable applicability to our very own field of second language writing.

I have come to the notion of "promises" by taking the position that an institution has a moral and ethical responsibility to provide English language courses and/or other language assistance to the nonnative English speaking (NNES) students it accepts into its various degree programs. In theory, this responsibility should apply to all NNES students, but it is especially demanded, I believe, in relation to international visa students, who typically pay supplemental tuition fees, often quite high, to study in North America. I recognize that from other perspectives, education can be seen as an economic transaction where tuition dollars are exchanged for an eventual degree. But I also see a more transcendent transaction, a sacred one if you will, where I believe it is as if a school, in accepting any given student, promises that student whatever assistance would be required to help him/her achieve their educational goals in an optimal fashion. For NNES students, this often translates into the fact that they need specific assistance with their English language skills so that they can better accomplish their academic purposes and maximize their learning experiences.

With this in mind, I would like to suggest that the "promised land"—from our perspective as teachers, researchers, and scholars in the field of second language writing, and specifically for those among us who are based at North American institutions of higher education—is one in which each and every NNES student at an English-medium campus would have access to programs of study and support systems that are designed to promote mastery and excellence in academic English in ways that most address the local and specific needs of those students, whoever they may be and at whichever campus they are studying. Unlike the original notion of a single Promised Land, our use of this metaphor allows for multiple types of promised lands. Still, I would argue that the metaphor is relevant in its plural form as long as we are referring to the search for ways to meet our sacred responsibility to our students: to provide optimal learning environments.

Regrettably, however, despite the vast number of institutions where NNES are located, it would appear that only a very small percentage could be accurately designated as "Promised Land Institutions" (PLI's). Clearly, this is a politically charged issue, and I concede that rather than an "all or nothing" designation, individual institutions deploy themselves along a continuum ranging from total success to total failure in serving their NNES student population(s). In this brief chapter, I would like to provide a broad analysis of some of the reasons why it often proves much more difficult and complicated to create new promised lands of writing despite our professional training that presumably orients us towards this goal and despite an abundant awareness of what "promised lands" might look like from the perspective of the NNES writer. Other chapters in this volume will detail specific institutional settings to provide an examination of how their present programs work to achieve a promised land of writing, miss the mark in one or more ways, and/or fail to provide adequate support to the

NNES writers for any number of reasons thus offering, in lieu of the promised land, a kind of perpetual wandering in the desert.

Setting Up More Promised Lands of Writing

Even with the *hope* that ALL our NNES students would be well-served, the *reality* is that creating PLI's is far more difficult than we might imagine. In exploring how new programs for NNES writers might be established (or extant programs might be improved), I would like to suggest that there are five layers of interlocking complications that make establishing a promised land of writing far more complex than might at first be apparent.

The First Complexity: A "Net" to Identify Students

HOPE: *All NNES students on a given campus who might benefit from English language assistance in one form or another would be identified prior to the onset of their studies.*

REALITY: No matter how NNES writers would be defined locally, in an ideal set-up, such students would be subject to placement testing, and, barring exemption, required to participate in one or more special courses (or supplementary programs) designed to strengthen the English writing and overall language skills they demonstrate at the start of their studies.[1] Providing specialized services, after all, would be a *sine qua non* of promised land design, and success could only come if the targeted students were identifiable. Then we must begin by asking *which* students in any given institution's student body should be identified as NNES writers. At the very least, an ESL writing specialist on any given campus would need to convince the office of international students to require incoming visa students whose prior schooling was not conducted in English to be tagged in some way and held for a placement test.

More difficult would be to secure the cooperation of other bureaucratic institutional divisions which would have to participate where any given school wanted to find a way to identify potential NNES who do not hold foreign visas, but who nevertheless may exhibit weakness in English writing resulting from their limited prior educational experiences in English-medium institutions (e.g., graduates of American high schools who have been in the country fewer than five years). To be more specific, it is quite likely that in places like California, Texas, and New York, with large populations of immigrants, the number of non-visa holding NNES students at any given school may far exceed the number of bona fide "foreign" student visa holders.[2] Setting up a net or tagging system, therefore is complicated by the need to identify who the NNES students really are. Further, such a net can only serve students if something like an office of admissions and records is able to put a "hold" on all registrations for the tagged students until results of the placement instrument were recorded. Otherwise, the net could be invalidated if students do not register for the classes they have been placed into.

Sadly, I suspect that many ESL writing specialists have neither the time nor the skill to fully identify let alone penetrate the multiple layers of institutional bureaucracy that would be required in order to create such a tagging system where one is not already in place. So, in the absence of an evolved procedure, reality trumps hope in the sphere of identifying who among the student body on our campus may most need the focused attention of ESL writing specialists. These unserved students will surely wander in the desert rather than reach the promised land.

The Second Complexity: Placement Testing

HOPE: *A well-designed and rigorously scored placement test would determine how to sort the target population of NNES test-takers into courses or programs designed with their needs in mind.*

REALITY: Quite connected to the suitable identification of target student populations, the quest for a promised land of writing and the courses which it would have require a well-designed and institutionally relevant placement test. Schools that have such instruments in place are able to refine them on an ongoing basis, but schools which lack a placement test are not in a position to mount a suitable program until they overcome this obstacle.

The design of a new placement instrument should not be put in the hands of a single person but rather should fall to a committee of knowledgeable faculty. Not only would the instrument itself need to be designed with great rigor but so too would its scoring guidelines so that decisions about where students are placed offer them the optimal path towards improvement in skill level. This would present a huge stumbling block on campuses with a limited pool of full-time faculty who have expertise in teaching English to nonnative speakers, let alone expertise in second language writing, and let alone expertise in testing and assessment. Many such faculty are likely to consider themselves overworked with their combination of teaching load, advisement responsibilities, departmental committee work, and so forth. And, of course, most institutions continue to rely on part-time faculty to deliver the majority of teaching in writing courses, faculty less likely to have the requisite academic expertise needed to develop an appropriate placement instrument. Even in the best case scenario of a faculty pool with training and expertise in L2 writing and assessment, reality may intervene in the form of lack of compensation for the additional work required to create (let alone score) a placement test. This is exactly one sort of reality that helps to keep the promised land elusive.

The Third Complexity: Placement into What?

HOPE: *PLI's would have available a suitable combination of courses in ESL writing, English for Academic Purposes (EAP), tutorial services, and second language writing specialists as teachers, tutors and advisors.*

REALITY: Where a multi-course and/or multi-program curriculum is designed and where NNES students whose performance on the placement instrument indicates the need for more than one term of work on their language skills in whatever way(s) an individual campus program is structured, such students can rest assured that they are not wandering in the desert. They have found their way to a Promised Land Institution.

But too often, complications in setting up a valid placement procedure connect to a sub-complication that creates more difficulty in the establishment of new promised lands of writing, namely the curriculum of the course(s) into which students would be potentially placed. If only one level of class is available, then the test results would have to be two-tiered: exempt or held to the requirement of taking the course. Performance on the placement instrument would then be a pretty high stakes issue and the one course would likely offer a curriculum that meets only some of the learning goals that could be identified. In such a case, faculty across the campus might accuse the NNES-oriented program of failing to adequately prepare students; it is rarely possible for a single course in academic writing to satisfy the very different notions of what students should be able to demonstrate across the curricular spectrum.

When more than one course might be required, concerns arise as to the credit-worthiness of such courses in the overall accumulation of credits towards a degree, and administrators begin to question the importance of insisting that NNES fulfill "service course" requirements above and beyond what native English speaking students are asked to do. Debates may arise as to whether a given three-unit course should "count" towards the total number required to earn a degree; students too can be resistant to seeing the value of courses that carry what is referred to as "workload" credit (i.e., must be paid for) but not graduation credit.

Gather a group of L2 writing specialists and they would have no trouble stipulating the course design of any number of 40 or 45-hour ESL writing and/or EAP courses targeting either undergraduate or graduate students or both. Examples of many excellent programs are provided in Leki (2001) and elsewhere in this volume. But the reality is that few such specialists work in environments where their first-rate course design skills are put to the test. Rather, there is more typically a conflict between what second language writing specialist faculty perceive to be student needs and what administrators are willing to support. Thus, the would-be courses remain chimeras.

The Fourth Complexity: Enforcement

HOPE: *All NNES students targeted for placement testing and not demonstrating sufficient English-language/writing skill to merit exemption would be required to register for mandatory courses and/or tutoring services.*

REALITY: Assuming a net was created and a placement instrument with suitable scoring guidelines was set up so that students could then find a promised land home in a course designed to meet their needs, the next complication is one of enforcement. Departments and programs across campus would have to buy into the idea that their NNES students would *so* benefit from taking these ESL writing and/or EAP courses that they would insist on it as a graduation requirement for the major. Indeed such is the case at many tertiary institutions, the best exemplars of PLI's. However, I can envision that in the worst case scenario, departments or programs or even entire schools within a college would petition to waive this requirement for their students, thus short-circuiting the efforts of having created a net, a valid placement instrument, and a curriculum. Reluctance to insist on this requirement comes from forces who believe that growth in English performance is best achieved through time and/or those who do not believe such a goal is central to the academic goals of a future X, Y, or Z (disciplinary professions omitted to obscure their identity).

For example, according to numbers released in 2003 by the Office of International Students on my home campus, a large public university in the Western United States, the six schools or departments with the largest concentration of NNES students from among our 1,200 visa holders are: business, computer science, engineering, cinema-television-arts, psychology, and art. To create commitment towards establishing a promised land of writing on a campus such as this, would one focus on lobbying the deans of schools or department chairs with the largest enrollment, or focus instead on lobbying advisors in disciplines, such as applied linguistics, philosophy and history, where fluency in written English plays an undeniably central and crucial role for students? As for campuses where programs are already in place, what can second language writing faculty do to prevent faculty in other disciplines from short-circuiting their efforts by working to get their majors exempt from the well-designed programs in place? Yet again, the reality of some faculty's lack of belief in the value of providing English language support might trump the hope of second language writing faculty to successfully serve students on a given campus.

The Fifth Complexity: Fiscal Impact

HOPE: *The cost of sustaining whatever courses or services are provided to NNES students would be absorbed into a given institution's general tuition package.*

REALITY: The fifth and final complication is a fiscal one. Let's assume that nets are set up, placement instruments are in place, courses are created to deliver curriculum that will provide students the learning opportunities they need (and faculty are available to teach these courses), and no obstacles to enrollment exist, we might still find that there is an additional wrinkle in our promised land quest, namely the cost to students. On many campuses, students pay for their courses on a per unit basis, and each new course that gets added to the curriculum translates into a specific price tag for the student. For example, in the 23-campus system where I work (the California State University system), international students pay additional per unit fees for each course they enroll in while non-visa students pay only a set fee based on their status as undergraduate or graduate students *and* in accordance with how many total units they carry. Currently, for each unit of coursework an international visa student registers for on my specific campus, there is a charge of $339 in addition to regular university fees. That means each three-unit course—whether it is a required component of a program or an elective of some sort—costs the international student $1,017 in addition to whatever tuition fees he/she pays. Similar surcharges apply on many other campuses as well.

In terms of our discussion, it appears that the entrance fee to the promised land can thus be in the neighborhood of $1,000 or more. How many second language writing specialists would feel comfortable with guaranteeing to students that a course in something like Advanced English for Academic Purposes, perhaps not even a requirement in their field of study, justifies such an investment? Is this "Promised Land" flowing with enough "milk and honey" for us to feel confident in asking NNES students to pay such a tariff? Clearly this is an uncomfortable question to pose and a more difficult one to answer.

Conclusion

Despite the vast differences that North American tertiary institutions have in their individual missions, in the nature of their student body, in their particular locales, in their very specific set-ups, and in the state of their financial stability, they deal with NNES students in one of two ways: Either (1) such students are provided with special programs and/or services designed with their language learning needs in mind or (2) NNES students become members of the general student body without much (or any) institutional concern about their English language development. This binary distinction is not meant to obscure the very real differences between individual programs but rather to highlight that some students enroll in institutions whose policies and/or programs recognize NNES as a distinct population with identifiable language needs—true promised lands—while other institutions more or less fail to create what we might refer to as designated special learning spaces for NNES students and instead condemn their students to wandering in the desert.

As I have sketched out in this discussion, creating a promised land of writing where one does not exist is not an easy task. Teachers, scholars, and educators always operate within institutional constraints, and their professional understanding of student needs doesn't always translate into an operational ability to create and/or operate suitable programs. Given that reality, I salute all those faculty who have successfully navigated their way through a complicated web of nested factors to create a promised land of writing. It is a daunting task indeed, but surely a worthy one.

Notes

* I appreciate the funding provided by the Faculty Fellows Program, sponsored by the Dean of the College of Humanities, California State University, Northridge, which helped to support the preparation of this chapter.

[1] I shall ignore the legitimate debate about whether to provide separate sections or mainstream NNES with native English speakers (see Braine, 1996, Dooley, 2004, and Silva, 1994, among others on this topic). My point here is that schools are not in a position to provide ANY services to NNES students if they are unable to identify them. A given school might prefer to offer tutorial help, for example, rather than specifically designated classes, but it still needs to know whom to offer ESL tutoring services to.

[2] For the sake of this overview, I shall collapse all L2 students studying at North American institutions into a single NNES category, ignoring the very real differences between EFL-backgrounds, Generation 1.5 students, and other ESL students.

References

Braine, G. (1996). ESL students in first-year writing courses: ESL versus mainstream classes, *Journal of Second Language Writing, 5*, 91–107.

Dooley, K. (2004). Pedagogy in diverse secondary school classes: Legacies for higher education. *Higher Education, 48*, 231–252.

Leki, I. (Ed.). (2001). *Academic writing programs.* Case Studies in TESOL Practice Series. Alexandria, VA: TESOL.

Silva, T. (1994). An examination of writing program administrators' options for the placement of ESL students in first year writing classes. *WPA: Writing Program Administration, 18*(1/2), 398–428.

Contributors

Kimberly Abels, Ph.D., serves as the Director of the Writing Center at the University of North Carolina at Chapel Hill. Her research interests include writing across the curriculum, writing center pedagogy, and ESL

Deborah Crusan is associate professor of TESOL/Applied Linguistics and Director of ESL Programs at Wright State University, Dayton, OH. She has published articles about writing assessment in *Assessing Writing, English for Specific Purposes, The Norton Field Guide*, and other recognized journals in the field. Her research interests include writing assessment particularly for placement of second language writers, directed/guided self-placement and its consequences for second language writers, and the politics of assessment.

Angela M. Dadak is the International Student Coordinator for the Department of Literature at American University, where she works with faculty and their multilingual students in the College Writing Program and the Writing Center. She also teaches courses on writing and cross-cultural adaptation. Her interests include teacher education, academic literacy, cross-cultural communication, and increased collaboration between the fields of first- and second-language writing.

Kevin Eric DePew is an assistant professor at Old Dominion University where he teaches undergraduate and graduate courses in composition, rhetoric, writing pedagogy for grades 6-12 and first-year writing, digital rhetoric, and second language writing. He has edited a special issue of *The Journal of Second Language* on "Early second language writing" with Paul Kei Matsuda, as well as a special issue of *Computers and Composition* on "Second language writers in digital contexts."

Danling Fu is a Professor of literacy and language in the School of Teaching and Learning, College of Education, University of Florida,

Gainesville. For a decade, she has worked and researched in the New York City schools which house large population of new immigrant students. Her research focus is on writing development and literacy instruction for new immigrant students. She is the author of *My Trouble is My English* and *An Island of English*.

Guillaume Gentil is an assistant professor of applied linguistics in the School of Linguistics and Applied Language Studies at Carleton University, Ottawa, Canada. His interests focus on professional and academic biliteracy, an emergent field at the intersection of second language writing/reading, literacy studies, bilingual education, languages for specific purposes, and written communication in the professions. His ongoing research, funded by the Social Sciences and Humanities Research Council of Canada, investigates bilingual communication in the Canadian public service.

Jessie Moore Kapper is an Assistant Professor at Elon University in North Carolina. She teaches TESOL, professional writing and rhetoric, and composition courses in the Department of English. Her recent research focuses on second language writing and on service learning in TESOL courses. She also is active in TESOL's Second Language Writing Interest Section and the CCCC Committee on Second Language Writing.

Barbara Kroll, a professor of English and Linguistics at California State University, Northridge, is a frequent presenter on topics related to teaching ESL/EFL writing and training L2 composition teachers. She is the editor of *Exploring the Dynamics of Second Language Writing*. Her first EFL teaching appointment was in the original Promised Land, at Ben Gurion University of the Negev, Beersheba, Israel, an experience she wrote about in *ESL Composition Tales,* a collection she co-edited with Linda Lonon Blanton.

Ryuko Kubota is an associate professor in the School of Education and the Department of Asian Studies at the University of North Carolina at Chapel Hill. Her research interests include culture and politics in second/foreign language teaching and critical pedagogies. Her articles have appeared in such journals as *Canadian Modern Language Review, College ESL, Critical Inquiry in Language Studies, English Journal, Japanese Journal of Second Language Writing, TESOL Quarterly, Written Communication,* and *World Englishes.*

Ilona Leki directs the ESL program and is chair of the Interdisciplinary Program in Linguistics at the University of Tennessee. She co-edits *Journal of Second Language Writing* and is author of *Academic Writing: Exploring Processes and Strategies* (Cambridge) and *Understanding ESL Writers: A Guide for Teachers* (Boynton/Cook). Her most recent research project will be published by Erlbaum as *Undergraduates in a Second Language: Four Case Studies.*

Marylou M. Matoush is an assistant professor of literacy education at Western Carolina University and in their teacher education program in Jamaica. Prior to beginning that position she spent over twenty years teaching children with diverse needs and trained teachers in a literacy program for at-risk first graders. Her research interests include visual literacy, emergent literacy, critical literacy, and education for social justice globally as well as locally.

Christine Norris is an Assistant Professor at the University of Nevada, Reno. Her research interests include theories of writing program administration and feminist historiography.

Christine Tardy is an assistant professor in the Department of English at DePaul University in Chicago, where she teaches courses in writing and the teaching of writing and ESL. Her research interests lie in the areas of ESL writing, academic writing, and the sociopolitical dimensions of teaching ESL/EFL. Her work has appeared in the *Journal of Second Language Writing, Written Communication, Journal of English for Academic Purposes,* and *ELT Journal.*

Stephanie Vandrick, Professor, Communication Studies Department, University of San Francisco, teaches ESL, writing, literature, and Women's Studies classes. Her research interests include critical and feminist pedagogies, identity issues, ethical issues in ESL, the use of literature in ESL classes, postcolonialism, and the use of personal narrative in academic writing. She is coauthor of *Ethical Issues for ESL Faculty,* coeditor *of Writing for Scholarly Publication,* and author of articles in TESOL, feminist, and peace journals.

Kerry Enright Villalva is Assistant Professor of Language and Subject Matter Learning in Adolescence at the University of California at Davis. Her research interests include academic language in secondary classrooms, multiple literacies of adolescent writers, and the schooling and language use of Latino youth. Her most recent publication, which appeared in *Written Communication* (2006), is entitled "Hidden literacies and inquiry approaches of bilingual high school writers."

Sara Cushing Weigle is Associate Professor in the Department of Applied Linguistics and ESL at Georgia State University in Atlanta, Georgia, where she is Director of ESL Test Development and Research and teaches graduate and undergraduate courses in linguistics, second language writing, teaching methods, research design, and assessment. She has published several articles in the areas of teacher education and assessment and is the author of *Assessing Writing* (2002) from Cambridge University Press.

Jessica Williams is a Professor of Linguistics at the University of Illinois at Chicago, where she also directs the ESL and Less Commonly Taught Languages programs. She has published on variety of topics, including second language writing, lexical acquisition, and the effect of focus on form. Her book *Teaching second/foreign language writing* (McGraw Hill) was published in 2004. An edited volume (with Bill VanPatten), *Theories in Second Language Acquisition* (Erlbaum), will be published in 2006.

Xiaoye You is assistant professor of English at The Pennsylvania State University, where he teaches courses in rhetoric, writing, and the teaching of writing. He is interested in comparative rhetoric and issues of English writing instruction in international contexts. His work has appeared in *College Composition and Communication, Journal of Second Language Writing, Rhetoric Review, Rhetoric Society Quarterly,* and *Studies on Asia* as well as edited collections in both rhetoric and composition and applied linguistics.

Wei Zhu is an Associate Professor in the Department of World Languages at the University of South Florida, where she teaches in the MA program in Applied Linguistics and the interdisciplinary Ph.D program in Second Language Acquisition and Instructional Technology. Her research interests include peer collaboration, academic literacy, and computer-mediated communication. Her work has appeared in *Language Learning, Written Communication, Journal of Second Language Writing, English for Specific Purposes, TESL Canada,* and *Journal of Asian Pacific Communication.*

Editors

Paul Kei Matsuda is associate professor of English and Director of Composition at the University of New Hampshire, USA. He is founding co-chair of the Symposium on Second Language and the chair of the CCCC Committee on Second Language Writing. He has co-edited several books and special journal issues focusing on second language writing. His work appears in journals such as *College Composition and Communication, College English, Composition Studies, International Journal of Applied Linguistics, Journal of Basic Writing, Journal of Second Language Writing*, and *Written Communication* as well as various edited collections in both composition studies and applied linguistics. http://matsuda.jslw.org/.

Christina Ortmeier-Hooper is a Ph.D. candidate in Composition Studies at the University of New Hampshire, where she teaches first-year composition, ESL, advanced composition, and teacher education courses. She is founding chair of the Second Language Writing Interest Section at TESOL and a member of the CCCC Committee on Second Language Writing. She coedited *Second-Language Writing in the Composition Classroom: A Critical Sourcebook* (with Paul Kei Matsuda, Michelle Cox, and Jay Jordan). Her dissertation project examines issues of identity and the development of academic writing skills among adolescent second-language writers in U.S. high schools.

Xiaoye You is assistant professor of English at The Pennsylvania State University, where he teaches courses in rhetoric, writing, and the teaching of writing. He is interested in comparative rhetoric and issues of English writing instruction in international contexts. His work has appeared in *College Composition and Communication, Journal of Second Language Writing, Rhetoric Review, Rhetoric Society Quarterly*, and *Studies on Asia* as well as various edited collections in both rhetoric and composition and applied linguistics. Currently he is working on a book manuscript tentatively titled *Writing in the "Devil's" Tongue: Rhetoric and English Composition in Chinese Colleges, 1862-2005*. http://www.personal.psu.edu/xuy10/.

Index

Abels, K., x, 75, 106, 306
academic reward system, 132, 140-143
accent, 171, 175, 177, 178, 181
accountability, 28, 40, 207
administration, 97, 101, 104, 106-108, 151, 156, 159, 161, 168, 169, 181, 207, 208, 238, 276, 281, 284, 285, 287
Albert, R., 187
Aljaafreh, A., 110, 121, 125
Amanti, C., 50, 52
Ame, C., 6, 27
Anderson, R., 6, 27
Anzaldua, G., 5, 27
Appadurai, A., 189, 201
Applied Linguistics, xii, 73, 74, 77, 86, 88, 89, 113, 114, 115, 119, 120, 148, 163, 231, 234, 273, 274, 277, 279, 303, 307, 309, 310
Ard, J., 171, 173, 186
argumentation, 224, 229, 232
Asenavage, K., 110, 122
assessment, viii, ix, xi, 39-40, 42, 61, 65, 66, 68, 91, 96-99, 108, 117, 118, 121, 123, 132, 134, 136, 145, 190, 193, 194, 197, 199, 205-207, 212, 215, 216, 217, 222, 223, 225-227, 231, 238-240, 270, 271, 301, 306, 309; authenticity, 224, 225, 232; external, 226; practical-ity, 236; process-based, 198; prompt, 101, 207, 216, 225, 228-230, 234, 236-239; reading, 232, 236, 238, 240, 241; reliability, 54, 140, 197, 206, 207, 224; self, 212, 215, 217; student-centered, 194; test preparation, 222, 223, 227-229, 231, 235-237; TOEFL, 78, 79, 83, 145, 214, 223; TWE, 223; validity, 206, 215, 224, 225, 232, 239; washback, xii, 223, 231, 235, 237, 238; writing, xii, 133, 205, 215-217, 223, 224, 230, 235, 237, 238, 306
assessment rubric, 40-43, 207, 233; holistic, 206, 228, 229, 233
Atkinson, D., 63, 70, 72
attitude, 65, 85, 212, 217, 285, 291

Bailey, K., 170, 186
Baker, C., 164, 165
Ball, A., 52, 206, 215
Barker, S., 131, 146
Barton, D., 31, 51
Becher, T., 131, 132, 146
Bell, J., 117, 121
Berg, C., 110, 121
Berlin, J., 71, 72
Bernhardt, E., 232, 239
Bianco, J., 84, 92

bilingual: education, 164, 165, 191, 307
bilingual, 5-12, 16, 17, 25-26, 30, 33-34, 37, 43, 45, 47-48, 51, 53, 61, 112-113, 148-149, 154, 159, 162, 164-166, 168, 191, 250, 307, 309
bilingualism, 5, 8, 9, 17, 25, 28, 43, 52-53, 84-85, 163, 165
biliteracy, 10, 25, 27, 150, 165; academic and professional, xi, 148, 151, 162; continua model, 149; K-12, ix, 7, 8, 9, 24-26, 28, 148, 149, 150-151, 154, 161, 166, 307; sequential, 9; spontaneous, 9, 10

Blakesley, D., xiii, 201, 208, 215
Blalock, S., 119, 121
Blau, S., 110, 122, 125
Bouquet, E., 109, 114, 122
Bourdieu, P., 150, 165
Boyer, E., 11, 27
Braine, G., 105, 107, 130, 145, 278, 305
Brandt, D., 129, 145
Brehony, K., 132, 145
Bresnahan, M., 172, 186
Brinton, D., 88, 92
Bronfenbrenner, U., 32, 33, 39, 51
Brooks, L., 110, 124
Brown, J. D., 226, 239
Brown, L. F., 109, 122, 123, 125, Brown, S. C., 281, 293
Bruffee, K., 112, 122
Buckley, J., 158, 167
Burton, L., 70, 73

Canagarajah, A., 148, 165, 270, 278, 286, 292
Capell, F., 225, 239
Carino, P., 114, 122
Carnegie classifications, xii, 247, 256, 259

Carroll, L., 70, 71, 72
Carson, J., 65, 66, 72, 126, 129, 130, 145, 225, 232, 239, 254
Carter-Tod, S., 110, 122
Casanave, C., 148, 165, 281, 292, 293
case study, 31, 34, 126, 177, 281
CCCC, 59, 60, 74, 100, 104, 107, 108, 290, 307, 310; Statement on Second Language Writing and Writers, 104
Charney, D., 225, 239
Chase, D., 66, 72, 225, 232, 239
Chase, N., 66, 72, 225, 232, 239
Cheng, L., 223, 239
Chernekoff, J., 208, 215
Chin, E., 129, 145
China, ix, xi, 7, 10, 17, 22-23, 61, 177-178, 188-196, , 199-2001, 264, 271, 310; Ministry of Education, 189, 191, 194, 201
Christensen, L., 206, 215
Clark, I., 119, 122, 132
class size, viii, xi, 104, 138, 142, 143, 199
classrooms, 129-131, 133-135, 138, 142-144
Cogie, J., 109, 122, 125
Cole, M., 149, 167
collaboration, xii, 75, 102, 106, 112, 118-119, 121, 156-158, 172, 180, 183, 184, 227, 238, 259, 264, 267, 278, 283, 299, 306, 309
Collier, V., 8, 27, 29, 91, 93
Colombi, C., 148, 165
Combs, M., 91, 93
communication, xi, 6, 7, 11, 27, 60, 70, 80, 96, 111, 116, 122, 124, 126, 132, 137, 141-142, 153, 155-159, 168, 171, 174-175, 177-178, 180, 190-191, 197, 200, 273, 282-283, 287-

Index 313

288, 307, 309; intercultural, 80, 103, 106, 190, 192, 306; oral, 80, 137, 169, 173-174, 176; written, 137, 144, 152-156, 158, 159, 174, 307
Communication Studies, 282, 308
Connor, U., 110, 122, 254
Connors, R., 67, 73
Conrad, S., 110, 120, 123
context, 130, 150, 262; non-English dominant, 188-189
Cope, B., 164, 165
Cornell, C., 42, 70, 208, 215
Crawford, J., 8, 28, 84, 92
credit, viii, xii, 55, 60-61, 68, 71, 80, 90, 97, 98-99, 153-154, 156, 212, 237, 263, 266, 268-269, 285, 287, 302
criticism, 177-179
Crow, A., 70, 73
Crowhurst, M., 225, 239
Crowley, S., 60, 69, 71, 73
Crusan, D., xi, 205, 211, 212, 216, 306
culture, 5, 6, 17, 25, 33, 43, 47, 63, 80, 85, 97, 130, 153, 170, 172-174, 188, 193, 211, 307; multiculturalism, xii, 92, 285
Cumming, A., 110, 122, 150, 165, 226, 239
Cummins, J., 8, 9, 28, 164, 166
curriculum, 35, 37, 38, 43, 46, 60-61, 67, 69, 70, 72, 100, 104, 123, 132, 144, 145, 151, 157, 159, 162, 165, 174, 180, 182, 186, 193, 201, 217, 227, 239, 282, 287, 293, 301, 303
Curry, M., 148, 166

Dadak, A., x, 94, 306
Damon, W., 119, 122
De Guerrero, M., 110, 122
DeCiccio, A., 118, 122

Deem, R., 132, 145
delivery, 179, 181, 262
Depew, K., xi, 168, 186, 306
DeShaw, D., 118, 122
Detterman, D., 68, 73
dialogue, xii, 78, 92, 124, 188, 209, 262, 264, 278
Dias, P., 65, 69, 73
discipline, xi, xiii, 68, 70, 71, 123, 129, 130-131, 133, 135, 138, 140-144, 146-149, 151, 153, 157, 161-162, 164-165, 169, 172-173, 175-176, 183, 186, 191, 194, 258, 260-262, 264-267, 273-274, 276-279, 287-288, 290, 292-293, 303; division of labor, 123, 148-149, 186, 274, 277, 279, 292
Donald, J., 131, 145
Duell, O., 131, 146
Durst, R., 67, 73
Dworin, J., 8, 28
Dyehouse, J., 119, 122

ecological framework, ix, 31
empirical research, 110
English: academic, vii, 12, 17, 50, 65, 168, 298; for academic purposes (EAP), x, xi, xii, 75, 77-79, 82, 86, 88-89, 91, 95, 97, 129, 142, 144, 147, 153-155, 158, 160, 162-163, 190, 239, 262, 264, 278-279, 301-302; for specific purposes (ESP), 193; international language (EIL), 200
English Only Movement, ix, 5
enrollment, xiii, 34, 43, 70, 78, 80, 139, 144, 206, 224, 256, 258, 281-282, 286, 303
error, 122, 125
ESL: as remedial, 86; specialist, 101, 114-116experiment, 104,

194-195, 197, 200
exposition, 229

faculty, x, xiii, 11, 39, 43, 47, 51, 59, 65, 69, 70-71, 73, 75, 76, 78, 80-81, 86, 88-89, 91, 95, 99, 100-101, 103-104, 106-107, 109, 113-114, 121, 125, 131-132, 133-144, 153-156, 159, 161, 163, 168, 171-173, 176, 180, 184-185, , 217, 226-227, 229, 231, 257-258, 263, 276-277, 280-285, 287-283, , 300-303, 305-306
Feak, C., 158, 167, 232, 274, 279
feedback, xiii, 40-41, 43-45, 47, 121, 123, 125, 160, 178, 220, 268, 275-276
Fettes, M., 31, 52
Fitch, F., 170, 172, 174, 175, 186
Fleischer, C., 206, 215
Foucault, M., 184, 186
Fox, H., 125
Fox, J., 236, 239
Fox, W., 125, 171, 185, 186
Freedman, A., 52, 65, 73
French, 61, 149, 151, 152-156, 159-163, 165-167, 288
freshman composition, 73
Frus, P., 208, 216
Fu, D., ix, 5, 28, 306
Fu, Z., 189, 201,
Fujieda, M, 189, 192, 201
funding, 6, 59, 77, 84, 89, 163, 168, 194, 215, 236, 259, 305

Gadbow, K., 109, 122
Ganobcsik-Williams, L., 72, 73
Gates, D., 158, 167
Gay, G., 171, 185, 186
genre, 62, 63, 64, 71, 157, 158, 181, 266, 271, 274
Gentil, G., ix, xi, 147, 148, 150, 154, 155, 161, 165, 166, 307

Gibson, S., 66, 72, 239
Gilewicz, M., 118, 122
Gillam, A., 109, 122, 123, 125
Gilles, R., 215, 216, 217
Gillespie, P., 109, 122, 123, 125
Glew, M., 236, 239
globalization, xi, 105, 189, 190, 192, 200
Goldstein, L., 27, 28, 110, 120, 123
Gonzalez, N., 50, 52
grammar, 54, 178, 188, 227, 275

Hake, R., 225, 239
Hale, G., 129, 130, 145
Hall, J., 110, 122, 125, 146, 167, 217, 279
Halleck G., 174, 186
Hamilton, M., 31, 51
Hamp-Lyons, L., 205, 216, 225, 226, 239
Haneda, M., 110, 123
Hansen, J., 110, 123, 276, 279
Hargrove, M., 66, 72
Harklau, L., 30, 52, 112, 123, 163, 166, 175, 186, 253, 261
Harrington, S., 215, 216
Harris, J., 123
Harris, M., 109, 110, 114, 125, 126,
Harris, R., 163, 166
Harvey, E., 208, 215
Haswell, R., 205, 206, 207, 213, 215, 216
Heath, S., 31, 48, 52
Heller, M., 162, 166
Henning, G., 225, 239
Herrington, A., 131, 146
high school, ix, 310
history: institutional, x, 91, 155, 223, 281; pedagogical, 180, 189, 201; second language writing, 147, 280; writing center, 114, 122

Index

Hoekje, B, 174, 186
Horn, H., 205, 216
Hornberger, N., 149, 150, 161, 165, 166
Howard, R., 64, 73
Huot, B, 205, 216, 217, 225, 239

identification, 113
identity, xii, 177, 262, 280, 289-290
individualized learning, 98, 192-193, 198
institution, vii-xii, 30-33, 39, 44, 47, 51, 61-62, 71, 75-76, 82, 86, 91-92, 106, 111, 113-114, 118, 120, 122, 125, 129, 131, 133, 142-144, 146, 148, 149, 151, 154, 156, 161, 164-165, 168-169, 171, 176, 188, 192, 194-195, 199-200, 209, 215, 217, 247, 257-260, 262, 264, 267, 275, 277-278, 281, 289, 291, 298-300, 304-305; departmental divisions, 159, 162; imagination, 199-200; K-12, ix, xii, 3, 77, 91, 103, 248, 256, 258-260; post-secondary, xii, 222

international, x, xi, 75-86, 88-92, , 94, 96, 98-99, 101, 102-103, 105-108, 112, 113, 126, 133, 144, 147-148, 150, 155, 164, 168-169, 177, 180, 184, 186-187, 189-190, 196, 200-201, 211, 227, 248, 250, 254, 256, 258-259, 261-262, 280, 282, 285-286, 290, 297, 304, 309-310; internationalism, x, xii, 94, 105, 108, 285
interview, 31, 35, 40-401, 49, 55, 79, 111, 113, 131, 133, 135, 137-138, 140-144, 155-156, 158, 185, 194-195, 265, 268, 270, 272, 281

Janzi, P., 64, 74
Jenkins, S., 173, 187
Jennings, M., 236, 239
Jensen, L., 88, 92
Jeong, Y., 189, 201
Johns, A., 70, 73, 146, 226
Johnson, K., 110, 123
Jones, C., 117, 123

Kachru, Y., 188, 201
Kachru, B., 263, 279
Kalantzis, M., 164, 165
Kaplan, R., 171, 172, 178, 186, 254
Kapper, J., xii, 247, 307
Kennedy, B., 109, 123, 126
Ketter, J., 206, 215
Kim, M., 172, 186
Kinkead, J., 109, 123
knowledge, vii, 8-11, 17, 26-27, 47, 50, 52, 64-65, 97, 106-107, 111, 113, 115, 118, 131-132, 136, 143, 145, 148, 150, 160-161, 167, 172, 181, 184, 190, 192-193, 197, 199, 200, 206, 208, 212, 228-230, 247, 257-258, 260, 266, 271-273, 276, 279, 293
Kohnert, K., 5, 28
Kramsch, C., 31, 52
Krashen, S., 9, 28
Kroll, B., vii, viii, x, xiii, 91, 92, 114, 123, 145, 167, 207, 216, 225, 239, 257, 292, 293, 297, 307
Kubota, R., x, 75, 84, 92, 106, 107, 307

Lantolf, J., 52, 110, 121, 125, 149, 166

Law, J., 109, 123
learning center, 81, 84
Leather, J., 31, 32, 52
Lee, J., 131, 132, 146
Leki, I., x, 59, 60, 66, 69, 73, 74, 126, 188, 201, 225, 232, 239, 254, 257, 289, 302, 305, 308
Leung, C., 163, 166
Lillis, T., 148, 166
literacy, 164; English, xi, 189-190, 192, 195, 199, 200; global, 192; instructional, 169, 170, 175-176, 180, 184; pedagogical, 184; technological, 179
Liu, J., 110, 123, 201
location, 248
Losey, K., 112, 123, 163, 166, 253, 261
Lueddeke, G., 132, 146
Lukes, M., 84, 93

Maguire, M., 148, 150, 166, 167
Mahoney, S., 189, 192, 201
mapping, xii, 248
material condition, 188, 189, 195
Matoush, M., ix, 5, 308
Matsuda, P., 105, 108, 112, 114, 123, 147, 165, 167, 169, 176, 186, 216, 248, 254, 257, 261, 274, 279, 289, 291, 292, 293, 306, 310
Matsuura, H., 189, 192, 201
McLeod, S., 73, 205, 216
Medway, P., 65, 73
Meier, D., 37, 52
Mendelsohn, D., 226, 239
mentoring, xi, 39, 44-45, 49, 169, 170, 173-176, 180-181, 183-185, 276
metaphor, x, 297, 298; Promised Land, vii, viii, x, xiii, 75, 91, 297, 298, 299, 301, 304, 307
Meyers-Scotton, C., 10

Mlynarczyk. R., 66, 73
modal, 173, 174, 176, 177
Moder, C., 174, 186
Moll, L., 7, 9, 27, 28, 50, 52
Moore, M., xii, 172, 178, 187, 247, 307
Moran, S., 170, 172, 174, 175
Morrison, F., 164, 167
Moser, J., 109, 123, 126
motivation, 67, 198, 237, 263
Mullin, J., 118, 122
Murphy, S., 59, 73, 109, 123
Myers, S., 28, 110, 114, 116, 120, 123, 126

narration, 229
narrative, 174, 194, 225, 280, 292-293, 308
nationality, 177
native speaker, 108, 114, 124, 126, 226, 292
Neff, D., 50, 52
Nelson, J., 118, 124, 126, 226
Neumann, R., 131, 132, 143, 146
Ng, M., 110, 125
No Child Left Behind, 8, 29, 31
non-native speaker, 108, 124, 126, 225, 229, 237, 292
Norris, C., xii, 262, 264, 308
North, S., viii, ix, xi, 61, 70, 76, 92, 121, 123, 151, 163, 164, 249, 250, 262, 297, 298, 304, 305, 306, 307

Ortega, L., 84, 92
Osborn, T.A., 85, 93
Ovando, C., 91, 93

Pare, A., 65, 73
Parks, S., 148, 167
participation, 43, 97, 99, 101, 120, 154-155, 265
Paulus, T., 110, 123

Index 317

Pawley, C., 164, 167
pedagogy: traditional, 193
Peng, J., 189, 201
personality, 166, 172, 177
Phelps, E., 119, 122
Piazza, C., 129, 146
Piller, I., 163, 167
placement, viii, xi, xii, 31, 35, 37, 67, 80, 100-101, 108, 112, 157, 159, 198, 205-217, 224, 231, 234, 267, 291, 299-303, 305-306; online, xii, 213-215
plagiarism, 64, 65, 125
Plakans, B., 178, 186
policy, 171
Polio, C., 236, 239
politics, ix, xi, xii, 5, 10, 33, 39, 51, 150, 161, 182, 188-189, 205, 227, 264, 281, 283, 289
Powers, J., 109, 110, 118, 124, 126
pre-college, 34-35, 38-39, 41-42, 45-46, 48, 51
profession, 172
proficiency, 8, 37, 61, 109, 116-117, 124, 165, 174, 178, 211, 233, 235; communicative language, 8; limited, 7, 34, 153, 248, 252, 256
program: bilingual, 8; cohort-based, 34, 39, 40, 46-48; dual language, 8-9, 16, 26; ESL center model, 86; ESL/bilingual transition, 26; TESOL graduate certificate, 86, 88
Purdue University, xii, 92, 108, 186, 201, 257, 261, 262, 289

Quellmalz, E., 225, 239
questionnaire, 177, 179, 185, 208-209, 213-214

Ramanathan, V., 63, 70, 72
Rampton, B., 163, 166

Rawley, L. A., 105, 108
Ready, D., 164, 167
Reagan, T.G., 85, 93
recommendation, 76, 82, 88, 91-92, 96-97, 104, 174, 180, 183, 207
Reichelt, M., 148, 167, 278, 279
Reid, J., 126, 207, 216, 217, 254, 257, 259
Reyes, M., 9, 10, 28
Reynolds, E., 208, 215
rhetoric, 62, 66, 82, 102, 129, 170, 177, 185, 188, 201, 206, 225, 227, 229, 239-240, 272, 274-276, 279
Rhetoric and Composition, 262, 273-275, 277, 293, 309, 310
Ritter, J., 110, 114, 120, 124, 126
Roemer, M., 67, 73
Ronesi, L., 109, 110, 124, 126
Royer, D., 207, 214, 215, 216, 217
Rubin, D., 135, 146, 171, 172, 187
Rubin, H., 135, 146, 171, 172, 187
Rubin, I., 135, 146, 171, 172, 187
Russell, D., 63, 67, 69, 71, 73, 150, 167

Saez, R., 8, 28
Samraj, B., 130, 131, 146
Santos, T., 226, 240, 254
Schendel, E., 215, 217
Schleppegrell, M., 148, 165
Schommer-Aikins, M., 131, 146
Schultz, L., 67, 73
Scribner, S., 149, 167
second language writing: *Journal of SLW*, 52, 67, 74, 107, 121-126, 147, 165, 167, 186-187, 201, 216, 239-240, 248, 274, 289, 292-293, 305, 307-310; research, vii, viii, xii, 11, 27, 72, 146, 170, 173-174, 247-248, 250-252, 254-257, 259-

260, 277, 290; Symposium, vii, xiii, 75, 92, 104, 108, 147, 259, 261, 289
self-discipline, 199
self-esteem, 198
September 11th, 178, 286
Severino, C., 70, 73, 74, 119, 121, 123, 124, 125
Shannon, D., 172, 178, 187
Shaughnessy, M., 24, 29
Shin, S., 109, 124, 126
Shohamy, E., 205, 217, 239
Siegal, M., 112, 123, 163, 166, 253, 261
Silva, T., xiii, 59, 69, 74, 105, 108, 109, 114, 123, 126, 150, 167, 216, 254, 257, 278, 279, 289, 305
Sims, E., 208, 216
Sizer, T., 37, 52
Smeby, J., 131, 132, 142, 146
So, S., 110, 122
society: justice, 47, 286, 308; space, 151
Spack, R., 126, 157, 167
Standard English, 7, 12, 24, 25
Stanley, J., 102, 104, 108
Stay, B., 109, 122, 123, 125
Sternberg, R., 68, 73
Sternglass, M., 66, 74
Stevenson, I., 172, 187
Storch, N., 110, 119, 124
Strain, K., 109, 122, 125
strategy: compensatory, 173-174, 186; contextual, 174; language learning, 190, 192; pedagogical, 175; pragmatic, 174; process, 185; rhetorical, 170
Strong-Krause, D., 212, 217
student: bilingual, 30, 33, 37, 43, 51, 61, 148, 154, 159, 162, 165; generation 1.5, xi, 99, 124, 126, 164, 168, 253;
immigrant, xi, 6, 43, 85, 112-113, 164, 168, 285, 307; international, x, 75-78, 80-86, 88, 90, 94, 96, 98, 101-103, 105-108, 112, 126, 133, 147, 155, 164, 168, 211, 248, 250, 254, 256, 258-259, 261, 263, 280, 285, 290, 304; L2, x, 60-71, 112, 117, 122, 157, 159, 163, 168, 184, 213, 289, 305; multilingual, 105, 165, 168, 292, 306
support: language, ix, 75-77, 79, 82-90, 95, 106, 107, 160, 303
survey, 79, 99, 124, 133-135, 138, 140, 142-143, 212
Swain, M., 110, 124
Swales, J., 158, 167, 274, 279
Sweedler-Brown, C., 226, 240

Tardy, C., xii, 181, 187, 262, 264, 308
Tassoni, J., 110, 124
teacher, 11, 238
teaching assistant: international, xi, 169-181, 183-187

technology: computer, 69, 79, 144, 149, 164, 170, 174-175, 177, 179, 184, 192-193, 195, 200, 213, 263-264, 285, 303, 309; information, 192-193; PowerPoint, 174-176, 178-179, 181, 208
tenure, 89, 100, 113, 156, 163, 259, 270, 281, 282, 284, 290
textbook, 65, 196
Thomas, W., 8, 29
Thonus, T., 109, 112, 117, 119, 120, 122, 124, 126
Tocalli-Beller, A., 110, 124
Tomasello, M., 9, 29
Tompkins, P., 208, 217

Tong, J., 196, 202
topic, 18, 23, 27, 43, 48, 62, 64, 97-98, 100, 102-103, 191, 196, 228-229, 238, 307, 309
tradition, 31, 38, 44, 51, 69, 72, 118-119, 133, 189, 193-197, 199-200, 207, 212, 230-232, 235, 238, 240, 266, 277, 285
transfer, 68, 69, 101, 236; general, far, 68; specific, near transfer, 68
Trimbur, J., 112, 125
Troyka, L., 158, 167
Tsui, A., 110, 125
tuition, 170, 210, 212, 297, 303
Twale, D., 172, 178, 187

unionization, xii, 280, 284

van Dam, J., 31, 32, 52
van Lier, L., 32, 52
Vandrick, S., xii, 95, 280, 292-293, 308
Vignola, M., 148, 167
Villalva, K., ix, 30, 33, 51, 53, 308
Villamil, O., 110, 122
voice, 17, 27, 71, 174, 264
Vygotsky, L., 149, 167

Waggoner, D., 34, 53
Wald, M., 102, 104, 108
Wall, D., 223, 235, 240
Watanabe, Y., 223, 239
Weigle, S., xii, 126, 222, 225, 229, 232, 234, 240, 309
Wertsch, J., 149, 150, 163, 167
Whalen, K., 150, 167
White, E., 205, 206, 215, 217, 224, 225, 240
Wiley, T., 84, 93
Williams, J., x, 72, 74, 102, 109, 110, 114, 119, 120, 125, 126, 174, 178, 186, 187, 289, 293, 309
Williamson, M., 206, 217
Winn, M., 102, 104, 108
Wittgenstein, L., 149, 167
Woodmansee, M., 64, 74
World Trade Organization, 189, 190, 201
writing: academic, ix, xii, 39, 47, 50, 74, 80, 124-125, 129-130, 134-135, 143, 148-149, 152-153, 155-156, 165, 225-226, 232, 237-238, 240, 262, 265, 271, 274, 276-277, 292, 301, 308, 310; across the curriculum (WAC), 69, 70, 72, 73, 237, 306; as a social activity, 129; cross-cultural, 105; developmental, ix, 6-7, 10, 12, 24-26, 33, 50, 141, 148, 150, 184, 210, 263-264, 276, 307; EFL, 188, 201, 307; ESL, xii, 105, 122-123, 186, 212, 216-217, 226, 239, 261, 263, 275, 277, 279, 280-281, 287-292, , 299-302, 308; first language, x, 7, 12, 59, 62, 67-70, 147-148, 158, 162, 210, 212, 280, 282, 289; foreign language, 148, 309; in the disciplines (WID), 70, 72, 73; second language, vii, viii, ix, x, xii, 26, 30-32, 60-62, 67-70, , 74, 107, 110, 115, 123, 129, 144, 147-148, 165-167, 169, 180, 183, 184, 188, 200, 207, 208, 211-213, 215-216, 239, 247-250, , 252, 254-256, , 259-260, 262-262, 274-275, 277, 280, 286, 289, 291, 293, 297, 298, 301-304, 306-307, 309, 310

writing center, x, 67, 70, 74, 78-79, 81, 84, 86, 89, 96-97, 99,

101-103, 106, 109, 110-126, 153-159, , 163, 216, 306; clientele, 110; consultants, 98, 102-103; L2 writers, 67; peer tutors, 122, 125; tutors, 46, 67, 81, 89-91, 97, 99, 101-103 106, 110-111, 113-116, 118-120, 123-227, 301

Writing Center Journal, 109, 118, 121-126

Writing Lab Newsletter, 109, 122

writing process, 24, 40-41, 47, 158, 160, 223, 227

Yagelski, R., 206, 215
Yancey, K., 118, 125, 206, 215
Yook, E., 187
You, X., ix, 188, 189, 194, 199, 201

Zamel, V., 213, 217, 291, 293
Zhang, Y., 190, 191, 193, 197, 198, 202
Zheng, S., 196, 202
Zhou, G., 189, 196
Zhou, X., 189, 196, 201, 202
Zhu, W., xi, 59, 74, 129, 130, 146, 309

www.ingramcontent.com/pod-product-compliance
Lightning Source LLC
Chambersburg PA
CBHW021753230426
43669CB00006B/71